W9-BNL-772

Whitetail Hunting
Tactics of the Pros

Books by Lamar Underwood

On Dangerous Ground

Books Edited by Lamar Underwood

The Greatest Fishing Stories Ever Told

The Greatest Hunting Stories Ever Told

The Greatest War Stories Ever Told

The Greatest Survival Stories Ever Told

Lamar Underwood's Bass Almanac

Man Eaters

The Quotable Soldier

Whitetail Hunting Tactics of the Pros

Expert Advice to Help You Be a Successful Hunter

EDITED BY
LAMAR UNDERWOOD

THE LYONS PRESS

Guilford, Connecticut
An imprint of The Globe Pequot Press

The Lyons Press is an imprint of The Globe Pequot Press.

Printed in the United States of America

10 9 8 7 6 5 4 3 2 1

Library of Congress Cataloging-in-Publication Data is available on file.

Acknowledgments

Articles in this book by the following authors originally appeared in books and are reprinted here by permission of the authors.

Charles J. Alsheimer: "The Rut's Timing Is Everything" and "Hunting Strategies for the Rutting Moon" from *Hunting Whitetails by the Moon*. "Understanding Whitetails" and "Gearing Up" from *Whitetail: The Ultimate Challenge*. Both books published by Krause Publications, 700 E. State St., Iola, WI 54990-0001. Reprinted by permission of the author.

"About the Whitetail" and "How to Use Deer Calls Effectively" by Peter Fiduccia originally appeared in the book *Whitetail Strategies*. Reprinted by permission of the author.

"Portrait of a Tracker" by Jerome B. Robinson is from *In the Deer Woods*, The Lyons Press, 246 Goose Lane, Guilford, CT 06437. Reprinted by permission of the author.

With the exception of the four articles listed below, the other articles in this book originally appeared in the following magazines published by Harris Publications, Inc., 1115 Broadway, New York, NY 10010 and are reprinted by permission of the authors and Harris Publications.

Whitetail Hunting Strategies, Guns & Hunting, Deer, Remington Country, Sportsman's Hunting Yearbook, Deer Hunter, Sportsman's Bowhunting Annual, The Complete Rifleman, and *Deer & Big Game Rifles*.

Articles originally appearing in magazines other than those published by Harris Publications include:

"The Rack" by Jay Cassell originally appeared in *Sports Afield* and is reprinted by permission of the author.

"Shedding Light on Moon Phases" by John Wootters originally appeared in *Outdoor Life* and is reprinted here by permission of the author.

"Whitetail Wisdom for the Ages" by John Wootters originally appeared in *Sports Afield* and is reprinted here by permission of the author.

"Shotgun Slug Savvy" by Wayne van Zwoll originally appeared in *Petersen's Hunting* and is reprinted here by permission of the author.

Contents

Introduction

Growing up as an "army brat," I did a great deal of traveling to my father's far-flung assignments, but home base was Georgia, the town of Statesboro to be exact, and that's where most of the action in my fledgling days as a fisherman and hunter took place. Deer were not very high on my agenda back then, the main reason being that bagging a buck was almost rare enough to get your picture in the paper. Things have changed, of course, and Georgia hunters today, like those everywhere else, are enjoying bountiful whitetail herds. My lack of experience in deer hunting, failure to pay my dues and initiation fees, had the effect of turning my early whitetail hunts into desultory and sloppy patrols into deer haunts, mainly creek and river bottoms. There I was so eager to blast a squirrel, rabbit, or—glory of glories—a jumped mallard that I no doubt spooked every deer into the next county.

My first real opportunity to get down to some serious deer hunting did not come until my early twenties, when a December dawn found me settled against the trunk of an enormous white oak in the heart of classic whitetail country among the folded hills and ridges of Pennsylvania.

Buck hunters pray for such a morning. At first light, the horizon was cut from steel—black lumps of white pines, the knife-like rim of a distant ridge looming above the forest. Without wind, the stillness seemed almost electric as I shivered in the cold, nervous to the raw edge at the thought of the buck I hoped would be mine.

When the crows began to patrol, their raucous cries announcing that it was time for things to get moving, I detected the rustle of squirrels in the branches overhead. As the light came on, I began to hear occasional gunshots, echoing from the distant ridge.

Suddenly, the sound of a limb breaking jerked my attention toward the trees to my left. I strained to see. Nothing! The sound came again, louder still, and followed this time by the dry rustle of leaves being shuffled. Another hunter, I thought. Perhaps if he sees me, he'll move on.

I stood up, and in that instant an enormous buck exploded away, his head adorned with what William Faulkner once described as, ". . . that rocking chair he toted."

I had blown it! I sat down, numbed, shocked. Certainly such an opportunity might never come my way again. For the next couple of hours, my mind seethed with self-recrimination.

Gradually, though, the feelings of inadequacy subsided. The forest came back to me—the sights and sounds of the birds, the feeling that possibilities still existed here. At noon I noticed that the squirrels were moving as industriously as they had at dawn. Strange, I thought. There must be some dirty weather around. I can't see it moving, but they can *feel* it coming.

I knew I was back in the groove then, focused on nature instead of myself.

That night it snowed, and two days later I shot a fork-horn buck. For the first time in my life—though certainly not the last—I found myself saying to the other fellows, "Well, boys, you can't eat horns!"

That the task of bagging a whitetail buck—any buck!—requires skill and patience is obvious to the brethren of the Hunter Orange. Non-hunters, especially *anti*-hunters, know about as much about real nature and whitetail deer as I know about nuclear physics. They point to their deer-ravaged shrubbery and smashed car fenders and headlights with the comment, "The things are a plague. They're everywhere! What's the big deal about hunting them?"

Well, the "big deal" about hunting them is that they are the most elusive and fascinating game animal on the North American continent. The devilish buggers that descend on your garden like locusts become an entirely different creature after opening day.

Opening Day. The pre-dawn explodes with noise, like a bomb going off. A deer, and especially a veteran "survivor" buck, would have to be deaf not to know what's going on. The cacophony includes the sounds of engines being revved up, wheels spinning in the mud, truck and SUV doors slamming, the *snick-snick* of gun actions being worked, and a myriad of shouts: "Hey, Joe, you goin' to the Oak Tree stand?" "I'll meet you at noon by the apple orchard." "Oh no, I forgot my shells!"

Trudging into this arena, with hope in his heart, the hunter knows the odds are stacked against him. Perhaps, he thinks, he'll get lucky. Happens all the time. To other people. Just stop by any check-in station, and you'll see guys with big bucks who can barely spell Whitetail and wouldn't know a scrape from a hog-wallow.

True enough, but you'll also see some steely-eyed, beaming gents and gals who do indeed know exactly what they're doing in the deer woods, who played their cards just right without going into debt to Lady Luck.

Years ago, to my delight and surprise, I had the opportunity to appear on "The American Sportsman" television show with outdoor writer and personality Grits Gresham. During all the years I had watched the show, I never had the remotest dream that one day I would appear on the show myself. And I had never dreamed that one day I would become editor of *Sports Afield*, which was the reason why I was invited to be on the show with Grits, fishing for bass on Florida's Lake Kissimmee.

One day during the filming, a real lunker showed himself behind the spinner I was buzzing on the surface. I slowed my retrieve, hoping for a smashing strike. Instantly, the bass sank into the depths.

"Grits," I asked, "when you know a bass is behind your bait, do you slow the thing down or speed it up?"

"It doesn't make a bit of difference," he said emphatically.

"How come?" I asked, surprised.

"Because whichever one you do will be wrong!"

Experience in the field has shown me that Grits' droll sense of humor is right on the money, whether applied to bass with lockjaw or the miscues that await the buck hunter. A lot can go wrong out there. You can expect it. Murphy and his law rule.

But the heck with the odds. We aren't going out there to admire the scenery or joke and drink with the boys in camp. We want a buck. Any buck will do, although, frankly, we wouldn't mind bagging one for the wall. But since we can't depend on Lady Luck, just what can we do to give ourselves an edge?

Trust me on this: Help is on the way! Just a few pages away, you'll start finding the answer to every deer-hunting frustration you've ever know—all the hours and days when your hunts were a blank. When the only action you got was the occasional glimpse of does.

I know it may sound corny, but I'd like to think that this introduction puts us on the front porch of a warm and friendly deer camp. Many of our old friends are inside, and the strangers will soon be buddies. They are people who have shaken more dirt off their deer-hunting boots than most of us will ever walk over. They know something!

Join me inside, and we'll hear what they have to say.

— Lamar Underwood
March 2001

Part One
Understanding Whitetails

What You Don't Know *Can* and *Will* Hurt You!

In his often quoted, *THE ART OF WAR,* the legendary Chinese military tactician Sun Tzu advises: "Know the enemy and know yourself; in a hundred battles you will never be in peril."

While things aren't all that desperate and serious in the whitetail woods, the gist of Sun Tzu's remark is worth remembering: You're better off knowing something about what you're up against.

While they are animals of fairly rigid habit, whitetail deer are interesting and complex creatures prone to a witch's brew—for hunters, anyway—of contradictory behavioral patterns that are sometimes hard to understand and impossible to predict. Just when you think they are going to *zig,* they *zag.* And vice versa. When you think you've got a lock on where they're feeding, they move to some other dining hall in another part of the forest or croplands. The white oak patch where you scouted a buck feeding a week before turns out to be empty on opening day—except for its colony of squirrels. This list of failed game plans could go on and on.

You think you know what the deer will be doing. Perhaps you do. But all too often it seems like they're doing it somewhere else—somewhere you don't know about!

Nevertheless, the fact remains that consistently successful whitetail hunters know a lot about their quarry—what the deer will be doing at different times, under varying conditions. And why! When they mix that savvy with heavy doses of woodsmanship and detailed knowledge of the terrain they're hunting . . . well, it's only a matter of time before they'll be filling out their tag.

Knowing the game; knowing the terrain. That's taking your best shot!

1 Understanding Whitetails

BY CHARLES J. ALSHEIMER

In this excerpt from his excellent book, WHITETAIL: THE ULTIMATE CHALLENGE, veteran hunter, photographer, and whitetail expert Charles Alsheimer gets our "crash course" in deer behavior off to an illuminating start.

My earliest recollection of nature, when growing up on a potato farm in Western New York, was seeing a whitetail bound across the field next to our house. The beauty of its measured leaps made a lasting impression on me, and fueled my desire to pursue a career of hunting, writing about, and photographing these animals. For over thirty years I've pursued wildlife with gun, bow, and camera throughout North America and no animal captivates me quite like the whitetail.

In a sense America grew up with the whitetail as well. When the first settlers arrived on the eastern shores of North America, they found a paradise teeming with a variety of wildlife, with the white-tailed deer being the dominant big game species. Prior to the early settlers' arrival, the Indians had relied heavily on the whitetail for centuries as a source of food, clothing, and tools.

It's not known exactly how many whitetails inhabited North America when the Pilgrims landed at Plymouth Rock. Some have estimated that their populations were as high as 40 million, while others claim there were fewer than today's 19+ million. At any rate, the early whitetail numbers did not remain high for long.

After the Civil War, Americans became adventuresome. Many began moving westward, clearing the land for farming and industry. In the process both whitetail habitat and numbers decreased dramatically. With open seasons, no bag limits, and a demand for venison in the cities, market hunting became popular in many parts of the East. And by the late 1800s, whitetail numbers were fewer than 500,000 throughout North America—just a fraction of what they once were.

Around the turn of the century, a plea went out from sportsmen throughout America and game seasons were closed. Unfortunately the damage was done and it took decades for huntable whitetail populations to return to the eastern portion of America.

Biology

Today, the white-tailed deer numbers over 19 million and is the most plentiful big game animal in North America, with thirty recognized subspecies. These various subspecies range from as far north as the 52nd parallel in Canada to the equator in the south. The size of these subspecies varies greatly over their range. Generally the farther north one goes, the larger the whitetails are. For this reason, the Northern Woodland and Dakota subspecies are considered the largest.

In the northern reaches of the whitetail's range, a mature buck will be about forty-two inches tall at the shoulder, while in its southernmost region, a buck will be little more than half as tall. In many parts of North America, bucks that dress out over two hundred pounds cause a great deal of excitement. Though two hundred pounds seems to be a benchmark for big bucks, several dressing out at over three hundred pounds have been recorded.

In November of 1955, Horace Hinkley shot the heaviest buck every officially recorded in Maine. The buck had a dressed weight of 355 pounds. It appears that the heaviest whitetail ever killed in the United States was taken by Minnesota hunter Carl Lenander, Jr., in 1926. It dressed out at 402 pounds and the state conservation department estimated the buck's live weight to be 511 pounds.

But perhaps the heaviest whitetail ever killed fell to archer John Annett of Ontario, Canada, in 1977. It dressed out at 431 pounds on government-certified scales. Unfortunately the buck was processed before Canadian authorities could examine it. Nonetheless, these weights show how big northern whitetails can be.

Though some states consider weight to be the key ingredient in determining how big a whitetail is, antlers are what make whitetails so popular. In the last two decades, more and more hunters have become knowledgeable about the Boone and Crockett scoring system and what it takes to grow a trophy buck. For over eighty years, Jim Jordan's ten point Wisconsin buck stood as the largest-racked whitetail ever killed, scoring 206-1/8 Boone and Crockett typical. Then in November of 1993, Milo Hanson of Bigger, Saskatchewan, killed a huge fourteen point buck that scores 213-1/8 typical.

It is generally accepted that a 140 class Boone and Crockett whitetail is a true trophy, wherever it is found. For a whitetail to be able to grow 140 inches of antlers, it usually needs to be at least 3½ years old. Though a white-tailed buck may sport a trophy set of antlers at 3½ years of age, it doesn't reach maturity until 5½. And with the proper genetics and habitat, a 5½-year-old buck can easily be in the 160–175 typical class.

With the huge interest in hunting mature white-tailed bucks, hunters are branching out across North America in search of a trophy animal. Rather than staying home to hunt the back forty, serious hunters are going to Texas, Kansas, Illinois, Ohio, Montana, and the western Canadian provinces in search of their trophy of a lifetime. (See Chapter 11 on Whitetails North and South.)

Spring and Summer

Spring is a time of birth and rebirth for all of nature. With spring green-up comes a dramatic change in the life of white-tailed deer. After a gestation period of approximately 202 days, the doe in the North gives birth around the end of May. From the age of 2½ on, does may give birth to twins, if they are healthy and the winters are not severe. When twins are born, one will usually be a buck and one a doe.

Compared with other times of the year, summer is relatively uneventful for whitetails. During this time does are busy nursing and caring for their young, in preparation for the upcoming winter months. In June and July fawns grow by leaps and bounds and command center stage for those who love nature. I love to photograph fawns during the summer months, not only because of their beauty but because of their innocence. They are playful, therefore they exhibit some unusual behavior. Also, it is quite easy to call them within camera range, using a fawn or doe bleat.

With the arrival of the summer months, both bucks and does are busy gorging themselves on the preferred foods found in their home range. It's not uncommon for adult deer to consume between ten and twelve pounds of food each day.

Except in the most remote portions of their range, whitetails are grazers during the summer months, relying heavily on wild strawberries, alfalfa, clover, and other grasses. As summer blends into autumn, they begin browsing more frequently in preparation for winter. During the early autumn months beechnuts, acorns, corn, and apples are among their favorite foods. When the frost has taken its toll on grasses and the fruit and mast crops are gone, whitetails turn to browsing. White cedar, apple, red and white oak, red maple, striped maple, staghorn sumac, witch hobble, and basswood are preferred browse in the North.

As the days of early spring become longer, a phenomenon known as photoperiodism causes a whitetail's antlers to grow. The increased amount of daylight activates the pineal gland that triggers growth hormones in a whitetail's body. It is this gland that determines when whitetails grow antlers, shed their antlers, change their seasonal fur coat, and breed.

In the northern region white-tailed bucks begin growing their antlers in early April. Growth is relatively slow throughout April and May; however, when the long days of June and July arrive, antler growth becomes significant. As the antlers grow, they are encased in a network of blood vessels and skin tissue called velvet, which nourishes the antlers throughout the growth process. By the end of August the buck's antlers are fully grown, have hardened down, and the velvet is ready to peel. During the summer months white-tailed bucks are secretive and move very little. They tend to bunch up and form bachelor groups and it's not uncommon to see four or five hanging together.

I've always been fascinated by the whitetail's annual antler cycle, from the time the bucks start to grow them in the spring until they cast them in winter. As a hunter and photographer, I've observed and photographed all stages of this cycle many times during the past fifteen years. However, one aspect of the antler process, the peeling of velvet, is something few have observed.

On August 31, 1989, while photographing on a large preserve, I was able to record this phenomenon on film. When I first located the buck at 7:00 a.m. in a swampy area, a small piece of velvet had already started peeling from one of the antler tines. From the time I started photographing, it took the buck fifty minutes to completely strip the velvet from his antlers.

During the fifty-minute period, I was amazed at the buck's behavior in attempting to strip his antlers clean. Throughout the process, he periodically licked all the blood off the alder bush he was rubbing before he peeled more of the velvet from his antlers. As more and more velvet began hanging from the antlers, the buck became violent in his attempts to remove the velvet. Several times the buck stopped, panted, and once staggered backwards, appearing to be exhausted. On two occasions he actually stopped and rested before continuing. After he freed all the velvet from his antlers, the buck scented the ground to locate the pieces that had been peeled off. Then, to my surprise, the buck picked up the velvet and ate it. I have since learned that bucks commonly eat their velvet, perhaps a behavioral trait to prevent predators from locating them.

One thing that sticks in my mind is the speed at which the buck removed the velvet and the violence involved in the velvet-shedding process. I've photographed several buck fights over the years and none was as violent as this buck's behavior. The annoyance of blood dripping and velvet hanging in its eyes probably contributed to this behavior.

Autumn

Though I'll elaborate more on the rut and whitetail behavior in later chapters, it's important to give a quick overview of autumn's happenings before going further into the text. By the time late September and early October arrive, the nights are cool and the year's crop of apples and mast start falling from the trees. Conditions are at their peak, and it's the grandest time of year for whitetails. In September, white-tailed bucks begin rubbing trees, and by October they start making scrapes throughout their territory. Bucks also begin sparring with each other to determine pecking order. The combination of rubs, scrapes, and sparring matches are preludes to the rut.

Autumn is also a time of chaos for the yearling bucks (1½ years old). When October arrives, they usually break from their summer bachelor group and begin searching for their first home. At the same time they experience the first sex drive of their life. In many cases this hormonal infusion causes them to travel great distances. As a result, their process of looking for a new home range and dealing with their first mating season makes them vulnerable. Because of this, they are by far the easiest whitetail to hunt.

Some of the older does will come into estrus (the time when does are able to be bred) in mid-October, creating what is known as a false rut, which causes bucks to go into a frenzy. From this point until mid-November, when most does come into estrus, bucks become very active as they search for receptive does. In the process they rub, scrape, and fight. Though the peak of the rut varies throughout the United States, the activity associated with it is the same whether one hunts Texas, New York, or Alberta.

Winter

It's not uncommon for white-tailed bucks to lose up to 30 percent of their body weight during the rut. Therefore, once the rut is over bucks go into a feeding frenzy, trying to replace lost body fat before the harsh winter months arrive.

Winter throughout the whitetail range is incredibly varied. In the northern reaches January often brings harsh weather. For the next ninety days whitetails are subjected to ice, freezing rain, and snow, where snow depths exceed three feet in some regions. Significant snow depth forces a situation called yarding as deer bunch up and gravitate toward traditional food sources and cover. Unfortunately most yards' food has long ago been depleted, making it impossible for whitetails to find their daily requirement of seven pounds of browse. In addition to starvation, northern whitetails must also cope with the constant possibility of predation. As a result they are susceptible to coyotes, wolves, and dogs during the winter months when their strength is at its lowest. In many areas of the North, predation is significant. Unlike the North, snow and cold is not a factor for whitetail winter survival in the southern areas of North America.

Throughout most of the range, white-tailed bucks cast or shed their antlers between December and March, before beginning the growing process again in April. When the end of March arrives whitetails are far from sleek looking, and throughout most of their range they look gaunt from the rigors of winter. Also, to compound their gaunt-looking condition, they begin to molt in preparation for spring's arrival. But in spite of all winter is able to throw at whitetails, the majority survive quite well and live to see another season. The fact that they are able to survive from the equator to North America's far northern forest is testimony to their strength and survivability.

2   About the Whitetail

BY PETER FIDUCCIA

Respected whitetail hunting authority Peter Fiduccia helps you learn more about the whitetail's lifestyle with this excerpt from his landmark book, WHITETAIL STRATEGIES.

J ust the mere mention of the name whitetail leads most to think about one of the deer's most recognizable physical characteristics—its large brown tail with its completely white underside. Many hunters and non-hunters alike have witnessed this graceful animal fleeting across an open field in long graceful bounds as it displayed the white underside of its tail held high in the air swaying from side-to-side as the deer retreated to safety.

As with most animals, specific physical traits are modified through the process of evolution to enhance the survival of the species. It is the external factors that generate changes in its physical evolution. The whitetail is no exception. The whitetail evolved into the graceful, fleet, alert deer that it is, to overcome predation, climatic changes and food source modifications.

The deer also evolved its well-honed sense of eyesight, acute sense of smell, and its superbly camouflaged and thermoregulatory coat to aid in its attempt to survive. Even a buck's antlers have evolved to act as weapons against other competitive bucks, predators (to some degree), and as a form of courtship to aid the buck with the visual attraction of females. All these physical traits aid the deer in its attempt to survive predation (man or animal), climatic changes, and to perpetuate the species.

The three most proclaimed physical characteristics of a deer is its eyes, ears and nose. Each of these sensory organs is used daily by the whitetail for a profusion of reasons including where to find its food sources, to locate and avoid danger and to seek out the opposite sex during the breeding season.

The Eyes

Let's take a closer look at all three of these sensory organs, beginning with the deer's eyes. A whitetail's eyes contain more rods than cones—allowing for better night-time vision. A whitetail's eye only needs ⅛th of the available light a human's eye needs to see in the dark! The white hair which lies directly under the eyes of the whitetail also help it see better at night. The white hair reflects as much light that is available during low light situations. Unbelievably, whitetails can see at least 310 degrees of a full circle (360 degrees) and at least 50 degrees of the 310 degrees can be seen in binocular vision.

Whitetails have evolved to detect motion and depth perception. The eyes of a deer have both monocular vision to each eye and binocular vision to the front, giving the deer a wide field of view (Moen 1982). The design of the orbit (the bony socket in which the eye lies) and the size of the retina (the sensory membrane that lines the eye and is connected to the brain by the optic nerve) allow all ruminant animals (those animals that are cud-chewers and have 3- or 4-chambered complex stomachs) to see back along their flanks and to also detect objects behind them.

Although, for years, it has been said that deer are color blind, recent research now suggests that deer can see shades of color. This research is based on the fact that animals that are predominantly active at night, have eyes that are dominant with light-sensitive rods. To the contrary, animals active during daylight, have eyes principally made up of color-sensitive cones.

In fact, one of the most controversial subjects regarding a deer's eyesight has also revolved around its ability to detect Ultra Violet (UV) light. I strongly believe deer do see shades of color. I have come to that conclusion not from a scientific basis but rather through thirty years of hunting and observing whitetails. I find the UV argument hard to swallow, however. I guess this is as good a time as any in this book to explain to you why I feel this way.

Over the last few years, the subject of Ultra Violet light and how animals see it, has received significant attention within the hunting fraternity. Many hunters are concerned about the effect ultra violet light has on "untreated" hunting clothing under low light conditions. The information about UV light in articles and in other forms of media, is packed with technical-looking information and misleading graphs detailing how animals, and particularly deer, are able to detect hunters when they wear "untreated" hunting garments, including blaze orange and camo clothing.

Although these articles strongly suggest deer do see UV light and colors, exactly how animals interpret UV and the spectrum of colors is very debatable. For instance, in an article I read about UV light, the article began by stating, "Laboratory experiments prove that deer see many things we cannot see, especially ultra-violet light at the blue-white end of the color spectrum." As far as I know, from my involvement in videography and photography, white is not a color and is not on the spectrum!

The question is, are animals, especially deer, able to pinpoint and react negatively to ultra violet light being reflected from hunters' garments?

It is true that most nocturnal animals are able to see as good in the dark as they can during the daylight hours. Because of several factors, they are able to see better in total darkness and, supposedly best, under low light conditions. Firstly, when the sun sets, a game animal's pupil opens wider to admit more light. Unlike humans, who only have cones within the central region of their eyes, deer's eyes contain both rods and cones. The rods, which are dominant within the deer's eye, are extremely sensitive to light—moreover dim light. In addition, human eyes have a filter that blocks out UV light, where deer do not have this filter present in their eyes.

But, the question remains, can deer and other game animals detect ENOUGH ultra violet light reflected from camo clothing, worn by hunters from DAWN to DUSK, that will require sportsmen to change their hunting strategies?

Some people think so. Kurt Von Besser is the manufacturer of a product called UV Killer by Atsko/Sno-Seal, Inc. Von Besser was the first to address the issue of UV light and clothing. In his booklet, "How Game Animals See," Von Besser supports his findings of how game animals see through research compiled by a vision scientist at the University of California. According to von Besser, hunters who wear camo clothing manufactured with or which have been enhanced by UV brighteners, are using camo which "has been working against [them]." He feels that the amount of ultra violet light reflected from clothing is detected by game to an extent which gives the hunter away or spooks the game. Thus, with his UV Killer (which is actually another dye to neutralize brighteners in clothing), sportsmen can eliminate UV reflection from their clothing and have fewer game detect them

If this is the case, where do the ultra violet brighteners come from? They come from standard detergents used to wash clothing. Therefore, if a sportsman washes his clothes in regular detergent, there's a greater chance his detergent has ultra violet brighteners in it. However, for the last 15 to 20 years, much has been written about scent, and how sportsmen should wash their clothing in a non-scented detergent or brown soap. Most of these "hunter's soaps" contain basic cleaning agents—free from ultra violet brighteners. Hunters who use these soaps, therefore, should be wearing camo clothing "safe" from UV brighteners, anyway.

In addition, because of the UV controversy, some leading manufacturers of camouflage clothing have had to take steps to comply with the public awareness of this new "scientific breakthrough." And, although most clothing manufacturers do not agree with theories revolving around the UV rage, they are spending time and money to assure the public their clothing does not contain any UV brighteners. According to the leading manufacturers, most camo clothing fabric houses do not use ultra violet brighteners in their dyes. In a conversation with Bill Jordan, from Spartan-Realtree, he stated, "All cotton fabrics used in Realtree clothing absolutely do not contain any optical brighteners." Jordan is a long-time, whitetail deer hunter. In addition, Jim Crumley, from Trebark told me, "There are no brighteners used in the ink dyes of Trebark fabrics." Crumley has been a successful turkey hunter for many years.

So what are the facts? The ability of deer to detect and react to UV light reflected from clothing, seems to be greatly exaggerated. Leading scientists, who are involved in extensive visionary research, do not support the claims that animals, especially mammals, detect UV light as being brighter than any other light they see. They all agree that since no documented research (using accepted psychophysiological methods specifically for deer) has been performed regarding deer's ability to detect UV light, little can be said to prove they can detect UV reflection from clothes.

John Coulbourn, President of Coulbourn Instruments/Megabucks Trophy Nutritional Products, who holds a degree in Behavioral Psychology and Zoology, states the following, "The notion that deer see ultraviolet wavelengths with significantly greater sensitivity than other mammals (including humans) is unlikely." Coulbourn feels the pictures displayed in the advertisements and articles are pointless. "No organism with a single lens eye could simultaneously focus on red and green and ultraviolet [which the pictures portray]. Either it would see an ultraviolet image and a blurred red-green haze or the reverse. Not being able to focus on an image or even detect target movement in this region of the spectrum means evolution would not select for this capability," said Coulbourn. In addition, the graph (by von Besser) depicting how game animals see is, "without labeled vertical axis and supporting data or reference. It is TOTALLY unsupported. Furthermore, the graph seems to have a fabricated curve because its shape implies that there is another unknown photo receptor with its peak at or below 300 millimicron. Such a major discovery would have set the visual research community on its ear!"

Coulbourn Instruments is primarily involved in manufacturing behavioral and physiological test instruments for drug and toxicology research. Having completed extensive studies regarding vision in animals, Coulbourn continued, "Mammals (in fact, most vertebrates) which have color sensitivity, are similar to humans; and any deviations from our green centered sensitivity tend to be to the far red, the opposite end of the spectrum from violet. This is ESPECIALLY true for *nocturnally* active animals." Coulbourn explained how deer's vision is different from our own, "While we concentrate on image formation and pattern-form discrimination, deer are more responsive to movement or target velocity across the retina. This is a common adaptation in prey animals which are attacked by swiftly moving predators."

Dr. Silas D. White, Professor of Psychology, at Muhlenberg College, finds that the concept of deer being able to detect clear images from ultraviolet reflection difficult to believe. Dr. White explained, "In vertebrate studies performed thus far, in no case does there appear to be much, if any, sensitivity to radiant energy in the U.V. end of the spectrum. This militates strongly against U.V. reflections being perceived as brighter than other wavelengths . . ." Because UV light has such a short wavelength, it is extremely unlikely deer can detect a clearly focused image of UV reflection. "It is unlikely that, if UV were indeed an adequate stimulus, which is doubtful, deer or humans would be capable of perceiving a crisp image resulting from reflections of such disparate wavelengths as those in the typical deer woods background and UV reflections."

In addition to the above, consider Coulbourn's point that nature has evolved all animals that are predated upon with vision that is super sensitive to motion rather than color. For instance, a rabbit who is feeding with eyes focused down, is able to instantly detect a hawk approaching simply by having the hawk's SHADOW trigger an instinctive response. It instantly reacts by hunkering down, pinning its ears back, and darting off. Similarly, a deer reacts much the same way when it sees something that visually suggests a problem. As hunters, we have all had this experience. The deer either stands still and remains motionless or approaches cautiously. With a single movement from the subject, however, the deer flees. My point is that deer's eyes have not evolved to react to color, but rather, as an animal that is predated upon by man and other animals, their eyes have evolved to detect movement.

And it is not only scientists outside of the hunting fraternity having doubts about the so-called "revolutionary" findings. Several seasoned outdoor professionals don't think deer can interpret reflections from U.V. light either. Glenn Cole, a Wildlife Manager in Region #3, for the New York Department of Environmental Conservation, has hunted whitetail deer for over 20 years. He expressed his thoughts about deer detecting UV light reflected from clothing this way, "The hard facts to support what an animal does—or does not see, under low light conditions are just not available. All the scientific literature I have read, says deer see in shades of grey. I have not seen any scientific material to the contrary. I can honestly say that any deer that has spooked from seeing me, reacted to movement or scent—and not because my camo clothing was reflecting UV light."

Game calling expert and avid hunter, Brad Harris, from Lohman Game Call company, said, "I do not feel that I am qualified to say whether 'UV Killer' is a benefit or not. I have heard many discussions for and against this product. I can say that over the past ten years, I have made my living calling game animals and have had many birds and wild game such as deer, elk, predators, turkey and small game within a matter of just a few feet on one or more occasions than I care to count." He attributes getting close to game by knowing the animal's habits and "being properly concealed with a good backdrop to break up my image."

In my personal experience, which includes harvesting 113 whitetail bucks, as well as photographing and videotaping many game animals up close, I can honestly say, to the best of my knowledge, I have never had an animal become frightened or run away because it spotted UV light reflected from my clothing. In fact, I have had, on many occasions, the opposite effects where deer APPROACH me. Over the years, I have done intensive in-field research with whitetails in the wild and at game farms. One such preserve, Davenport Game Farm, is a 250 acre enclosure deer research facility owned and managed by Stephen Novotny. While conducting my research it has been my experience that the overwhelming majority of the deer that I have "spooked" either in the wild or under controlled conditions, occurred from the deer either winding my scent or detecting my movement.

To support this point, think about your own hunting experiences. How many times have you had deer, or other game animals, very close to you while wearing "untreated" hunting clothing? What about the deer who stared you down, trying to decipher what it was looking at, and after many moments of staring, decided that what it saw was not a threat and either began to feed or calmly walked away undisturbed? If it detected a "glowing" would the deer have remained within the area? My point is, too many hunters have had too many of these exciting close encounters over the years to suggest that deer are frightened from possible problems from UV light being reflected from our clothing.

Other than eliminating human scent, camouflage has been the second most important factor in getting me closer to deer—undetected. I have harvested and videotaped bucks while they were staring directly at me, unable to decipher what they were looking at. Over the years, many of my hunting companions have told me of their experiences of deer coming within touching distance of them while wearing "untreated" camouflage clothing. All this "hard evidence" clearly indicates that the UV issue, related to deer hunting—is primarily designed to sell product.

So, to summarize, many seasoned outdoor professionals, biologists, scientists and plain every day hunters are skeptical about the subject of UV light and how it supposedly scares deer. Until there is more viable and conclusive evidence about how deer react to ultra violet light reflected from camo clothing and its affect on our hunting, there can be no emphatic statements made about the subject. The answer lies in trial and error and in documented long-term research conducted with deer.

I intend to continue hunting in "untreated" clothing, not because I want to continue to prove the UV theory wrong, but because I don't want to change my long-time winning formula. Until the time comes when ALL the facts and figures are gathered and carefully analyzed and evaluated, it seems to me and many other folks, that the UV reflection issue is mostly bogus. What is most important to re-member is a deer's eyes are designed (because it is an animal that is predated upon) to pick up the slightest movements. Keep that fact uppermost in your mind and you will not have to worry about UV!

The Ears

That brings us to the next sensory organ, the deer's ears. The whitetail's ears are quite sensitive and respond to unusual sounds immediately. Each ear has about 24 square inches of surface in which sounds are able to glance off of. They use their ears constantly in a radar-like swivel fashion to aid them in determining if anything unfamiliar is occurring in their surroundings and, to monitor the where-abouts and the behavior of other animals that share their domain, especially preda-tors. By closely observing how the whitetail holds its ears you will be able to tell what the deer is thinking and what it is about to do. I will cover this more in Chapter 10 on Body Language.

The Nose

Their sense of smell is their number one defense system. Each nostril is lined with epithelium, a membranous cellular tissue which is composed of mucous membranes and sensory nerve endings. Kept moist by the deer's tongue and the internal tissue itself, the epithelium of the nose can pick up odors much better. The nose also aids them in defining exactly who's who—individually—in the deer world. A whitetail also uses its nose not only to locate its food, but also to deter-mine if it is going to be palatable enough to eat. Of course, it is used ultimately to detect danger and to locate a receptive doe in estrus.

I believe—bar nothing—the deer's sense of smell is its key to survival and a hunter's key to success in bagging whitetails consistently. You will hear me repeat throughout this book a couple of phrases—The first and the one you should never forget and that you can "take to the Deer Hunting Bank," is this, "In order to be a consistently successful deer hunter, bust the bucks ability to use its nose against you, and you will bust the buck."

The amount of membranous cellular tissue which lines the nostrils found in man is about 1/8,000 of the skin's total surface. And, about 1/80 of the skin's total surface in deer which is the same as found in a dog. Obviously, because deer's nose has more epithelium membrane tissue than a human's (in proportion to total skin surface), it is much more capable of sensing the slightest of odors. Although deer can detect odors from as far away as ¾ of a mile or more, by the time the olfactory sensory organs pick up the scent, it is dispersed enough not to make a significant impact on the deer. Many biologists agree that a whitetail has to be no more than about 50 to 100 yards away from the source of a scent to react one way or the other. Of course, these figures are altered by wind currents to some degree.

The Stomach

As I have mentioned, the whitetail is a ruminant, which simply means it has a four-chambered stomach. Each of these chambers are shaped differently and have different linings. In addition, each compartment is capable of only holding a certain amount of food and serves a different and a specific function. The large paunch or compartment, which lies on top of the intestines, is the *rumen*. Its primary function is to store the deer's unchewed food. It holds about two gallons of material. The rumen allows the deer to quickly swallow the food it eats in large chunks. When a deer is eating it's head is down which does not allow for the deer to see as well. In this particular feeding position the deer is more vulnerable to predators. But being a ruminant, the deer can gather its food quickly and retreat to a safe area of cover. A useful and practical gift of the evolutionary process from Mother Nature. Once in a secure area the deer brings the food back up into its mouth again and chews it more thoroughly. This is known as cud-chewing. The rumen is a digestive or fermentation compartment of the stomach unique to ruminants. It acts as a holding area for unchewed food. Fatty acids then ferment the food which the deer regurgitates to chew and then re-swallows. The rumen consists of small papillae varying from ⅛ to ½ inch in length. Papillae look very similar to small lengths of spaghetti; there are 1600 papillae to the square inch.

The second compartment of the deer's stomach is known as the *reticulum*. It looks very similar to a honey comb. The reticulum forces liquid into the rumen deferring small food particles which are carried back to this compartment and then on to the third chamber called the *omasum*. The reticulum is about the size of a large orange.

The omasum primarily serves as a dehydrator. It removes excess water from the food. This section has about 45 to 50 flaps of different sizes which strain the food as it passes through. This is the compartment where digestion really begins to take place before moving on to the fourth compartment called the *abomasum*.

The abomasum secretes digestive enzymes and is the final area where digestion takes place for the deer. The abomasum is similar to the stomach of non-ruminants in that it is smooth and sleek. With about sixty to seventy feet of intestines. This is where all non-absorbed foods are then prepared to be passed out in the form of excrement—or deer dung. The entire digestive process can take about 24 to 36 hours for food to be eaten and then passed out as dung in an adult deer.

Other Body Information

This chapter would not be complete without the following statistical information and biological facts about the white-tailed deer that every dedicated deer hunter should know.

The Tail

On a Northern whitetail the overall tail length is about 12 inches from its rump to the end of its tail. When spread, the white hairs on the underside of the tail can reach 10 to 12 inches wide. When a doe holds her tail straight out and off to one side, she is visually signaling that she is now "ready" to accept the advances of an accompanying buck. Hunters who observe does exhibiting this type of tail flagging behavior should keep a keen eye open for a trailing buck. Seldom will a doe showing this "ready" tail signal have a buck far behind her! I use this behavior as a decoy tactic which I will explain more about in the decoy chapter.

The Hooves

The deer's feet are actually two extended toenails. The whitetail's prehistoric ancestors had five toes on each foot. Over time this proved to be disadvantageous for the deer. It hindered the deer's ability to run fast enough to escape their enemies. So once again, Mother Nature stepped in and through the process of evolution the other three toes changed. The first toe completely vanished. The other two slowly began to regress or atrophy. Today we see them as dewclaws. The two remaining toes have slowly developed into the two main toenails or hoofs that we see on the modern deer of today.

The whitetail's hoof has also evolved into a highly efficient "foot" for the firm type surfaces of woods, fields and the like. However, it is not very functional at all on ice surfaces like a frozen lake or pond. Once a deer falls on ice it may never be able to regain its footing. In fact, many deer have died from exhaustion after falling on ice and not being able to recover their balance quickly.

The deer's hoof is also used as a protective weapon. Both bucks and does use their hoofs to fend off predators. The deer stands on its hind legs and in an aggressive manner flails out its forelegs and strikes the intruder. The blow is powerful enough to crush the skull of a wolf, coyote or domestic dog. If the deer fails to connect with the head, just a glancing blow to the body could inflict a tearing deep wound to the flesh of its adversary. Does usually use this form of antagonistic behavior with other deer only when all other types of aggressive body language and vocalizations and the more docile foreleg kick have failed to get the desired results.

Much has been written and said about the deer's hooves. Some argue that a hunter can tell the difference between a buck and a doe by the size of its hooves, by its tracks, or by the distance between each track.

When it comes to trying to identify a buck from a doe by how deep the track is in the ground, the track's size and shape, or the distance left between tracks, remember this—information left by deer tracks is all relative! There are no absolutes or positives about what a hunter can or cannot tell from tracks. Not unless you see the deer who is in the tracks at the time. Here are some basic facts about hooves and the tracks they leave.

A deer's front hooves are usually larger than the rear hooves. Deer are also knock-kneed. This fact accounts for why the outside of the hoof is most often larger than the inside of the hoof on each foot. Deer are inclined to walk on the inside "lobe" or "toenail" more often, accounting for the unique angle we see when we look at tracks left by deer.

Much has also been written and argued about the size of a deer's tracks. Old timers as well as some so called "experts" emphatically state that a hunter can identify the sex of a deer by its tracks alone. I have never seen either prove their abilities to me about this subject with any consistent success. They go on to say that a buck will leave deeper, wider tracks, that the buck track will have a rounded hoof, and that the angle of the track also is specific to whether it was left by a buck or doe. At the risk of sounding righteous, this is pure nonsense. The only absolute way—notice I said absolute—to determine whether a buck or doe left a particular track is to see the deer standing in the track itself. Take that fact to the Deer Hunting Bank!

Many mature older does can attain large body weights, especially in states where does are protected during hunting season. These old females leave deep tracks with rounded lobes that are often associated with buck tracks. Remember, throughout the country, most bucks, a majority in fact, are shot before they reach 2½ years of age. Most does are much older than that before they are shot—if they are even hunted at all. In my home state of New York, does that reside within the Northern Region of our state are protected from hunting because the population density in this region has been traditionally lower than the western or southern portions of the state. Does of the Northern region often reach live weights of 140 to 170 pounds.

It is "OK" to speculate about a track belonging to a buck as long as you are practical about it and remember that it is only a conjecture at best. That way after you have followed a "buck" track for miles over hill and dale for 8 hours and it turns out when you catch up with the deer as its making the tracks you are following, it turns out to be a doe—you are more than ready to accept the misjudgment you made without frustration.

One of the only half-way reliable track indications that I know of is usually visible after a light snowfall of one to two inches. In this instance, the buck's hoof tracks are accompanied by a drag mark of several inches. Traditionally, a doe will pick up its feet clear of the snow and leave just the hoof track itself. A point to remember, especially for novices—button bucks, spikes, and mature bucks all leave drag marks. Size of the track becomes an important factor here. If you follow a track with a drag mark, thinking you have definitely found an antlered buck, you may discover you've been following a button buck or a yearling spike—which may not be the buck you hoped he was going to be regarding the size of his antlers.

After hunting whitetails for 31 years I can tell you that if you absolutely depend on a track to indicate the sex of the deer that left it—you're making your deer hunting more difficult than it has to be. And, you are not hunting with good ol' common sense on your side. Common sense is a major relevant factor to consistent deer hunting success!

One other fact about this subject. A whitetail's walking stride which is calculated at a steady walk of about 3½ to 4 miles per hour (which is just a little faster than man's) is 18 to 19 inches. Their trotting gait which is a speed of about 10 to 12 m.p.h. is 30 to 36 inches.

The Coat

A whitetail's coat comes in many different shades and in a few instances even different color phases. Different shades of the coat are mostly dependent upon in what section of the country the whitetail lives. Changes in their primary color such as **melanism** (all black), **piebalds** (patches of white and brown or all-white with brown eyes), or **albinism** (all white with pink eyes) are hereditary. In general, the overall color of a deer's average coat is made up of black, a few different shades of brown and white hairs.

The deer's coat is an evolutionary thermoregulatory marvel. In summer the whitetail's coat is reddish in color and is made up of solid, straight, thin hairs with no undercoat. Although the thin coat helps to keep the deer cool during the heat of summer, the downside is the thinness of the coat offers little protection from insects allowing the pests to easily bite through it. Interestingly, however, the summer coat of a whitetail is compiled with more hairs per square inch than a winter coat.

To the contrary, the hair of the winter undercoat is soft, thin and kinky. The upper coat is hollow, longer and thicker, with each hollow hair filled with air cells. Offering the whitetail two layers of superb insulation. Confirmation of just how good the winter coat insulates the deer can be found by watching a deer during a snow storm or on a frosty morning. In each case the deer's coat will not melt the frost or snow that has accumulated on its back. Verifying how little body heat the whitetail actually loses through the top of its coat.

Any hunter who has ever seen where a deer has previously bedded down in the snow can attest to the fact the snow in the bed has melted. It does so because any heat that has escaped is trapped by the snow beneath the animal and the earth. However, snow falling on any other part of the upper body will not melt as long as the deer keeps the hair standing on end. When the hair is laid flat against the body, snow will melt rapidly on the deer. Interestingly, the hair on the front of the chest (brisket) points forward while all other hair on a whitetail is directed back or down.

It is also important for hunters to know that on different sections of the whitetail's body, the hair is of different color and texture. I have used this hair color and texture information many times in determining exactly where I shot a whitetail that ran off—especially when I am bowhunting.

The color, or colors of the hair will give insight to what part of the body it came from. For instance, hair falling from the lung area will be coarse, brown and it will not have black tips. Hair from around the kidney area will be long, dark and brown, and sometimes it will have black tips. Knowing how to identify what hairs come from what portions of a deer's body is critical when tracking wounded deer.

Through hair identification, you can determine more accurately just about where on the body you hit the deer. This will also give you a clue to what type of blood trail to expect and how long to wait—or not to wait—before going after the animal. It should also give you a good idea about how far the deer should travel before expiring from its wound. All very important information in the recovery of deer which run off after being shot—especially for archers.

3 48 Little-Known Facts About Whitetails

These unusual scientific facts about America's favorite big-game animal not only are intriguing but may help you fill a tag, too.

1. A mature whitetail buck makes an average of 225 antler rubs on saplings every fall.

2. Fawns are born completely odorless, which for the first month of life is their major defense against predation.

3. Deer are ruminants, possessing four-chambered stomachs. This enables them to feed without much chewing so that they can quickly return to the safety of heavy-cover bedding areas. There, the animals can regurgitate the food for further mastication.

4. Using radio-telemetry equipment, biologists have determined that east of the Mississippi, a whitetail buck's home range is 2½ square miles and oval shaped. West of the Mississippi, in those regions where there are wide expanses of open ground separating the cover configurations, home ranges may be as large as 7 square miles.

5. In a nationwide study of whitetail stomach contents, it was determined that the animals regularly feed upon 614 different varieties of plants.

6. Not only is venison delicious, but nutritionists have found that it's higher in protein and lower in fat and cholesterol than any domestic meats.

7. The hollow hairs comprising a deer's winter coat are equal in their insulating qualities to the most sophisticated high-tech fibers mankind has ever developed.

8. Bucks restrict their movements in spring and early summer because their rapidly growing antlers are rubbery, tender, and very susceptible to damage.

9. Just because you find occasional piles of deer pellets when you're scouting doesn't mean there are plenty of deer in your area. Scientists tell us that a whitetail defecates an average of 13 times every 24 hours.

10. The "Minnesota Giant" taken by James Rath in 1977 is one of the country's rarest trophy whitetails because it made the Boone & Crockett record book in both the typical and nontypical categories, scoring 199 6/8 and 231 2/8, respectively.

11. There are more than 30 known subspecies of whitetails in North and Central America, all of which are believed to have evolved from the "type" species. This primary strain is the Virginia whitetail (*Odocoileus virginianus*).

12. No one knows why, but studies have shown that deer respond most frequently to grunt calls and antler rattling when doing so means that they must travel uphill or at least remain on level ground. They seldom respond if it'll require downhill travel.

13. Ninety percent of all antler rubs are made on aromatic or resinous tree species, such as cedar, pine, spruce, shining sumac, cherry, dogwood, or sassafras. The reason is that the oily cambiums of these species will retain the buck's forehead-gland scent for longer periods of time, even during inclement weather.

14. Research by Georgia deer biologist Larry Marchington has revealed that during a given year, a buck will make from 69 to 538 antler rubs on trees, with a mature buck averaging 300.

15. Deer possess a supranuclei ganglion—also known as an internal sleep clock—in their brains. The mechanism allows them to fall into restful sleep just as humans can. But unlike humans, deer can spring into total alertness in only a third of a second.

16. The size of a scrape is a reliable indicator of the size and age of the buck that created it. Mature bucks paw scrapes that are minimally 18 inches in diameter, and sometimes up to 4 feet.

17. Deer are excellent swimmers and will not hesitate to cross rivers or lakes any more than you'd hesitate to cross a street.

18. The greatest deer-research breakthrough in the past 25 years may be the finding that deer are not limited to black-and-white vision but can see a wide range of colors, including ultraviolet light, which is invisible to humans.

19. By the conclusion of the rut, an average mature buck will have lost as much as 25 percent of his body weight.

20. Radio-tracking studies have shown that the largest bucks make the largest antler rubs on trees, and they begin engaging in their rubbing behavior a full month before younger bucks do. *Tip:* Find the big, early rubs and you'll have found your trophy.

21. The widest record-book buck rack ever taken is known as "Big Red." Taken in Kentucky in 1982 by Denis Nolen, the rack scores only 172 4/8 but has an incredible 37½-inch outside spread.

22. Hunters who are skeptical about the effectiveness of deer calls should consider that biologists using sophisticated audio recording equipment have identified 15 distinct vocalizations that whitetails make to communicate with each other.

23. For generations, hunters believed cold air temperatures triggered the rut. We now know it's shorter day length and reduced amounts of sunlight entering the eye that cause changes in a deer's endocrine system, spurring the onset of breeding.

24. Many hunters have long wondered why they've never found shed antler velvet in the woodlands. The reason is that bucks eat most of it; what remains on the ground quickly disintegrates. Biologists studying penned deer commonly observe this behavior but have no explanation for it.

25. The largest body weight ever achieved by a whitetail is 511 pounds, by a Minnesota deer taken in 1976. This is followed by deer of 491 pounds and 481 pounds from Wisconsin in 1980.

26. Laboratory studies of deer suggest their sense of smell is at least 10 times more acute than that of a human, and that they are able to separate and analyze seven different odors simultaneously.

27. Can you examine a pile of deer pellets and learn anything from them? Yes! The largest individual pellets are most likely from a buck, because mature bucks are larger in anatomical body size than mature does. Moreover, New Jersey biologist C. J. Winand's research has revealed that a mature buck will leave a pile of 75 pellets or more.

28. When looking at distant objects, the human eye uses binocular vision while the whitetail eye uses wide-angle vision. This is why we are less adept at spotting movement around the periphery of our visual scope than deer are.

29. When running, does are far more likely than bucks to "flag" with their tails. This behavior enables the doe's offspring to follow their mothers in dim light or when the mother is fleeing through cover.

30. Eons ago, when North America was largely swampy, deer walked flat-footed with five toes. As the habitat dried, the deer evolved. One toe disappeared entirely, two toes migrated to the rear and became dew claws, and the remaining two toes hardened and became pointed into hooves.

31. When making rubs, mature bucks deposit priming pheromones from their forehead glands. These pheromones induce late-estrus does into coming into heat and also chemically intimidate younger bucks into submission so they are less inclined to attempt to breed.

32. In bitter-cold weather, deer feed heavily upon staghorn sumac. They instinctively know that this plant is higher in fat than any other native food and thus helps generate body heat.

33. Deer have a so-called odor comfort zone of 300 yards. Beyond this distance, foreign odors are not likely to alert or alarm them, because the scent molecules comprising that odor have become diluted and are no longer capable of triggering the chemoreceptors of the animals' olfactory system.

34. A whitetail's tarsal glands carry its unique "signature," just as fingerprints do among humans. A doe released into a pen with 50 fawns can thus instantly find the one that's hers.

35. Vermont biologist Wayne LaRoche's research has revealed that the width of a deer track—not its length—is the most reliable indicator of the animal's age. The reason is that because a deer's body weight steadily increases with age, the animal requires a progressively wider base platform to support that weight.

36. A doe is able to sniff a scrape, chemically analyze the tarsal scent left there by the buck that made it, and then evaluate the health and virility of the animal to determine if he would be a worthy sire.

37. A lone bed measuring 45 to 50 inches in length is most likely that of a big buck. If the bed you find barely reaches 45 inches and is accompanied by one or two smaller ones, it's undoubtedly that of a doe with offspring.

38. Studies of penned deer have shown that they have an attention span of about three minutes, after which they forget whatever alerted them. Consequently, if you snap a twig while stillhunting, stop and remain motionless for at least three minutes before you take another step.

39. Immature bucks commonly check their scrapes by walking right up to them. Mature bucks normally scent-check their scrapes from 30 to 50 yards downwind while remaining in thick cover.

40. Although a whitetail's home range may span several square miles or more, radio-tracking studies indicate that mature bucks have a core area of approximately 40 acres where they spend up to 90 percent of their time.

41. A scrape is always found near a low, overhanging tree branch that has been chewed and broken by the buck that made the scrape. The buck deposits saliva and forehead-gland scent on the branch to pass along olfactory information telling other deer that this is his breeding area.

42. The reason hunters commonly find pairs of shed antlers near each other is not because they naturally dropped at the same time. Rather, when one antler falls, the imbalance created by the remaining antler annoys the deer so much that he kicks at it with a hind foot, or knocks it against tree trunks, to dislodge it.

43. Whitetails are relatively immune to bitter-cold weather. The species lives as far north as the 59th parallel (which cuts across northern Manitoba and Saskatchewan), where the winter temperatures commonly plummet to −60°F.

44. Unknowledgeable hunters often mistakenly refer to deer antlers as "horns." Horns remain with an animal for its entire life, as in the case of pronghorn antelope. Antlers are shed every year.

45. Whitetails have a vomeronasal organ in the roof of the mouth, which allows them to "taste" odors detected by the nose. After this chemical analysis is performed, the information is then transmitted to the brain for deciphering.

46. The smallest whitetail inhabiting North America is the Key deer (*O.v. clavium*), a protected species that lives in southernmost Florida. A mature adult stands only 22 inches tall and weighs 45 to 65 pounds, about half the size of a Labrador retriever.

47. Radio-telemetry research has revealed that, in a whitetail buck's home range, he will lay down his scrapes in a star configuration, with one scrape line having a north-south axis that intersects with a second scrape line having an east-west axis.

48. When a doe enters estrus just prior to breeding, she chases away her buck and doe yearling fawns. After breeding, any doe fawns are permitted to rejoin her, but the young buck is now on his own, searching for his own home range elsewhere. This is nature's way of preventing inbreeding among family members the following fall.

4   They Are Where They Eat

BY JEFF MURRAY

A whitetail deer travels on its stomach—it's got no other choice. That's why a solid food source strategy can't be beat whether it's bow or gun season.

W hat aspect of whitetail anatomy impacts deer hunting the most? Chances are you've got sex on the brain. After all, hunting rutting bucks is one of the most discussed strategies in whitetaildom. While the results can be eye-popping, I believe hunters would see more consistent results throughout the season—and over the years—by focusing elsewhere. Recent research on the heart rate of whitetails indicates that a deer's biggest weakness is probably its stomach. And here's a dandy contradiction: A deer's stomach is also the main reason why so many hunters experience so few daylight opportunities.

This irony is best explained by the fact that a deer's heart pumps less while at rest, enabling researchers to determine exactly how much time the animals are active and inactive. Cornell University's Dr. Aaron Moen discovered that the typical whitetail spends more than two-thirds of its life—approximately 70 percent—bedded down. You do the math: Deer are up and moving only about 10 to 15 percent of the time during daylight hours.

The implication is that to see more deer, hunters need to know where deer are most likely to be feeding throughout the season. But before we can make this connection and incorporate it into meaningful strategies, we need to know more about how a deer's stomach functions.

"A deer's stomach pretty much dictates a predominately sedentary lifestyle," says Todd Stittleburg, an animal nutritionist whose life passion is studying whitetail diets. "It's kind of ironic, considering the graceful, bounding image we typically associate with whitetails. But in reality, a deer's daily routine essentially revolves around feeding and bedding with not much action in between."

The main reason for this is that a deer is a prey species. As such, the animal's digestive system is designed to reduce exposure to predation. While a deer's stomach is as important as its nose for avoiding danger, astute hunters have learned to turn these strengths into weakness. One key to unlocking this weakness is understanding how deer process food.

Deer are broth browsers of fibrous stems and branches and grazing ruminants (like cattle). A four-part stomach (rumen, reticulum, omasum, abomasum) allows whitetails to digest and metabolize foods that many other animals can't.

27

Food—from forbs to fruit, from legumes to tree limbs—is consumed so rapidly that it's practically swallowed whole. Then it's stored in the rumen, the stomach's largest chamber. Once the rumen is filled to capacity, the animal beds down and "chews its cud" over the next eight to 10 hours.

As the nutriments are regurgitated, remasticated and reswallowed, microbial breakdown is promoted by moving food back and forth from the rumen to the reticulum. It's the microbes living in a deer' stomach that keep it alive; however if a deer doesn't feed regularly, the microbes will die, thus making a deer a virtual slave to its stomach.

Incidentally, by applying slight pressure to its sternum, a prone position helps a deer to regurgitate its food. So deer "lie around" twice as much as humans because of their digestive system and not because of muscle fatigue. In other words, deer must bed down or they can't "process" vital nutrients from their food; interrupting this natural process can be life-threatening.

In fact, a satiated deer deprived of the opportunity of chewing its cud is courting death, as enterprising Ukrainian deer hunters in the mid-Canadian provinces of Saskatchewan and Manitoba have discovered. After locating a mature buck feeding in a wheat or oat field, a Canuck hunter intentionally allows the animal to fill its stomach for a half-hour or so. Then the chase is on. Once on the track, the hunter doesn't stop for a second, not even for a quick cup of coffee. As often as not, by the end of the day he gets his buck.

What Deer Really Prefer

That whitetails dine on a seemingly endless list of forbs, stems, nuts, flowers, fruits and grains is legend (about 2,000 plant species have been documented in the rumen of whitetails). Equally alarming is how deer often target a single food source to the exclusion of all others, then switch seemingly overnight. As complicated as this all may seem, we can break it down into a simple hunting principle, thanks to a food preference study conducted at the Auburn Deer Research Facility by Mssrs. Waer, Stribling and Causey. The absolute bottom line, the researchers concluded, is that deer prefer "rapidly growing plants that are at their highest in crude protein and lowest in fiber." Controlled feeding experiments revealed that:

- During the cool season, small grains—such as ryegrass, oats, wheat and barley—were preferred.
- Crimson clover was chosen when it was most lush, followed by ladino clovers when their peak growth occurred later on.
- Deer spent about the same amount of time feeding on carefully planted forages (including those mentioned above) as they did on volunteer "weeds" such as blackberry, evening primrose and bahiagrass.

In a practical way, deer are very much like humans: we both like variety. Which is good because it ensures a balanced diet providing our nutritional needs.

Additional research reveals a second principle governing whitetail food sources: Deer tend to choose a food source based on the food's relative convenience as much as its nutritional value and its taste. Toss this variable into the whitetail salad, and we come up with another hunting strategy that relatively few hunters know about. Specifically, all deer foods can be segregated into primary and secondary sources. This, you're about to see, drastically affects hunting locations.

Security Food vs. Nocturnal Food

When researchers talk about a food's convenience, the net effect is that what deer eat during the day and what they consume after dark is rarely the same. Think back to the whitetail's basic survival instinct of predator avoidance, and ask yourself where's the safest place for a whitetail to be after dark. The answer is out in the open (where a deer can use its superior light-gathering vision) and preferably in low-lying pockets (where scent settles and a deer can use its nose to full advantage). It just so happens that this is where lush vegetation is most prolific, thanks to a generous supply of direct sunlight. Consequently, deer typically feed on primary food sources after dark.

Conversely, the safest place for a deer during daylight hours is just the opposite—within heavy cover (deer actually experience a visual disadvantage in bright light) and at higher elevations (where scent rises during the day). This location favors secondary food sources that are usually lower in crude protein—primarily browse with some nuts, berries and forbs—that grow in shady areas where photosynthesis is reduced. As a result, deer feed on essentially two types of food sources in two distinct places during any given 24-hour period. And the hunter understanding this key distinction is well ahead of the pack.

Primary Food Sources

If you wish to intercept deer on the way to, or coming from, primary food sources high in protein, you need some assurance that deer will feel comfortable visiting these areas during shooting light. That's a tall order in many areas of the country. Here are some parameters.

- Remote fields are a good starting point. Once deer are disturbed near a food plot or open cropland, they instinctively hold back till the wrap of darkness.
- Fresh droppings—pasty green as opposed to dried brown—indicate current visitations. An absence of fresh droppings, however, is a telltale sign that deer have probably switched food preferences and are feeding at a different location.
- Natural forest openings located near food plots and croplands increase deer visitations because of the added variety of plant species. (Remember the study showing deer feeding alternately on "weeds.")
- The availability of nearby water—drainages, creekbottoms, even stock dams and farm ponds—enhances the value of an open source. The extra daylight increases evaporation, which, in turn, accelerates dehydration of deer.

Another important component of a primary food source is its layout. Some are simply more huntable than others. Over the years, for example, I've been most successful hunting T-shaped fields. In hindsight, I think it's because this configuration tends to corral deer predictably into closer quarters. Additionally, smaller strips with irregular tree lines tend to be more productive than larger rectangular-shaped fields with woods edges that are straight as an arrow. If you think like a deer, the reason is simple. A field formation with lots of corners and pockets is a lot safer during daylight hours.

Finally, incorporate staging areas into every primary food source hunt. In spite of the above conditions, mature bucks often refuse to expose themselves in the open till it's too dark to hunt. But these same bucks also like to vacate the thickets before twilight, because they know darkness and thick cover are not a good match. Reclusive staging areas—where the terrain is neither open nor thick, neither wooded nor grassy—is a very special place indeed. Here, bucks can dine in waist-high cover that's both secure and fairly nutritious.

Identifying staging areas is a simple three-fold process. First and foremost, look for areas meeting the above description situated between security cover and the open food source. Second, double-check for fresh droppings (the better areas will also be marked up with rubs). And third, if bucks are visiting them often, there should be a few trails (although bucks do not travel trails to the degree does do, making an abundance of large tracks a solid clue).

Secondary Food Sources

Like most deer hunters, I would rather set up near a field than in the middle of the woods; fields are easier to hunt and easier to access. But reality dictates that if I want to see more bucks I better be hunting some sort of cover. Why not boost the odds by hunting cover that also provides a nutritious diet? Here are some options:

- In the North, aspen shoots are hard to beat. The late Gordon Gullion, nationally renowned grouse researcher, discovered that certain aspen leaves contain a remarkably high phenol content that allows them to stay "green" long after hard frosts. While the rest of the forest has withered and wilted, aspen "suckers" (shoots springing up from one- to three-year-old slashings) still hold their leaves. Every deer in the immediate vicinity knows this and will make this a part of its diet in mid- to late-October. Keep in contact with private logging companies and forestry officials to find out what's been cut, when and where. Where hunting pressure might be a concern, zero in on the tracts with the most difficult access.

- In the Midwest and some mid-Atlantic states, greenbrier is a dependable deer food in the transitional month of October. Deer like greenbrier so much, in fact, that they often form trails within the patches. You'll know when you've found a honeyhole if some of the greenbrier branches fork at the end—evidence of browsing in previous years. You might have to get down on all fours to find clues to browsing activity, however, because deer often nip these vine-like branches right to the ground.

- In the South, the key is likely to be honeysuckle. This vine grows in the oddest of places, and deer visit these thickets year after year. And why not? They've got food, comfort and safety all in one neat package. Contact a Soil Conservation extension field agent about this deer favorite.
- Texas is a land with its own deer laws. Granjeo, prickly pear and persimmon especially rule in some parts of the Lone Star State. According to Bob Zaiglin, biologist and deer management consultant, Granjeno is 21% crude protein. Some bushy varieties (such as lime prickly ash, an aromatic, thorny bush) also provide shade in hot, semi-arid regions. Talk about a comfortable, nutritious bedding area! Prickly pear (cactus) also offers cover and food. Some bucks even return up to the same pear flats year after year, so it pays to plot their whereabouts.

The game of intercepting deer will always be a game of chance. But because deer have to eat every single day, knowing where they're most likely to be dining out can tip the odds your way. In fact, you can bet on it.

5 Why Deer Move When They Do

BY CHARLES J. ALSHEIMER

Is deer movement a mystery to you? Time has come to shed some light on the puzzle.

Hunters are forever asking me what I think is the most important ingredient in whitetail hunting. Without fail my answer surprises them when I say understanding the environmental factors that go into the whitetail's world. I quickly follow up by telling them why I feel weather, temperature, barometric pressure and lunar phases rate as high as scents, scrape hunting or rattling.

Down through the years I've come to realize that understanding how various environmental factors influence whitetails can mean the difference between success and failure in the deer woods. I'll even say that once a deer hunter understands the various hunting techniques, his application of them to various environmental factors will be a key to success.

Let me set the stage for what follows by offering an example of how environmental factors can effect whitetail movement. A few years ago, cool temperatures coincided with the peak of the whitetail's chase phase of the rut here in western New York. Things kicked in as expected with great buck movement. For two straight days the sky was clear, with temperatures ranging from 25 degrees in the morning to a high of 45 degrees during the day. It was a bowhunter's dream. Then with no ominous storm front approaching, the temperature rose, ranging from 45 degrees in the morning to low 80s during midday. For the three days this lasted, deer activity was nearly nonexistent. Obviously the rise in temperature caused the whitetail shut down. More specifically, the cause of what took place was the whitetail's inability to function in such warm conditions. Their thick winter fur made life intolerable for them.

Biology

In order to understand why whitetails move as they do during the autumn months it's important to take a look at how they are physically equipped for this period of time. For a whitetail, photoperiodism is a marvelous phenomenon. As winter fades and spring approaches, all whitetails begin shedding their thick winter fur. In its place grows a thin coat of hair that allows deer to survive the swelter-ing summer heat. If you were to view this fur change from close quarters you'd be able to see that when the summer fur grows in you can actually see the skin of a whitetail and in most cases there is no hair at all on a whitetail's ears during this time.

As the days of summer grow shorter and July eases into August, the first signs of thicker hair can be seen on northern whitetails as the photoperiod causes the winter coat to begin growing. By late October, a whitetail's winter parka will be complete and in the north it enables whitetails to withstand the arctic blasts of the harsh northern winters. In the whitetail's southern range the process is very similar but the fur is not as long or as thick.

Unlike humans, who have a fine-tuned network of sweat glands to help cool the body when a heat-up occurs, whitetails must cope other ways. Without sweat glands as we know them, whitetails cool down by venting through their mouth or by being inactive, with the latter being the primary means. For this reason, a whitetail's "fur factor" dictates under what conditions they move.

After years of intensive study, it's my feeling that four interrelated factors: air temperature, barometric pressure, weather patterns, and lunar phase have the great-est cause and effect on whitetail movement. When the fur factor is added into the mix, how a whitetail moves or doesn't move becomes very interesting.

Temperature

Of the four factors I've listed, temperature has perhaps the most powerful in-fluence on deer movement. Certainly the other factors work in concert with tem-perature, and may sometimes override temperature's influence on deer movement. But unless the temperature matches a whitetail's comfort zone, movement gener-ally will not happen, at least not during hunting season. To experience optimal deer activity during northern deer seasons, at approximately the 40th–50th lati-tude, I've found that daytime air temperatures should not exceed 55 degrees. On the other hand there is a low end to a whitetail's comfort zone. At the same lati-tude, temperatures below 20 degrees will generally curtail activity, unless the rut is full blown. An exception to these figures would be if there have been several days of extreme heat or cold. Then any snap of as little as 10 degrees cooler or warmer, respectively, will be enough to trigger movement. But as a rule I've found that the most deer activity will occur when the temperature falls in this range in the north. The south is a different story.

In places like Texas, where exists a different subspecies, deer operate under an entirely different comfort zone. It's not uncommon to see good deer movement in the south Texas brush country when temperatures are in the 80s, providing the rut is on and a storm isn't raging. Whitetails in this environment have much shorter hair and can tolerate the heat much better.

Far northern whitetails in the bush of Canada (at the 52nd latitude) seem to have a comfort zone of about 10 to 15 degrees different than whitetails found in the United States. Several years of hunting big Saskatchewan whitetails has shown me that their comfort zone ranges from about 10 to 45 degrees during the month of November.

Once the mercury rises above or below a whitetail's comfort zone, deer will generally shut down and move little on their own unless a storm front is approaching. A hunter would do well to find out what normal temperatures are for the area being hunted. Armed with this information it's easier to plan hunting strategies.

Barometric Pressure

Study after study has shown that a rapidly falling or rising barometric pressure triggers increased deer movement. And when the moving barometer (especially falling during autumn months) coincides with temperatures in the whitetail's comfort zone, the number of deer sightings increases dramatically.

A scientific study from White-tailed Deer: *Ecology and Management* illustrates the point well. "In the mountains of North Carolina, Barick (1952) was able to increase trapping success greatly by setting deer traps when the barometer was falling, with a forecast of rain or snow within 24 hours. On one area he caught 68 deer in four nights by trapping ahead of the storm fronts, compared with only 65 deer captured in a 10-week period the previous year."

Certainly there is enough evidence to justify why hunting is great when barometric pressures are dropping rapidly. However, there is much to be said for what occurs after. Once the storm arrives deer are generally inactive, regardless of whether the air temperature is in their comfort zone. Whitetails move when they feel they have an advantage so when hard rain is falling, high winds are gusting or a heavy snowfall is in progress very few whitetails will be out and about.

However, once the storm ends and the barometer begins rising, deer activity will increase dramatically, providing air temperatures match the whitetail's comfort zone. A number of studies have been done regarding the effects of barometric pressure on whitetail activity. One done by Illinois biologist Keith Thomas found that the highest whitetail feeding took place when the barometric pressure was between 29.80 and 30.29. The point to remember here is that when the barometer is falling or rising through this range, deer activity should be the greatest. So, be a weather watcher to ensure you have the upper hand.

Weather

With knowledge of how a whitetail's thick winter fur dictates a deer's willingness to move, it's wise to become a student of barometric readings and the weather. When the barometer is rising or falling, try to determine what kind of weather is coming. If you can master this, or at least get a feel for what's in the offing, you'll have a better handle on how to plan your hunt.

During the course of a year, weather causes all kinds of disruptions, and frenzies, in the way whitetails feed and move. Knowing this has made me more and more of a weather watcher during the last 15 years, especially during deer season. I live in the East, and due to prevailing weather patterns, the Midwest and upper

Midwest weather takes about 18 to 30 hours to reach our area. So, during the deer season I make it a point to watch the weather to the west so I'll know what kind of weather is approaching. I also watch the barometer to see if it is falling as the front moves closer.

An example of what takes place when the barometer falls rapidly and a weather front moves in can be illustrated from one of my recent deer seasons. After a flurry of deer activity early in the shotgun season, sightings had become fewer and fewer as the last week of the season arrived. The last Monday of the season was pretty much a repeat of the previous 10 days with little activity. On Tuesday afternoon, the temperature dropped and snow began falling. With it came high winds, making hunting difficult. Rather than brave the elements I decided to sit out the storm.

The next morning dawned clear and cold, with two inches of fresh snow on the ground—perfect for deer hunting. I decided to take a stand near a well-used stream crossing. I wasn't in my blind long enough to chill down before I heard snow crunching on the other side of the stream. I brought my gun to my shoulder and waited. In single file a doe and two fawns crossed the stream, walked past my stand and out of sight. Within 20 minutes, two more does and a spike buck followed their trail. I decided to pass on the spike buck hoping something bigger would come by.

For the next hour the woods became quieter as only chipmunks and gray squirrels moved about. As the sun rose, the freshly fallen snow began to melt. Behind me I heard a twig snap in the direction the does, fawns, and spike buck had gone an hour before. At first I wasn't sure what was coming but through the snow-laden branches I began picking up patches of brown. I brought the shotgun to my shoulder and peered through the scope. Five does and fawns and what appeared to be the spike buck I passed up were feeding back past me.

Just as the group was about to go out of sight, I picked up more movement. Another deer was trailing them. In one motion I threw my gun to my shoulder and scoped the deer. Sun reflected off antler tines and immediately I knew the buck was worth shooting. As he passed by 30 yards from me, I clicked off the safety and pulled the trigger. At the 12 gauge's roar, the buck jumped and ran 20 yards before falling within view.

As I sat in the woods admiring the buck, I reflected on all the deer movement I had seen in the first 2½ hours that morning. It was obvious that the sudden change in weather had caused all the movement, for there were no other hunters in the woods.

It's important for the hunter to realize that it is not the sudden drop in temperature that often accompanies these fronts that causes whitetails to head for the thickest cover. Rather, it's the unsettled weather associated with the leading edge of the low-pressure front that causes movement, with the greatest movement occurring if the barometric pressure drops rapidly. With few exceptions, little deer movement will occur once the front arrives. Then, as the front passes through and the weather returns to normal, whitetails and other wildlife start to move again in search of food.

When the front finally moves on and it clears off, deer hunters will almost always find some of their best hunting. If a hunter is in the woods within a few hours of the front moving out of an area, the hunting can be fantastic.

Lunar Phase

With each passing year, hunters and researchers are learning more and more about the moon's effect on whitetail movement. It's been my experience that when a full moon is rising at the same time as the sun is setting (and visa versa), deer activity will be above normal, providing temperature is in the normal range and storm conditions do not exist.

Since 1995, Vermont researcher Wayne Laroche and I have been involved in a lunar research project dealing with how the moon relates to whitetail breeding dates. (See separate story.) Our findings have shown that the second full moon after the autumn equinox (this equinox occurs approximately September 23rd each year) triggers the whitetail rut in the North. Basically what happens is when this moon, which I call the Hunter's Moon, shines full the seeking/chase phase of the whitetail rut swings into action. Then about seven days after the Hunter's Moon, the primary breeding takes place, with the breeding window lasting about 14 days. In 1998, over 75% of our research does bred right on schedule, just as we predicted. The beauty of this kind of information is that hunters can look at the calendar and predict when every aspect of the rut will occur.

The environment's impact on the whitetail is immense. I'm convinced that if more whitetail hunters studied environmental factors as much as they do the various hunting techniques success rates would be much higher than they are. Mastering the various techniques associated with whitetail hunting is a challenge but one thing is certain: knowing how to hunt in whatever Mother Nature throws at you can add precious memories to the hunting experience.

6   Predicting Deer Movement: Some Surprises from Science

BY JOHN WEISS

New deer science has revealed the times when deer move the most! And it's not when you thought—matter of fact, it's at different times in different parts of the season!

South Carolina's Francis Marion National Forest offered up one of my biggest bucks, more years ago than I can remember. Yet that day, which turned out so happy, certainly didn't begin that way.

I'd picked a prime location for my portable stand overlooking a trail intersection deep within a black oak swamp and planned to begin my vigil one hour before daybreak. Yet the following morning, bright sunlight glinting through my motel room window brought me to an abrupt sitting position. My alarm clock hadn't gone off and, mother of all horrors, it was nine o'clock!

As it happened, by the time I showered, dressed, packed my truck and made the long drive to the forest, I didn't arrive at my stand location until almost noon. Understandably, I didn't expect to see a thing, rationalizing that at least I had arrived plenty early enough for the evening watch.

However, only 30 minutes later I heard a rustling in the leaves and very s-l-o-w-l-y turned around in my seat. Not more than 30 yards away an impressive eight-pointer was methodically pawing through the ground litter in search of acorns. Moments later, when I saw my arrow fletching bury itself just behind the deer's shoulder, the warhoop that rang through the woodlands must have sounded like an Apache on the warpath. I knew the deer, although still on his feet, would quickly go down and, sure enough, he fell into his tracks just a short distance away.

Learning a New Language

As pleased as I was with how the day had made an unexpected turn-around, that experience caused me to begin seriously questioning a lot of my previous beliefs. Aren't whitetails, especially mature bucks, supposed to be bedded during midday?

Well, recent scientific evidence has revealed that mature bucks, even those subjected to hunting pressure, are not as nocturnal as most hunters believe. In biological parlance, nocturnal means strictly night-oriented. Bats are nocturnal creatures, for example.

The opposite of this are creatures that exhibit diurnal lifestyles, in that they are exclusively day-oriented such as quail and turkeys.

Deer, on the other hand, are classified as being polyphasic. Poly means "many" and phasic means reoccurring over and over again. Polyphasic therefore means deer may be up and around at any hour of the day or night, depending upon weather conditions, mating urges, and a host of other variables. This knowledge diminishes the idea that hunting success hinges upon being on stand either at the crack of dawn or later in the day at evening dusk. Actually, hunters can and should expect to encounter deer engaging in travel, feeding, and other normal activities almost any time.

Bedding, for example, is not something all deer engage in at the same time, or is it exclusively a midday activity; rather, it's done on a whim, whenever individual deer or small groups of deer so choose.

There are, however, certain times that reveal higher deer activity levels than others, but they are not during the hours of dawn and dusk. In recent months, biologists have pegged some of these times through what is called "diel-period tracking."

This study method involves live-trapping deer, outfitting them with radio transmitter collars, then releasing them and using the signals from the radios to plot their activities around the clock. In other cases, deer may be held captive in large fenced enclosures—several square miles—and their activities and travel patterns monitored by both radio tracking and visual sightings.

By keeping tabs on the deer 24 hours a day, often for several months at a time, researchers are able to learn plenty about their behavior throughout the year.

Change Is the Only Constant

One major breakthrough is that whitetails have been found to exhibit entirely different travel and feeding patterns during the warm-weather months than later in the year.

In the spring and summer, whitetails are crepuscular, meaning their activity levels are highest during the twilight hours of dawn and dusk. Since the average daily air temperatures during these months may range from mild to searing hot, it's simply more to a deer's liking to idle away the midday hours sequestered in shaded cover or along breeze-filtered ridges where there is some respite from tormenting insects.

Yet about the time fall hunting seasons begin to open, deer begin showing a reversal in their behavior patterns. The very early and late hours of each day are cool and, to conserve energy, deer begin feeding and traveling later each morning and cease traveling earlier each afternoon.

By the time midwinter approaches, with the onslaught of frequent polar blasts assaulting states north and south alike, whitetails begin concentrating the bulk of their feeding and movement during midday when the sun is brightest and the air temperature the warmest.

Every year we observe these seasonal changes in deer behavior on our southern Ohio farm where corn and ladino clover—two premier whitetail foods—suck deer out of adjacent woodlands like a vacuum cleaner hose inhales lint. We've also noted which of our invited hunting guests are consistently the most successful, and more often than not, the times of day they take their deer are quite predictable.

Ohio's bowhunting season is the first to open in early October when temperatures range from balmy to cool. During the initial weeks, those archers who are out early and late in the day invariably do best. Yet as the season wears on, fewer and fewer deer are taken in early morning's dim light.

Next comes Ohio's slug-shotgun season, beginning in late November, with temperatures becoming colder and sometimes dipping below freezing. Now, it seems, hunters collect most of their deer later still, during the mid-morning hours.

Ohio then stages a blackpowder season beginning the day after Christmas and lasting a week, whereupon the bowhunting season reopens until January 31st. Almost unanimously, the most successful muzzleloaders and late-season bowhunters I know say they don't even begin thinking about heading for their morning stands until about 11 a.m. and they know in advance that nearly all deer activity will come to an abrupt halt around 3 p.m.

Stand-Hunting the Rut

Through diel-period tracking, biologists also have uncovered startling new data regarding the rutting period, which in most states north of the Mason-Dixon line occurs sometime between late October and late November. In the deep south, all of this is delayed somewhat, with late December and early January seeing the greatest levels of mating activity.

Yet whether north or south, the radio-tracking studies have revealed that a majority of whitetail mating behavior does not occur late at night after full dark, as most hunters have long supposed, but right during the middle of the day!

At the Fred T. Stimpson Wildlife Sanctuary in Alabama, for example, hundreds of deer were studied in a diel-period tracking experiment conducted by biologists from Auburn University. The scientific data acquired from the investigation revealed two primary periods of rutting activity each day.

The first took place from 10 o'clock in the morning until 11 o'clock. Yet, shockingly, this first mating activity was followed by a second, far more intense flurry of mating behavior from 2 o'clock in the afternoon until 3 o'clock!

Moreover, from the conclusion of the first mating period at 11 o'clock until the onset of the second mating period at 2 o'clock, a majority of the study deer remained on the feet and engaging in feeding.

Consequently, even if a hunter does indeed elect to head for his stand in pre-dawn darkness, he's almost certain to miss whatever peak deer activity the day has to offer if he does not tough it out until at least 3 o'clock in the afternoon. By the same token, if these same hunters like to occupy their stands for the evening watch, 3 o'clock is the generally accepted time most begin heading for their posts.

Make It an All-Day Vigil

Yet aside from conclusions we might draw from these rock-solid biological investigations into the lives of deer, the most predictable thing about their behavior mannerisms is their confounded unpredictability. Just when you think you've got a handle on where they should be, what they should be doing, and at what time of day, they do something entirely unexpected and leave hunters muttering unprintables.

As a result, I'm now of the belief that the only real way to milk the deer season for all it's worth is this: park the seat of your pants in your stand before morning's first light and do not leave until legal shooting time has passed.

In fact, if I have my druthers, instead of hunting the two-hour-long dawn and dusk period every day for a week, I'd rather pick just one day when weather conditions are predicted to be the most favorable and remain on stand that day for 14 continuous hours.

Clearly, this is not easy hunting. But the undertaking is more comfortable if a hunter takes a soft cushion to sit upon and a daypack filled with sandwiches, snacks, and beverages. Even take a small paperback book to occupy your time, if you like. And by all means, alternate sitting and standing periods to stretch tired muscles.

Admittedly, eating, drinking, stretching and reading causes a bit of occasional movement and noise. But these periodic activities are far less conspicuous than climbing down from your perch during mid-morning, hiking back to camp, then hiking back through the cover to your stand in mid-afternoon.

Weather—Or Not

However, there is one type of situation in which all-day hunting can be a futile endeavor.

It's when there are strong, half-gale winds of the type that gust erratically from all compass points and threaten to lift the hat right off your head. Under these conditions, you can count on deer diving into the heaviest cover they can find and not even twitching their noses.

Wind sharply reduces a deer's ability to make effective use of its senses. With stalks of vegetation, tree branches, and other cover swaying in the swirling air movements, they even have a difficult time visually classifying which movements are natural and which may be associated with danger. Their hearing, as well, is likewise greatly impaired.

I've seen bucks so paranoid by high winds that after retreating into thick cover and lying down, they stretched out their necks and laid their chins down upon the ground. With their senses rendered inoperative, they simply had no other recourse but to hide, and hope.

This is why, as I said earlier, my decision as to which day to endure a 14-hour period on stand is always made in strict accordance with a weather forecast.

Stand-Placement Is Critical

As effective as hunting can be during midday, any hunter should look upon stand-placement as a crucial consideration. Even though deer are likely to be up and around throughout the day, midday will typically see them on higher ground and close to thicker cover than during the dawn and dusk periods.

Two factors account for this. First, thermal currents during midday begin rising toward the crests of ridges and drifting uphill into the heads of long hollows. As a result, the animals seem to know instinctively that higher ground is the place to be if they are to accurately test the air currents to detect anything on the prowl below them.

Second, the time period from 10 in the morning until 3 in the afternoon is usually associated with bright light and increased people activity. Not only are many hunters themselves on the move, but in the fields and forests there may be farm workers, loggers, surveyors, linesmen for utility companies, and others, which prompts shy whitetails to slowly begin gravitating in the direction of "security cover" as the day wears on.

This is not necessarily meant to imply the deer are intent upon finding bedding locations; only that as the day progresses they shift their feeding, mating, and social interactions from the more open-meadows and bottomlands to higher ground and heavier cover within the immediate region.

This makes it logical to assume that a multiple-stand approach would be best, with the hunter occupying a low-elevation stand early in the day and then sometime around mid-morning traveling to a high-elevation stand for the remainder of the day. Yet this defeats the entire go early, stay late effort because the hunter simply joins the legions of the many other foot soldiers in the area and helps push deer to those stalwarts who have remained glued to one stand for the entire day.

I've found it much better to rely upon just one stand that is located somewhere in between low and high ground, in moderately thick cover, and especially in the vicinity of scrapes if the rut is in progress. In this manner a hunter capitalizes upon morning deer passing his stand as they slowly travel to higher ground, sees midday deer as they mingle around in the intermediate elevations, and he'll be in position to bushwhack late afternoon deer descending past him as they gravitate toward lower elevations at dusk.

Throughout the season there are sure to be many weeks when a hunter's schedule allows him to maintain not just one but perhaps several all-day vigils on stand.

In this case, I strongly suggest a multiple-stand approach so that the hunter does not find himself returning to occupy the very same stand each and every time. Mature bucks quickly become sensitized to human intrusion into their home areas, and an all-day 14-hour period on any given stand will contaminate the immediate area with so much human scent that each stand should be rested and weather-washed for at least two or three days before a return visit is made.

I personally like to have three all-day stands in place, none closer to each other than a half-mile. This also gives the hunter the option of picking which stand he'll occupy on a given day, depending upon the wind direction.

But whether bowhunter or gun hunter, I'm convinced that midday is no time to be snoozing back in camp. Go early, stay late and you'll see deer during time frames you never thought they'd be up and around.

Part Two
Most Likely to Succeed

Prime Locations, Prime Times to Be There!

Like gold, deer are where you find them. They can be in a lot of other places too. Especially during the hunting season. Especially bucks.

Picking the right patch of ground to take your stand or make your stalk is usually the decision that will make or break your whitetail hunt. As I mentioned in this book's introduction, it's entirely possible for you to take a stand at a certain spot and stay there without having the slightest idea why that particular location might pay off. A buck ambles by, and you shoot it. Easy as pie. Happens all the time.

Do you feel lucky? Could be that's all you'll need to bag a buck? On the other hand, you'll find it's a lot more interesting to really become a buck *hunter*, not just a buck *shooter*. There's a big difference. Buck *hunters* have more fun. And they take more deer.

In this section, we're going to start getting into position to make real *buck hunting* happen.

7 Hunt Corridors, Not Trails!
There's a Big Difference!

BY CHUCK ROBBINS

Most so-called "Deer Trails" turn out to only be "Doe Trails." Here's how to spot the corridors bucks really travel!

To be sure, clueless hunters who trust their chance to lady luck kill lots of bucks each year. In today's crowded whitetail woods, where, in some places, opening day of buck season more resembles a carnival than a real deer hunt, luck works—at least sometimes.

It's no secret that some of the best hunters now spend more time patterning hunters than bucks. Where there is excessive hunting pressure, success often becomes a matter of numbers and the odds are pretty high when a buck gets moving that someone is bound to see him and get a shot. In such intense hunting situations a lot of bucks get killed in a short time (Pennsylvania hunters kill 80% of maybe 150,000 bucks on the opening day, and most of those are taken in the first couple of hours of daylight), and it's often the less skilled hunters who do the killing. Buck hunting in the 90s is not always what it's cracked up to be. So, while you don't need to be a master class buck hunter to down a whitetail buck, striving to be a more savvy hunter can't hurt.

While many less skilled hunters fill tags each season, so do a lot of capable and serious buck hunters. And the truth is, in my hunting lifetime it's always been that way—some hunters rely on pure luck, while others take their buck hunting to a higher level, beyond luck. Many rely on trail and scrape watching, hunting over food plots (even bait where it's legal), and the use of gadgets to achieve success; while some of the best rely more on woodsmanship and careful observation to unveil the travel corridors bucks use daily and to escape hunting pressure.

"Nothin' to it, my boy," Uncle Bob said, in a sagacious overtone that was every bit intentional since it was directed at me, the young buck hunter he had taken on as a personal project. As I fondled the horns, while admiring the wide seven-point buck lying on the blood splattered snow at his feet, he continued, "Just a matter of being at the right place at the right time."

Well . . . maybe!

Making Your Own Luck!

Although I was young, way short on buck hunting experience, I wasn't dumb. To me, it was already apparent that where Bob's buck shooting prowess was concerned, "Being at the right place at the right time" was a too familiar routine to be mere happenstance. It was a rare season that he didn't down a buck—more often than not, the best on the camp roster. Maybe he thought of his success as a matter of luck, but I was skeptical. And now, with the wisdom and hindsight of 40 more buck seasons, I doubt that he did either.

The way I see it Bob learned through hunting the camp property frequently just where the bucks, the best bucks in particular, ran once the shooting started. His was the accumulated knowledge that comes with knowing and observing a place over an extended span of time. It was not something one might grasp fully in just a day or two of hunting, or even a season or two, for that matter. In addition to his vast hunting experience on the property, he spent even more time watching and learning the habits of bucks in the off-season, so that by the time opening day rolled around he knew some of the bucks on a first-name basis, so to speak. More importantly, he seemed to have a pretty good handle on what they might do when the woods filled up with hunters.

"There's a nice buck living near the Sand Spring," he would say. "He crossed the Little Woods every time I kicked him out this fall."

Opening day Bob would be backed up against a favorite stump, likely sitting on an old *Playboy* magazine (no better "hot seat," as far as he was concerned), and usually the outcome was just a matter of time.

Winter, spring, summer and early fall he observed the bucks living on our several hundred acres. Through subtle observation he determined that a certain buck favored a particular spot, watched what happened when he moved him, decided where he would most likely cross come opening day and parked his butt at the best ambush site along that route. He paid scant attention to well worn deer trails—"doe trails," he called them—and rubs, scrapes and other buck signs were a place to start his search and exciting stuff to talk about but had little impact on his final hunting scheme.

Proof that his way worked was written into the long string of consecutive buck kills archived in the camp rosters. The latest result lay there before us in the snow. Even as a wide-eyed, still wet-behind-the-ears young buck hunter, I realized knowing what Bob knew about our bucks would put me on the right track. But I'm a slow learner, and it took awhile before I understood just what all was involved.

In today's specialized world there are a lot of expert buck hunters. They tend to sound a lot like wildlife biologists, tossing out terms like patterning, core area and scent markers while discussing dominance and sub-dominance within the buck population. Many of them spend a lot of time in the trees learning all they can about the bucks they hunt. Often the experts fool with buck lures, cover scents and grunt tubes while banging large antlers together. They know a lot about deer that most of the rest of us don't, and it shows in the collection of impressive heads some of them own.

The "Expert" Observer

I doubt if Bob knew anything about those things until he was too old to care—and by then he was too set in his ways to change anyway. Besides, he killed a lot of bucks through the smoke of a warming fire so he probably had his own ideas about the need for lures and cover scents and the like. But he knew all about patterns, core areas, and scent markers, though he might have come up short on a modern terminology quiz. He operated on a plan where the bottom line was what counted: the buck lives *here;* when the shooting starts he will run *there;* and I will be *there* to intercept him. It's as simple as that. Come to think of it, today's buck hunting lingo might be a little different and there are sometimes a few more quirks in the plan, but the bottom line still works.

Even in places that get a lot of hunting pressure, bucks aren't always fleeing harm's way as they move through their home territory. As they move from bed to feed and back again in their daily routine, bucks travel in very predictable ways, though often not on well-defined deer paths. Over the years I've watched bucks move through low places, necks of dark timber, saddles and other terrain features walking parallel to distinct trails, but only rarely on them. Most times a buck will move through one of these natural funnels using the cover rather than walk on the "doe trails," as Bob called them. He put me onto this concept first, and later I became thoroughly convinced through the teachings of another early mentor, Dick Byrem.

Dick was the consummate woodsman. Nearly every waking thought, every word, seemed aimed at his favorite pastime, buck hunting. He was a crafty and successful buck hunter with gun or bow. His collection of big racks was even more impressive than Bob's. In addition, Dick was a little more progressive in his approach (he often perched in trees for one thing) and was willing to do whatever it took to get his buck, even if that meant changing his ways. While Bob was well acquainted with several hundred acres, Dick roamed several counties. A rather loose work ethic allowed him time to keep track of such a large territory.

It was this intimate knowledge of such a far-flung territory that really got my attention. No matter where we went he knew the back roads, the lay of the surrounding land and the whereabouts of the buck crossings—even more impressive, he apparently knew a whole lot about the bucks using them.

Eliminating Guesswork

Typically, we would leave home in the middle of the night, drive for an hour or more, mostly on dirt roads, park the car and walk through dark woods for a time. About when I was pretty certain we were hopelessly lost somewhere between the car and the middle of nowhere, and in the dark besides, Dick would call a halt and whisper, "This is a good place. Climb up. The deer should come from over there." He pointed off into the blackness.

I would settle on a limb like a hunting owl and almost without fail deer would start filtering by. And more times than not they wandered by from just where Dick said they would. While sometimes I admit to being slow to catch on, even dimwitted me could hardly miss that Dick had something special going for him—something beyond luck—that allowed him to find the best ambush sites. Still, at the time, it was all quite mysterious to me. In other words I knew that he knew stuff that I didn't, but was at a loss as to how he pulled it off.

One October afternoon we traveled 30 or 40 miles from home to place I'd never been before. As we strung up our recurve bows, he said, "There's a big eight-point hanging out here, I saw him this summer in Greene's hay field, and just last week crossing the road at dark. I think I know where he's staying during the day and where he should cross."

I didn't know Greene, or where he was talking about, but I knew better than to doubt and, besides, it all sounded good to me.

That evening, when dusk began to settle, we were roosted a hundred yards apart on tree limbs overlooking a neck of narrow woods between two deep brushy hollows, with alfalfa fields on either side. The place was cut by several well-used deer trails, making it obvious, even to my untrained eye, that deer walked through the neck fairly often. The fact that many of the saplings within sight were rubbed and that we'd passed several big scrapes on the ridge top coming in didn't seem to hurt our chances as we waited out the last minutes of daylight.

The tree he chose for me to stand in was a sugar maple, just small enough in diameter for me to get my arms around and shinny up to the first limb. It was off to the side of a well-used trail about 20 yards, but over top of brush and saplings that looked like a perfect place for a big buck to sneak through on his way to the green alfalfa.

Sure enough as the light began to dim, so that shapes in the distance began to lose their defining edges, several does walked quickly past on the trail, single file, in perfect bow range had I been out to collect venison. But it was antlers I was after. Shortly I heard a rustling to the other side of my tree. Soon a buck appeared, moving slowly through the brush, looking like a gray/brown apparition with glowing white bones floating above in the fast fading light. I wondered if it was the big buck Dick had targeted. No matter, though, because even in good light he was just beyond my self-imposed shooting limit of 20 yards. Given my customary, highly agitated state, whenever a buck was in the vicinity 20 yards seemed plenty far enough to loose an arrow.

As usual, at the sighting of the ghostlike buck, I was wired tighter than a banjo string. So tense, that when I heard a loud Snap! behind I nearly fell out of the tree. Thankfully, it was Dick, because had it been another buck, I doubt I could have ever have gotten off a decent shot in such an altered condition.

Not surprisingly, Dick had tagged the buck we'd come looking for, "Pretty lucky, huh?" he said, grinning wide in the darkness as we dragged the big buck the last few yards to the car.

"Some of us have enough luck, they could stand to spread it around to those of us who ain't got none," I answered, giving the buck a final heave to the edge of the road.

But that was all just talk, I knew there was very little luck to it. Dick's buck hunting skills went way beyond luck.

Terrain Details: The Ultimate Key to Buck-Hunting Success

Whether you hunt 10 acres, or 10,000, the more one knows about it the better the hunting chance. The best way to learn a hunting place intimately is to walk on it, study it, and spend time there in all seasons, in all kinds of weather and light. It's amazing how much the look of a piece of cover changes in snow, fog, or from dusk to dawn—and bucks are likely to use it differently as things change. Learn to recognize low places, saddles, necks of cover that run out into openings or connect larger tracts for these are natural deer highways.

Deer, especially bucks, like the security of overhead cover; dark timber and heavy brush provide this in spades. Bucks use the subtlest as well as the most obvious features to hide and disguise their movements. If the only way through is on an open, well-traveled deer path, of course the bucks will walk it. But if there is any cover at all, bucks, especially the best ones, will stick to it like flies to manure.

Taking cues from Bob and Dick, over the years I've stumbled upon useful buck hunting lore in surprising ways. Running my Brittanys through a particular piece of grouse woods that doubled as ideal bedding cover for the local bucks, one day a light came on as yet another buck lost his nerve at the jangle of the bouncing troupe and bolted his daytime hideout. Following along in the wide-splayed tracks just because they happened to be going in the direction I wanted to, I noticed the tracks passed through a low place in a relatively flat woods. As I pondered that, I remembered that every time we jumped deer from that cover they always ran through the same low place—hmmm. There was never much buck sign there, only an occasional large track, now and then a rub or two, usually no scrapes—in fact, not even a well-defined trail. Yet, despite what the low place lacked, I thought I'd seen enough.

Opening day of buck season I sat myself against a big white pine with a clear view of the low place. Not long after the first shots rang out along came Mr. Buck hightailing it right where he had on our previous grouse hunt. As he sneaked through, moving quickly and on full alert, he failed to notice but one thing—me. That started a streak of four or five buck kills there on opening day and a couple of misses, which are a whole other tale. The point is I found the natural escape alley while grouse hunting. I haven't hunted that place for a number of years, but if I was to go back tomorrow you can guess where I'd be set up. I don't have any misgivings that it might be the wrong place.

A saddle on a nearby ridge in a state forest has had a buck killed there the first day of the season for as far back as I can remember. I never hunt it opening day because it's too crowded, but I've had lots of action later on after the crowds dwindle.

Largely because I wanted to be like my mentors, studying whitetails and their habits developed into a serious hobby. I've spent countless hours watching deer trails that could easily pass for cattle paths; sat over scrapes and rubs until even my butt fell asleep; used my share of scents and lures; even tried grunt tubes and other deer calls, although each time I do I feel pretty foolish because I've yet to turn so much as a buck's ear with my renditions—not surprising, by the way, because I can't sing or play the fiddle either.

How to Find the Secret Corridors Bucks Travel

Anyway, all of these activities have been enjoyable and enlightening, and I've no doubt they work well for others more talented than I. But finally I've come to the conclusion that the bucks I hunt mostly use invisible trails that in reality aren't really trails at all, but rather travel corridors; that they make and visit scrapes and rubs mostly at night or when the season is closed; and that grunt tubes, scents and lures are things that work for other hunters. The bucks I hunt, especially the ones I kill, end up in my sights largely because I've made careful observations in every season of the year. And while I'll probably never achieve the lofty status of Uncle Bob or Dick, I feel confident in being able to recognize at least some of the travel corridors bucks use routinely or as escape routes when the hunting pressure is on.

Last season was a week old when I found a wide deer highway snaking its way through the open timber on the point of a ridge between two deep hollows. Fresh snow revealed the tracks of many deer going both ways. Fifty yards ahead, a thicket of mountain laurel and dark hemlocks traced its way parallel to the well-used trail. In the dawn light no tracks showed there yet, but I was pretty certain that if a buck crossed the point, especially this late in the season, it would use the cover rather than the morel obvious trail.

I scraped away snow and frozen leaves at the base of a large red oak and settled in to watch a 20-foot-wide opening in the thick cover. Before long I heard something coming behind, and I turned my head slightly as two does scooted by on the trail. Then a limb snapped in the opposite direction and quickly I swung back around and caught movement beneath a low hemlock in the laurel. Just then, a buck hurried into the opening in the thicket. The crosshair settled behind the front shoulder. I squeezed the trigger . . . and there before me lay further proof that hunting travel corridors, rather than pinning hope on the more obvious trails and sign, really can take your buck hunting to another level—and way beyond luck!

8 The Art of Patterning Big Bucks

BY GREG MILLER

Trophy whitetails become less predictable the older they get, but with these pointers and a lot of luck, you can greatly increase your odds of bagging a giant buck this season!

Can big bucks be patterned? Renowned trophy-whitetail hunter Stan Potts, from Illinois, says it's possible—to a degree. Don Kisky, a highly successful big-buck hunter from Iowa, agrees with Stan. It is possible to pattern big bucks, but only to a certain degree. I agree. One only has to study rub lines and scrape lines to see that even monster bucks have certain routes they prefer to use more than others. In fact, many mature whitetails I've taken over the years met their demise because I was able to pattern their activities somewhat. But in almost every instance, there was a bit more to the story behind the kill than merely waiting in ambush along preferred travel routes.

I believe it's sometimes possible to figure out where big bucks will travel through certain parts of their ranges. (The key word here is sometimes.) However, I doubt anyone can consistently predict the exact time or even the day when those deer will show up. Here's what Don Kisky had to say about the subject.

"First of all, I think this is a great subject to address," he stated. "Too many deer hunters are under the impression that big bucks can be patterned to the point where you can predict not only exactly where those deer are going to walk, but also exactly what time they're going to show up. I personally haven't seen a single instance where this was possible—especially with bucks that are 4½ years of age and older. At that point in their lives, big whitetails become even more unpredictable. For one thing, they don't leave behind as much sign as they did when they were younger. Also, whitetail bucks seem to wander more as they become more mature. You never know exactly where they'll be or what they'll be doing."

My brother, Jeff, and I spent the better part of five years chasing a couple monster bucks that resided on a 300-acre tract of farmland. There was lots of open ground on the property, which allowed us to sit back and safely observe deer activity. Even though the two bucks we were chasing were very mature, we quickly discovered they were also quite visible.

Anyway, our initial observations left us with high hopes that one of us would eventually get in position to arrow one of them. However, it didn't take long for those hopes to be dashed. Time after time we saw the bucks use particular travel routes when they accessed our property. And time after time we'd set up along those routes—only to see the bucks use a totally different route the next time around. Jeff and I continued to play this frustrating game for a couple years. Granted, we both came close to arrowing one of the bucks on several occasions. But each time the bucks managed to evade us simply because they used slightly different routes than the ones we'd seen them use previously.

My experiences with this sort of thing haven't been limited only to mature farmland bucks either. I've seen the same thing dozens of times when hunting big-woods whitetails. I'd be set up in a spot that showed the most promise, but then I'd see the big buck I was hunting use a slightly different route. Of course, I'd relocate my stand site within bow range of where I'd seen the buck, only to have the deer yet again use a totally different trail on his next pass through the area. I'd be willing to bet that almost all the serious trophy hunters reading this can relate to my experiences.

So What Should You Do?

Stan Potts made what I thought was an interesting observation on this whole patterning problem. "Anymore, I dedicate the majority of my scouting time to just trying to pinpoint the core areas of big bucks," he told me. "Like Don, I firmly believe that whitetail bucks become more and more unpredictable as they grow older. So the way I look at it, the best we can do as hunters is to figure out where big bucks live, and then periodically hunt a few spots within these areas that we believe those bucks use upon occasion."

Stan's strategy for hunting older-age bucks mirrors the approach I used to take my best whitetail ever. Although the big deer spent a great deal of time on our property, neither Jeff nor I could ever get in the right position to waylay the buck. Truth is, we spent almost two full seasons hunting the super deer before one of us even got a look at him. That "look" came on a brutally cold December evening when the monster non-typical walked out to feed in a snow-covered alfalfa field. After a tense, heartbeat-accelerating wait, the buck finally turned and offered me a clear shot at his vitals. The 18-pointer had a gross non-typical score of 202⅜.

That was the first time either of us had seen the big buck. Still, Jeff and I hadn't had any trouble keeping track of the deer's activities on our farm. This was one of those rare older bucks that left behind an incredible amount of rub sign. Basically, what Jeff and I did was to periodically set up along the rub lines we figured the buck was most likely to use when he traveled through the area. (My hunt actually took place near the confluence of two of the non-typical's most active rub lines.)

As I said, our hunt for the buck spanned nearly a two-year period. And I won't lie; my brother and I did become more than just a little frustrated during that time. But I believe any serious whitetail hunter would become frustrated with not being able to see a buck that consistently rubbed on thigh-sized and larger trees. I also won't lie about something else: I was totally surprised and even a bit shocked when the buck walked out to the alfalfa field on that cold December afternoon. After remaining virtually invisible for nearly two years, the buck appears in the wide open a full 45 minutes before dark!

But Maybe There's a Pattern Here

Don Kisky doesn't believe my experience with the non-typical was a fluke. "Actually, I'm of the opinion that the post-rut period is one of the best times to pattern older bucks," he said. "This is especially true if the weather turns cold and we get a substantial amount of snow. People have to remember that the older bucks usually are the most prolific breeders. These deer run off a lot of their body fat during the rut, and they can get pretty desperate trying to restore some of that fat. As a result, they sometimes get into very predictable feeding patterns. While they may not use the exact same trails every day, big bucks often will visit the same feeding areas on a regular basis. Our muzzleloader season here in Iowa is open during the post-rut period. If we get the right kind of weather, I'm very confident that either me or my wife will connect on a big buck." In fact, Don's wife, Kandi, did take a great whitetail during the 1999 Iowa muzzleloader season.

"The weather had been unseasonably warm throughout most of December, and we hadn't had much in the way of snow, so the bucks weren't hitting our food plots until after dark," Don told me. "But then in early January we got the break we'd been waiting for. It snowed a few inches, and the temperature also dropped a bit. Kandi and I decided to set up near the edge of a food plot where we'd seen the buck in the past. Actually, I had missed the buck close to that area earlier in the fall during the archery season. After my experience I kind of got a feel for where the deer was bedding and where he was feeding."

As luck would have it, the buck the Kiskys were after made an appearance on that cold January afternoon. Kandi made the one shot from her Knight muzzleloader pay off, and the trophy whitetail ran only a short distance before expiring. The monster eight-pointer achieved a gross score of 167 and a net score of 163. Making the deal even sweeter was the fact that Don captured the entire hunt on video.

Stan related a story that once again exemplifies the importance of locating big-buck core areas. "A buddy and I once hunted the same big buck for three seasons," Stan said. "The buck had a relatively small core area, and he'd hang tough to that area during the pre-rut. But once the rut started, he was gone. We wouldn't see him anywhere near his core area again until the rut was over. Then he'd show up again. My buddy finally arrowed him on a late-season hunt in December. The deer had a typical 625 rack that gross-scored 184."

Stan said the fact that the big buck spent a lot of time in a relatively small area didn't make their task any easier. "One of us would see the buck using a certain part of his core area one day, but then the next time we saw him he'd be using a totally different part. But that's pretty much the way it is with older-age whitetails. About the only set patterns they get into is that they may visit the same feeding areas on a daily basis during the post-rut period. But it's highly doubtful they'll use the exact same route two days in a row to get to those feeding areas. Hunters just have to keep moving around and hope they eventually end up in the right spot."

Stan and Don repeatedly told me that the biggest key to patterning big bucks is first finding their core areas. "Where I live we manage to pick up quite a few shed antlers each year," Don said. "Unless we have an extremely brutal winter, our deer won't relocate. So we usually can safely assume that the deer we find the antlers from are living right in the immediate vicinity. We then combine this information with our summer sightings and our experiences from the hunting season. In the end we're usually able to pinpoint the core areas of the bucks we're hunting. And then we can somewhat pattern how those deer will move around in their core areas."

Granted, Don's experiences with shed antlers are pretty much limited to farmland habitat. But my hunting partners and I have seen the exact same thing with big-woods whitetails. Provided big-woods bucks aren't forced to relocate because of harsh winters, they usually will drop their antlers somewhere within their core areas. Like Don, I've used the discovery of shed antlers and experiences from some of my hunts to pinpoint the core areas of quite a few big deer.

The Rare Exceptions

Of course, there are exceptions to every rule. Once in a while I hear a story about hunters who do manage to pattern mature bucks. Not only were the bucks quite visible, they also used the same travel routes and showed up in the same places at almost the same times every day. I've talked with quite a few of these hunters, and most were successful on their very first attempt. What's more, almost all these people were hunting in relatively unpressured areas.

Earlier I mentioned there was a bit more to the stories surrounding some of my big-buck successes than merely waiting along travel routes. Truth is, none of the big bucks I've somewhat patterned were taken on the first attempt. And darn few were taken along the routes where I first suspected they would appear. In almost every instance I've had to fine-tune my stand locations a few times before I ended up in the right spot.

It's true that we can dramatically increase our chances for success by spending all our free time hunting in areas where trophy deer live. But being able to pattern a mature buck to the point of predicting accurately when he'll show up in a specific spot is usually nothing more than a pipe dream. When it comes right down to it, racking up an enviable success rate on large-racked whitetails means spending a lot of time in the woods—and occasionally making the right guess!

9　Tweaking Treestands

BY GARY CLANCY

Small changes in treestand location can sometimes make huge differences in success.

L et me be up front with you right from the start. Unless you are really into hunting for whitetails, this article is probably going to bore you to death. Tweaking treestands is not exciting stuff. I'm not talking anything new or revolutionary here. But from my own experiences and those of other seasoned hunters, I'm convinced that often the difference between a shot and no shot, or a good shot and a poor shot, or just seeing deer and having opportunities at deer are, very often, the little things I'll talk about here. My definition of "tweaking" is to take something that is already good and make it better—to fine-tune it. An incident from last season reminds me how seemingly insignificant changes can have dramatic results.

On a farm I hunt a couple of hours from home, I had, after a thorough scouting job, hung three Ol' Man Tara strap-on treestands in what I felt were the three best locations on the 160-acre property. My Number One stand overlooked a spot where a five-strand barbed-wire fence had been significantly bowed by a fallen tree. The farmer had removed the tree but had not tightened the fence, obviously thinking it would still hold his herd of Holsteins. Deer, of course, can jump a five-strand fence anyplace they like, but they rarely will. Instead they'll walk along the fence until they find a convenient place to cross, and once they locate such a place they'll cross there regularly—which, of course, makes such spots super places for stands. Sometimes, with permission from the landowner, I will wire the top strand to a lower strand to create such a crossing, but in this case nature had done it for me.

On this farm deer meandering down from the high ridges, where they prefer to bed, would cross the fence on their way to feed on the abundant acorns on the little oak flat where my stand was; then later they'd mosey out to dine on soybeans, corn and alfalfa. I hung the stand 20 feet up a ramrod-straight basswood tree just 15 steps from the fence crossing. I felt confident that everything was perfect, and I couldn't wait to hunt the stand.

But on the first evening I quickly realized that everything was not perfect. The first deer to come along was a lone button buck, which hopped the fence and turned broadside to follow the heavily used trail just as I had envisioned. But the second group of deer was a different story. It consisted of a long-necked, hump-nosed, mature doe with a pair of fawns. (Big bucks get all the credit for being the "smartest" deer, but they don't hold a candle to mature does. Does are entrusted with the job of raising the young, so nature has instilled in them incredible wariness.) The doe came down the ridge and stopped in a small opening a good way out and stared holes right through me. Despite the fact that I was 20 feet up a tree, the ridge dropped off steeply and put the doe on my same level. I was dressed in camouflage, including a facemask and gloves, and hadn't moved, yet that old doe knew that the blob in the tree had not been there the last time she'd used that trail. The old gal stared for a long time and I was afraid she was going to go into one of those snorting and blowing sessions, but she didn't. Nor, however, did she continue down the trail to the fence crossing. Instead she took her twins in a wide loop around my stand. I hoped that this was just a fluke and continued my vigil.

But the next deer to come down the trail, which happened to be another doe with a single fawn, convinced me in a hurry that I was wrong. Just as the first doe had, when the second doe reached the opening on the steep ridge, she stopped and stared right at me. Eventually, she too worked her way around me.

It was prime time by now, the sun having just about disappeared behind the ridge, and I didn't want to move, but I knew I had to do something. What I did was to step off the stand, loosen the strap and swing the stand around to the backside of the tree. Then I screwed in another step to allow me to access the platform easily and climbed aboard. The whole operation took maybe five minutes.

Now my stand was facing directly away from where the deer approached. It wasn't ideal for sitting comfortably and being able to scan the area where I expected deer to come from, but even a fussy old doe can't see through a basswood tree!

It would make a great story if I were to tell you that 10 minutes later a monster buck came along, hopped the fence and met his destiny, but that didn't happen. What did happen is that three more deer used the fence crossing before the end of shooting hours, and although all three happened to be bucks, none were of the caliber I was looking for. And by the way, none of the three so much as glanced in my direction.

I ended up hunting that stand a half-dozen times last season and saw deer each time. The only deer that ever showed any sign of nervousness were those two does that picked me off the first evening.

I'm convinced that most hunters put too much emphasis on comfort when selecting stand sites. For example, when I put that fence stand up I knew that the basswood tree offered no cover in the way of branches, and that was a concern. However, I convinced myself that if I sat still, no deer would spot me. The key word here is "sat." I prefer to remain seated most of the time while on stand, and I like to be comfortable while I wait. I want a tree that is either straight or leans slightly away from me so that I can lean back and be comfortable. I want to be able to easily scan the direction from which I think deer will approach without craning my neck or making other contortions. And I don't want a knot or a sawed-off branch stub sticking me in a shoulder blade. There is nothing wrong with any of this, unless, of course, you pick your trees and the position for your stands based on comfort rather than maximum effectiveness. My stand in that basswood had to be placed on the backside of the tree, which meant that instead of sitting kicked back on the comfortable net seat, I had to stand the whole time peeking around the tree. It wasn't nearly as comfortable, but it was 10 times more effective.

Don't Be Too Quick to Move

Here is one I've been guilty of on more occasions than I care to admit. In fact, I did it again just last October. I was hunting a farm just minutes north of my home in southeastern Minnesota. Before the season began I had hung several stands on the farm, my favorite being one in a corner of the largest block of timber on the farm. An overgrown tangle of a fenceline—a natural travel route—intersected with the corner of the woods. The farmer who worked the land had cut a 10-yard-wide swath through the fenceline right where it joined the woods so that he could easily move machinery from one field to another. Deer moved through this opening with regularity. One deer in particular that was in the habit of crossing there was a dandy 10-point buck that I had watched fatten up on soybeans and alfalfa. After a rain one evening I walked out to where the buck had been feeding in the soybeans and got a good look at his track so I could recognize it. I found that track often in the soft soil of the cut through the fenceline.

But the first evening I hunted my stand, the big 10-point buck did not make his way down the fenceline; instead, right at dusk, I spotted him across the field where a blunt finger of timber jutted up from the river into it. He worked a couple of overhanging branches and was still along the far edge when it got dark.

The next morning I hung a stand along that other edge; and, you guessed it, right at dusk the 10-pointer sauntered through the gap in the fenceline right under my vacant stand. Frustrated, I snatched my Tru-Talker from inside my jacket and sent a series of tending grunts floating across the bean stubble. The buck heard me and came sauntering slowly across the field. With the light fading quickly, the buck finally made his way across the light-colored stubble, but by the time he stepped into the timber it was too dark to shoot. I kept track of him through the sound of his steps in the fallen leaves and knew that he was moving my way, no doubt searching for the buck he'd heard grunting. When he was only 10 yards away I finally saw the white of his throat patch as he lifted his head to sniff one of the scent wicks I'd hung around my stand. The buck hung around for five, maybe 10 minutes before I heard him walk off. I don't know if he detected something amiss and avoided that place the rest of the season or if he was taken by another hunter or what, but I never saw him again. If I had followed my own rule, which is to never move a stand on the basis of one sighting but to wait for a second to confirm the first, I would have had my opportunity at that buck.

Which brings to mind outfitter friend Mike Pavlick, who runs his Golden Triangle Whitetail (708-828-2378) operation on several thousand acres of prime deer habitat in western Illinois. When it comes to treestands, Pavlick is a standa-holic. All summer and winter he's scouting for new places to hang stands. Before a stand ever goes up, Pavlick is pretty darn sure that the location he's chosen is the very best for that situation.

"But invariably," Pavlick said, "one of my hunters will come in from hunting foaming at the mouth over the big buck he has seen just out of range. Of course, these hunters want me to move the stand to where they saw the big buck. I try to convince them to give the original stand another try and then if they happen to see the same buck or a different buck using the same travel route as the first, I will move the stand for them. Most go ahead with this plan and very often end up killing a good buck from the stand I originally hung. But sometimes a guest is emphatic that the stand has to be moved, so I go ahead and move it. I can only recall one hunter who's had a shot at a buck after I've moved his stand, but I've lost count of the hunters who've come back in with long looks on their faces to report that good bucks walked right past the original stands."

The bottom line on tweaking? Let the deer decide when it is necessary and when it is not. And trust your instincts and skills. If your experience tells you that the place to hang a stand is right there, then trust your experience and give that location a chance. But if the deer show you by their actions that your stand location needs tweaking, don't delay; do it now.

10   Stitch the Ridges

BY JOHN WEISS

You'll find more bucks if you leave the bottomlands and get up where you belong—on the ridges where the does are!

I t was long ago that Illinois deer biologist Harry Mixen taught me the wisdom of finding bucks during the rut. "Forget about hunting scrapes, rub lines and trails," Mixen said. "You'll have far more buck encounters if you simply find a prime food source. That's where the does will be—and where the does are is where the bucks will be."

Sounds easy enough, and for many years it worked. Consequently, most of my rut-hunting efforts were around cropland perimeters and hill-country bottomlands where lush native vegetation was plentiful.

But I began noting a pattern. Does were characteristically seen in these locations, feeding and occasionally being chased by bucks, but only during the early morning or just before dark. I wondered about the rest of the day, and was there possibly a hunting strategy that would work during both the pre-rut and peak-rut periods?

Finding the solution was easy. I called Harry Mixen.

"Locate doe bedding areas, because that's where you'll find the does. And where you find the does, that's where the bucks will be," he said.

Sounds easy enough, and it's working for me!

Where the Does Bed

It's been my experience that in rolling terrain, hill country and mountains, does generally bed about one-third to one-half of the way up the slopes. Depending upon the size of the area, this may be anywhere from a few hundred yards to a half-mile from the lower elevations.

It's only speculation, but I suppose this midday positioning allows them to watch for danger from above. And with their noses and the direction they're facing, they can simultaneously monitor breezes or rising midday thermals to keep tabs on what's going on to either side or directly below them.

Doe bedding areas are easy to find and recognize. They're usually in thickets, and if the weather is unseasonably warm, a majority of them will be on cooler

61

north-facing slopes. If the weather is unseasonably cold, expect to find them on sun-drenched south-facing slopes.

Invariably, does bed in clustered family groups. This means you'll see matted ovals in the grass or snow that will differ in size, representing deer of various ages. In time, as adult does begin coming into estrus, they'll chase away their daughters from the previous year and their offspring from the current year. So it's best to scout for doe bedding areas well before the rut begins and the family units are still intact.

It's not a very scientific technique, but I just randomly hike the hillsides, keeping an eye out for not only the beds, but the animals themselves as I flush them out. Then I move in and study the area where they were bedded. Doing this scouting early allows each bedding area to be "rested" for at least a few weeks, but it generally takes only a few days for the does to return.

Bucks on the Prowl

As does begin slowly climbing to the zenith of their estrous cycle, bucks begin using the sloping hillsides in a manner similar to the does. From my experience, most of them use a lateral band of terrain anywhere from 50 to 200 yards above the doe bedding areas. They likewise bed in thickets during midday periods and make particular use of thermals to monitor the rising, wafting aroma of does as they approach estrus. If nothing's doing, they may follow the lateral band of terrain in one direction or another and relocate immediately above another doe-bedding area elsewhere. After another brief monitoring period, they may relocate yet again where other does are bedding.

Of course, even a mild wind of only 5 mph cancels out thermals, preventing a buck from ascertaining the state of breeding readiness of the does below him. When this happens, bucks now engage in a common behavioral switch. With their noses no longer effective, they come downslope to the point where they can visually monitor the does' behavior.

A sure indication that a doe is entering estrus is her unique body language. It consists of what can only be described as nervous, edgy behavior, with the doe repeatedly standing, laying down, then standing again. She may also periodically bleat for a buck's attention and walk around in circles stiff-legged. And she may extend her tail straight back or off to one side, which is the universal "I'm ready" signal.

The Ridge Connection

With does bedded roughly a third of the way up a slope and bucks bedded or patrolling a third of the way above the does, it stands to reason that an enterprising hunter will want to, in turn, be working just above the bucks.

In this situation, many hunters effectively combine stillhunting with posting, and I especially like to work terraced hillside benches slightly below a ridgeline. By slowly poking along, it's possible to spot bucks below you.

One time I came upon a nice bedded six-pointer that was fully preoccupied with watching a band of does just beneath him. Because they were only 50 yards away and the cover was relatively thin, I could watch the does, as well, and the scenario that unfolded was both amusing and frustrating.

Occasionally, one of the does would stand to stretch, and at this the buck would catch the movement and quickly crane his neck to have a better look. Then the doe would lay back down, and the buck's attention would visibly subside. I was within bow range, but had no shot at the buck. So I simply played the waiting game, hoping he would eventually rise and give me an opportunity. When he finally did stand, more than an hour later, it caught me unprepared. Before I could raise my bow, he already was moving parallel to the hillside through thick cover, apparently to relocate to another doe-bedding site some distance away.

Sneak 'n Peak

When stillhunting parallel to a ridgeline, stopping every few steps to study the terrain below in hopes of spotting a bedded or patrolling buck, occasionally you will see a stretch of thin cover ahead. You know that the cover doesn't offer enough concealment for you to progress farther without being exposed.

When this happens, I immediately stop moving in that direction, turn left or right and slowly sneak up to the crest of the ridge and peer over the top for long minutes. What I want to ensure is that no deer are close and able to see my body form suddenly coming over the ridge crest. Then I slip down over the ridge and make my way downhill for whatever short distance seems appropriate and resume stillhunting on the opposite slope.

In this manner, a hunter can alternately zigzag along a ridge crest, hunting one side of the hill or the other for an almost indefinite distance.

In the Saddle

When a buck is patrolling for estrous does and generally paralleling ridgelines, it's common for him, upon coming to a saddle, to pass through it in order to check out doe activity on the opposite slope. After working along that slope for some distance, the buck may then come upon another saddle and cross through it back to the other side.

Consequently, when I'm stillhunting along a sidehill, whenever I come to a saddle I like to park there for a while. The best vantage is near the ridgeline—but not exposed above it—so the hunter can look down into the saddle almost the same as if he were in a treestand.

During last year's severe drought in the Midwest, the ground cover was so dry and crunchy that stillhunting was nearly impossible, so I spent most of my time stitching the ridges. In other words I'd find a saddle, post it for an hour, then quickly move to the next.

One time I could actually hear a buck approaching before I was able to see him. Then he suddenly stepped through the narrow slice in the terrain and right into the path of my arrow. Like a mugger lurking in a dark alley, I had capitalized on a travel tendency that deer have used for a long time.

The eight-pointer ran only 25 yards, skidded to a halt, then looked back over his shoulder in my direction, in what appeared to be disbelief. He covered a dozen more yards, stumbled and went down.

Mapping Out a Plan

As noted, in rolling or steep hill country, deer rarely travel straight up or down hillsides to gain access to the other side of a mountain or nearby bottom-land. Instead they walk the gentle slopes, particularly the benches and terraces, traveling parallel to the ridgelines until they come to a saddle or break, and then traveling through the cut.

The first time I hunted a saddle, scouting was done by first studying a topo map. All you have to do is find about six or eight contour lines that are fairly straight, run a long distance, and are so close together that they almost seem to form a single thick line.

This feature indicates a long and very steep ridge. Now simply run your finger along the length of those compacted contour lines, looking for an interruption where they suddenly become a bit wider before returning close together; the contour-line number at that location should reveal a rapid change of approximately 10 to 40 feet in elevation. This is the crossover location, and it's the proverbial pot of gold at the end of the rainbow.

The particular saddle I found was no more than 40 yards wide and choked with brush. Moreover, the cut was peppered with tracks, evidence enough it was used daily by deer.

Setting up was easy because there were only two considerations: I had to pick one side of the cut in accordance with the wind direction, and then find a bit of screening cover to hide behind that would allow me to watch both the cut and the adjacent bench.

In fact, preventing deer from scenting you in high country is easy. If there's no wind, just thermals, your human odor is rising straight up. If there is a discernible wind, doping out its most consistent direction is a no-brainer. In broken country, where there is a mix of varied elevations, the lowest of those elevations are the most likely to see swirling air currents in unpredictable directions due to the way those currents bounce off hillsides, sheer walls, points and other irregular contours. However, in higher elevations and especially along ridgelines where saddles are located, the wind flow is basically steady, uninterrupted and unlikely to suddenly change direction or swirl.

Fine-Tuning Your Strategy

Keep in mind that stitching the ridges during the rut is designed for midday hunting when bucks and does leave the lower-elevation feeding areas and climb to bedding locations. So if I were to pick times at which to be sidehilling it, they would be from 9 a.m. to 4 p.m. This means I'd be hunting a low-elevation feeding area at the crack of dawn. By about the time the sun had fully cleared the horizon, I'd abandon my stand and begin working the high country. In late afternoon, I'd then return to my bottomland stand near a feeding area.

Also keep in mind the simplicity of this approach because during pre-season scouting you only need to locate two things: known doe feeding areas and known doe bedding areas. Using this strategy, it is not necessary to try to find scrapes, rub lines or other typical buck sign. In fact, the only significance of finding buck sign is that it tells you one thing: that there are bucks in the immediate area. But otherwise, because that "area" may encompass a large chunk of real estate, narrowing the search becomes essential.

So after all is said and done, where are the bucks? "They are where the does are feeding or bedding," Harry Mixen said. "And because the does will be at their feeding sites for only a small amount of time each day, the odds of success are with the hunter who spends the larger portion of each day stillhunting the sidehills, posting where bedded bucks or bedded does are spotted, and stand hunting in the vicinity of saddles."

Try it, and you may find yourself saying it works for you, too.

11 Shedding Light on Moon Phases

BY JOHN WOOTTERS

Can lunar calendars tell you when to hunt? The author has the experience, and his own database, with the answer to that question.

Big and round, it hangs in the sky like a big pizza pie, as Dean Martin used to sing. It inspires all manner of "lunatics" from poets to lovers to songwriters to Dracula . . . to deer hunters. It is Earth's only natural satellite. And along about late summer, the moon starts to draw hunters' eyes irresistibly upward, seeking omens and portents for the coming season.

Mine, too. I'm a believer. Now in my 59th year of hunting whitetails, I've passed a thousand autumn days and nights in deer camps peopled by seasoned hunters. As a boy, I sat as the grizzled veterans spoke knowingly on deer behavior. Sooner or later, the discussion always got around to the moon. And in that aspect, little has changed. I've yet to know an experienced whitetail hunter, then or now, who doubted the moon's importance in determining hunting tactics and timing. That the moon matters is a given. Wind and weather can be predicted, if at all, only in broad generalities or for periods of short duration. But any feed-store almanac can tell us precisely when and where, and how bright, the moon will be on any given night.

If the moon's effect is so great, does it pay to plan hunts by that almanac? Maybe so—if only because it's the lone environmental parameter we can accurately predict. Perhaps only the timing of the local whitetail rut is of more use to hunters. But if everybody agrees that it is as cut-and-dried as that, and that deer react to moon phases and movements, why does the subject remain a perennial campfire topic? That's easy: Most of us agree there's an effect, but we don't necessarily agree on exactly how deer are affected. Everyone, it seems, nurses his own pet theory, but no scientific research (to my knowledge) has yet conclusively proved which one, if any, is correct.

Some of those theories are a little weird, or at least wishful. One author states bluntly that deer always move and feed when the moon is up. Period. No qualification. No equivocation. If you look up and see the moon during legal shooting hours, go hunting!

Wouldn't that be nice.

More widespread is the idea that deer need moonlight to find food at night and therefore are stuffed full and lie low on mornings following bright nights. On moonless nights, I suppose, they stumble around, bumping into trees in the dark and awaiting dawn with growling bellies. The problem with this picture is that whitetails' night vision is so good they can easily feed on even the blackest night. Biologists tell us that a deer can see about as well on a moonless, starlit night as humans do at dusk on an overcast evening. I don't know about that, but I do know I've swept favored feeding fields in prime deer country with headlights on pitch-black nights and have seen a hundred green-glowing deer eyes, yet found the same fields eerily deserted on full-moon nights. Not every time, but often enough to call into question any statement that a hard-and-fast correlation exists.

Still another school of thought holds that whitetails respond to lunar (and perhaps also to solar) positions more or less in the following manner: When the moon is either directly overhead or high on the opposite side of the Earth, regardless of what time it is, whitetails are on the move. This is an oversimplification of the theory, but a little analytical thought leads to the conclusion that this is essentially a tidal theory being applied to terrestrial mammals. It holds that all creatures—including humans—are subject to predictable major and minor periods of activity during which they run to the store, chase girls, stop by the icehouse for a beer, whatever. Since these periods occur at night as often as during legal shooting hours, the value of such tables (for hunters, if not fishermen) seems automatically somewhat limited.

Many will, of course, recognize from this description the venerable (and copyrighted) Solunar Tables, originally the creation of, and promoted by, John Alden Knight. At one point, I made a serious, good-faith effort for four full hunting seasons to correlate whitetail sightings with the Solunar Tables. Frankly, I wanted them to work. I even got a funny sort of clock that tells time in Solunar periods. How convenient—simply look up tomorrow's deer activity in a table! Locate your trophy in a column of numbers. Imagine all those boring, frigid hours on stand saved just by following these tables!

Alas, whitetails are a tad more complicated than that, as most of us probably suspected all along. I tried and tried, but I simply could not find any consistent relationship between observed deer activity and Knight's periods—major, minor or medium-rare. This is true of the many commercial offshoots, variants and permutations of what I describe as the "tidal theory" of deer movement that I've looked into. For fish, maybe they work. But not for deer—I've found them to be a bust.

Actually, a correlation might be discovered for deer, too, if all else were equal. But all else is not equal with whitetails; powerful influences act and interact continuously on a deer herd—weather fronts, hunting pressure, intermittent food availability and the almighty rut being among the most obvious. Take away those and other variables, and the tidal predictors of whitetail movement might, well, hold more water.

So if a computer won't do it, and you have to collect your buck with a bullet or arrow, not software, it comes down to personal observations. Verified by 20 years of written records, mine leave not the slightest question in my mind that a hunter will see more deer and more bucks on days following *moon-dark* nights. The database ratio—compiled from sightings over 19 years, the majority in South Texas—is close to four to one (mornings after dark nights versus after-full-moon nights). I will not presume to offer an explanation for this phenomenon, nor will I offer to tell you at what hour and minute a worthy buck may appear, or where. In my opinion, that's the stuff of the Psychic Friends Network. You still have to do your own hunting, in other words, but the odds are definitely on your side with a new moon.

This maxim applies as well in Maine as in Alberta, in Florida as in Texas.

Many of my findings concerning whitetails' responses to temperature, wind direction and velocity and other environmental factors can vary wildly with local climates, but the moon is the moon, regardless of latitude. And from my data I've discovered a fact that the strict interpreters of moonphase theories can't account for. It doesn't matter whether a night is dark because of a new moon or a cloud deck—in either case, the next day's hunting will be promising.

Finally a question: Do bucks and does respond similarly to lunar influence? My data leads me to believe they do.

The very best time to go deer hunting, as everybody knows, is whenever you can! Forced to make a choice, however, I invite you to join the rest of us "lunatics"—invest in an almanac and turn to the hunting-season month (or months) in your state. Find the date of the new moon and plan to be in the woods then. You still have to figure the rut and worry about where to go and how to shoot straight, but you have the "when" part licked!

Keeping a Hunting Log

A log of your time afield can be invaluable. Not only do universal patterns such as deer movement during moon phases become apparent, but localized patterns can show up after analysis of data kept over several seasons. Here's how I organize my records:

- I assign one "week" (actually three days before and three days after the moon's day of total fullness) to "full" status. A similarly split week around the new moon is regarded as "dark," and I designate both the second- and fourth-quarter moons as "half." It may not be statistically precise, but at least this practice provides a consistent format for data collection from year to year.
- My time-of-day data is divided only into a.m. and p.m., and I suspect that more divisions would yield a more sensitive index to the moon's influence on whitetail movement. For example: It's clear that buck movement on days following full-moon nights tends to begin later in the morning.

12   When the Snow Flies

BY JEFF MURRAY

Tomorrow we'll have a nice tracking snow. But today the sifting flakes are changing the wood-lands minute by minute. What are the bucks doing now?

So it finally happened. After patiently waiting, you're going to get your wish. You'd been praying for it along with every skier and snowmobiler in the country, and last night it really snowed. The woods and meadows are covered with a plush carpet of magic crystals!

But I wonder. How many deer hunters will really benefit from the change in scenery? In spite of Snow White's popularity, come deer season, I have a funny feeling that a fresh snowfall backfires on far more hunters than it helps.

I know that things haven't always worked out the way I'd dreamed they would. In spite of my euphoria, there have been times that a white blanket put a wet blanket on my chances for a particular buck. But nothing I've experienced rivals what once happened to the late Hans Gersbach. How would you like to miss out on a 450-pound, bushel barrel-racked whitetail because of snow? Take heed and profit from his loss.

Hans was a vanishing breed of North Woods old-timers—a gritty immigrant from the Old Country who was truly ahead of his time. Unlike hunters of his day, he hunted for sport, not meat. What a dream-come-true it would have been to kick back over a steamy pot of Russian tea, and let the conversation flow with the brew. What unpretentious deer lore to pick up on! But it rarely happened. Hans had a speech impediment, and his English wasn't very good.

But once—just once—one of those precious nuggets of wisdom slipped out between stammering lines. I almost wished it hadn't, though. You'll never hear a sadder deer tale.

Picture the halcyon days of logging camps and timber crews. It was a golden era when huge bucks with wrist-thick racks first roamed the big pine country of the Great Lakes states. The particular deer Hans was after this time around had a nickname, as do many legendary bucks. Only this one was no legend. He had caught glimpses of the monster two years in a row.

"Buster was not only da biggest dear I'd ever zeen," Hans reminisced one day, "but his brow tines ver zis tall." With an emphatic gesture he shoved a pair of stubby hands in front of my face, one at least a foot above the other.

That first year, Hans never saw Buster. But the following season he made the discovery of discoveries. He found a scrape line skirting an isolated cedar thicket, and it led to the "scrape of scrapes." It looked as if a hand grenade had exploded there, leaving a patch of ground the size of a living room torn up and shredded to pieces. And the immediate area reeked of buck musk.

Hans knew Buster would return to his calling card once the rut kicked into higher gear, so he decided to set up an ambush downwind and wait the buck out. It had worked before.

"Right avay I zaw two udder big bucks come to da scrape," Hans told me. "But dey vern't Buster. Dey came for tree dayz in a row, but den it znowed and dat vas dat."

What happened? Hans had to settle for deer track soup. He didn't see another deer—not even a doe—in that area for the rest of the season. Worst of all, the buck he thought he had patterned turned up as a road-kill only a few miles away. It became the talk of Minnesota's North Shore for many years to come.

"It was Buster all right," Hans whispered in a quivering voice. "After da znofall, he followed da does dat moved closer to da highvay. Vun night he was hit by a lumber truck. He vas smashed up pretty bad, but somevun scaled him anyvay. Can you accept 450 pounds?"

There are some valuable insights to be gleaned from this little tale. Two stand out especially loud and clear.

First, a doe's instincts tell her this is the time of the year to pack on as much weight as possible; soon, winter will settle in and heavy snows are sure to restrict travel and eliminate many food sources. Moreover, she'll need the extra nutrition for her developing young. Her predicament is similar to that of a pregnant woman at church bazaar. At first, she'll have the luxury of sampling many courses. Eventually, however, some dishes will be depleted, leaving fewer and fewer options. Still, she'll have her own list of "what to shift to next."

Indeed, it would be wise to know these shifts, as winter weather approaches, before they occur. Then, establishing new travel patterns as they emerge will keep you in the thick of deer concentrations.

Second, hunters need to know the relationship between snowfall and apparent breeding areas in their specific region. What happens, for instance, to a scrape once it's covered with snow—will a buck re-open it, or will he make a new one? Will does approaching estrus linger in areas where old scrapes are now covered over?

Before addressing the first point, let's rehearse some basic facts that might not be so basic to a lot of well-informed deer hunters.

Deer are considered ruminants, or cud-chewing animals. However, recent studies show that when given a choice, they will choose grasses over twigs and branches when available (assuming danger is not a concern). So, even though they are biologically classified as "browsers," they'd really rather be "grazers."

A recent study done on Wisconsin deer confirms this. The stomach contents of 76 road-killed whitetails were examined from April 15 through November 15. The bulk of the food inspected—a full 87 percent—was herbaceous material. Another 10 percent of the food volume was made up of fruits and flowers, such as acorns, mushrooms and blackberries. A scant 3 percent was woody twigs and stems. Over 70 different plant types were identified, with aspen leaves being the most important source of food for the deer sampled. Grasses were second.

Conclusion? Deer will switch from soft, leafy plants to harder, woody varieties only when they are forced to do so. Yet, many deer hunters look at "prime deer habitat" with its thick and brushy second-growth vegetation and remark. "Look at all the deer browse." They make a good observation but come to the wrong conclusion.

In the farming belt, the phenomenon of deer switching food sources is easy to keep tabs on. You just have to inventory those cultivated lands that harbor both standing and harvested crops. But don't expect all deer to favor unharvested fields over picked ones. The reverse is more often the case. Deer will key on the residue left behind until supplies have dwindled, or snow depths make pawing out today's meal impossible. Then they'll invariably shift over to standing crops.

Which crops? The exact order of preference is a source of much debate. Some veteran hunters and biologists feel that corn is always number-one. Other respected authorities insist that deer favor smaller-grained crops whenever accessible. My experiences cause me to lean in the direction of the latter camp. The lone exception I often observe is when colder temperatures accompany heavy snowfall and drifting occurs. At that time, corn usually wins out probably because it doubles as wind-breaking cover.

If you think the picture on the North Woods scene is more difficult to draw conclusions from, you're right. That is, if you don't know about slashings that might contain clover and aspen suckers. You probably know that clover is to a woods buck what alfalfa is to a farm buck. And you know that once clover beds are layered beneath a blanket of snow, the deer will abandon them overnight.

But did you know that aspen leaves on sucker shoots have a high phenol content and are extremely hardy? They're capable of resisting many freezing nights before turning colors and falling to the ground. The only trick is to pinpoint the exact locations of aspen logging operations of one, two and maybe three years ago. These clear-cuts will continue to attract feeding does long after other fields have been left behind for greener pastures—make that browner branches and twigs. All you have to do is pattern the entrance and exit routes, as well as identifying the bedding sites in thicker cover.

Buck Sign & Snowfall

The other consideration raised by Hans' whitetail of horrors concerns the relationship between buck sign and snowfall. The whole key is when the snow falls during a given deer season. A recent interview with Michigan biologist, John Ozoga, yielded some interesting footnotes.

In spite of all the research scrapes have generated Ozoga says that biologists still don't know exactly what a scrape is or why it exists. The closest we can get is that they are "some sort of display of dominance" and, perhaps, a source of priming does for the mating ritual. Whether one scrape is "hotter" than another depends mostly upon where it's located. There are isolated scrapes and clusters of scrapes. You'll have to draw your own conclusion, but scrapes should be able to tell you one thing: whether breeding bucks are still working a particular area. And a breeding buck is one that's more likely to make a mistake than one that's not.

Also, we know that scrape activity peaks just prior to peak breeding activity. After that, it's all downhill. According to Ozoga, an early snowfall will affect scrape activity far differently than one later on in the season. And there are differences worth noting between farm deer and deep woods deer.

"To begin with, you don't normally see a lot of snow when the rut is about to peak," he told me. "But when the two coincide, my bet is that a breeding buck is likely to either stay with a hot doe until he breeds her, or he'll continue to act pretty rowdy in his core rutting area. Usually, I don't think he'll follow after the does right away as they switch to different food sources. He'll lag behind a bit."

Snow later on in the season is an entirely different matter. Bucks will have bred most of the does in the North Country and a secondary estrus is not likely to occur. Consequently, scrapes are a rare commodity, come late November and early December. At this time of year, Ozoga feels that "scrape areas" are not nearly as significant as they might have been in late October or early November. But there is a minor exception, he says.

"In the lower Midwest agricultural areas, you will see a sudden upsurge in breeding activity in mid-December. That's when many fawn does will go into heat. Scrapes become significant again, and they should be taken into account, regardless of the snow conditions."

New Mysteries—& Some Answers

Now when you add Ozoga's thoughts to Hans' whitetail of horrors, you might come up with more questions than answers. Like, why did the other two bucks show up and not Buster? And, why not a single doe?

The answers will come once the final clue to locating deer in snowy conditions is plugged in: the yarding instinct.

Federal researcher L. David Mech has radio-tracked deer in northern Minnesota while investigating the many mysteries of yarding migrations. Some of his findings can affect deer hunting strategy. For example:

- Temperature is more of a factor than snow depth in triggering deer movements toward traditional yards.
- Moderating temperatures were observed to have influenced deer in a reverse role: rising temperatures drew deer out of their winter yards and back toward summer ranges.
- In some areas, the deer made a beeline for time-honored yards, traveling distances of 20 to 30 miles within a day or two.
- In other areas, more gradual migrations toward the densest cover of the non-winter range were observed, especially following significant snowfalls.

The hunter who is greeted with an early winter during the deer season, or the one who opts for late-season slug, bow or blackpowder hunter, needs to familiarize himself with how deer yard up in northern climes. He is particularly vulnerable to becoming "trapped" between deer movements, unless he correctly analyzes the unfolding conditions before him.

Start by asking your state conservation agency the right questions about your particular hunting area. Precisely where do deer yard up? Does he feel that deer tend to make a swift move toward a yard, or do they gradually move to heavier cover? As an example, in northeastern Minnesota, radical, long-distance movements are more common than in Michigan, where Ozoga generally sees a gradual shift toward heavy cover that "might not be ideal shelter, but offers better browse than the core of a yard."

Next, make note of the thickest cover in your hunting area. If you think you're already hunting the thick stuff, look again. Chances are, you've been compromising and choosing areas with small openings or those with scattered "shooting lanes." They just won't do this time of the year. The deer move into the kind of thickets that you almost have to walk backwards to get through. Those at the headwaters of a waterway, or riverbottom ribbons are always a good place to start your search. So are cedar swamps abutting hardwood ridges, pine plantations and hemlock stands.

Knowing where to hunt deer when the snow flies is helpful only if you know how to hunt them during this special time. There is really only one way: harder. Ironically, many hunters relax a bit and think it's easier now than without snow. They reason that a brown coat against a white backdrop stands out better than when it's against a brown or gray one, so they don't have to look so hard. Wanna bet? Don't forget that you, too, stand out more readily to the deer. They also know that snow muffles woods noise, and they'll turn to their eyes to help confirm their noses' suspicions.

You should follow suit. Instead of relaxing your eyes when the snow flies, work them overtime in hopes of seeing deer well before they see you. You'll rarely get a double-take from a whitetail, like mulies often do. And this is one time of the year they'll spook at the slightest movement, regardless of wind direction, if they've been pressured at all. What a sinking feeling is to find a fresh set of big tracks with 20-foot spaces between them.

This leaves only one option—don a pair of binoculars whenever it snows. If you hunt deep woods, carry a pair of compacts. For farmland deer hunting, tote along a larger, more powerful set. You'll appreciate the way snow reflects light and gives you added resolution and detail, even in dim situations.

To get the most out of your optics, slow down and check out anything that looks "different." I've found that a deer's nose sticks out best, followed by its eyes, ears and white throat.

Without binoculars, it's next to impossible to tell a big deer from an average one in dense cover. Once I spotted what appeared to be a nice buck, and was about to launch a 180-grain bullet from my .308, when I thought I'd take a closer peek with the glasses. The wind was right and I was well hidden, so why not? It turned out to be an overstuffed forkhorn, and I decided to let it go, which turned out to be a good idea—a decent 10-pointer showed up only moments later (that would have come by while I dressed out the smaller buck). I'll never forget that lesson!

Another trick for spotting deer before they spot you is to use your peripheral vision for picking up movement, rather than relying strictly upon head-on eyesight. There is a trick to it: avoid staring at the suspected target. Instead, look off to one side and let your peripheral vision tell you if there's something alive there. I'm continually amazed at how this part of the human anatomy functions, and it can be a great asset to a deer hunter.

What about hunting in the thick of a snowstorm? Standard whitetail dogma dictates that deer sit tight, as should you until the front passes through. I wholeheartedly disagree. Sure, the deer hunker down, but that can be to your advantage if you get off your stand. The only percentage shot for sneaking up on a wary, bedded buck is when it's snowing sideways. He'll have a heck of a time seeing you, and he certainly won't hear you. The main obstacles are making sure you see antlers, and getting off a quick shot. It won't be "easy" unless you first know where the bedding areas are. You must be able to concentrate at a very intense level without any lulls or wavering.

Deer hunting and fresh snow seem to be made for each other. But it can be a love/hate relationship if Snow White pays a visit during the deer season and you're caught out of position like one of her dwarfs. Remember, there's a big difference between responding to changing circumstances and reacting in a panic when the changes come.

13   Midday Monsters

BY GREG MILLER

Early risers don't always get the biggest bucks.

We were heading back to camp when we saw the monster whitetail. The time was 11:45 a.m. on a hot November day. Pat Reeve, chief videographer for Hunter's Specialties, was sitting next to me in the truck. Ever true to his profession, Pat took a quick look at the deer and immediately grabbed the bulky beta-cam video camera that rested on the floor between his feet. He hit the 'on' button and quickly shoved the camera out his open window.

The buck stayed on course and lunged across the gravel road just a few yards in front of my front bumper. I immediately turned the truck sideways and slammed on the brakes. This gave Pat a clear 'shot' at the deer as it loped across a cut soybean field. The massive-beamed monarch ran a couple hundred yards, then stopped and looked back in our direction. It was an awesome sight—and one that I can relive over and over again thanks to Pat's quick work with his video camera.

Midday Can Be a Hot Time

Our encounter with the above mentioned buck didn't come as a great surprise to either Pat or myself. Both of us have been playing this game long enough to know that rutting whitetail bucks have a reputation for being quite active during the midday hours. What did surprise us, however, is that the big buck was out and about with the weather the way it was. It wasn't warm, it was downright hot! If memory serves me right, the temperature at the time was pushing into the mid-70's. That's the main reason Pat and I had already called a halt to our morning hunt.

Like I said, the midday hours often prove to be extremely hot when it comes to rutting buck action. Let me assure you, that statement isn't based on just a few isolated experiences either. Rather, it's based on solid evidence provided by several different sources. The whole thing got started both because of my own experiences and the fact that I was continually hearing stories about big buck encounters during the midday hours. Of course, this only served to pique my curiosity—which led me to do a bit of personal research on the phenomenon. The first thing I did was to go back and review my notes from the many interviews I've done with hunters who have been successful at taking huge bucks during the rut. (I was most interested in the time of day these individuals harvested their trophies.) The next thing I did was to make it a point to start asking some of my seminar attendees when they saw the majority of big buck activity during the rut. Finally, I looked at the times when my hunting partners and me have had encounters with big bucks during the rut. This included actual kills, close calls and mere sightings of mature animals.

I put all the data together and was actually quite surprised when the final numbers came up. Better than 60-percent of all the rutting buck encounters I'd documented had occurred between the hours of 9:30 a.m. and 3:30 p.m. I had always suspected rutting bucks were somewhat active during the midday hours, but I would never have dreamed that the level of activity would be this significant. And I'd be willing to bet there are lots of other hunters who also would be surprised by my findings.

For those who might be skeptical about the midday buck movement thing, I ask that you search your memory banks just a bit. How many times have you spotted big bucks out and about while driving home from a morning rut hunt? How many times have you heard the rural mail carriers, milk haulers, farmers, etc. from your neck of the woods talk about seeing rutting bucks cruising around in wide open spaces during the middle of the day? And how many times have you heard or read about some other hunter shooting a huge buck during the midday hours? I'm sure the answers to those questions will convince most of you that I'm on the right track here.

So Why Are Rutting Bucks So Active at Midday?

I really wish I knew the true answer to that question. Not that I haven't heard my share of speculation and assumptions as to why rutting bucks are so active during the midday hours. Over the past several years some of my seminar attendees have provided me with a rash of 'theories' as to why big bucks display such behavior. Truth be told, I even have a theory of my own. But before examining mine, let's look at a couple of the more interesting theories I've heard from other hunters.

Actually, the first theory I'm going to cover has been suggested to me more often than any other. It seems there are an awful lot of people out there who believe that big bucks wait until later in the day to move because they know that doing so means there's less chance of encountering hunters. If this theory is indeed true, then it means that midday buck activity is dictated solely by hunting pressure (or more accurately, a lack of pressure). This could be the case in some areas, but I'm afraid the theory doesn't hold true across the board. Why not? Because I've seen bucks displaying the behavior even in areas where hunting pressure had forever been extremely light and/or almost non-existent.

Another theory I've heard concerns the amount of traveling mature bucks do during the rut. As one hunter told me, "The reason you see big bucks moving around later in the morning is because they were probably out all night chasing does in another area miles away. It then takes the bucks a few hours of traveling in the morning to get back to their home ranges." Like the one above, this theory might apply in some instances, but it certainly doesn't totally explain the midday movement thing. As many deer hunters know, big bucks make only periodic visits to their home ranges during the rut.

So what's my theory on the midday activity thing? To be very honest, I do agree somewhat that hunting pressure has forced bucks to adopt midday movement patterns. More than anything, though, I believe the behavior is a product of nature. Put simply, rutting bucks move about a lot during the midday hours because doing so allows them to more thoroughly check specific areas for estrous does—while at the same time expending the least amount of energy.

Countless times during the past 20 years I've watched big bucks scent-check doe/fawn bedding areas during the rut. The routine was pretty much the same each time. To begin with, the bucks almost always showed up later in the morning. They would slowly walk on the downwind side of the bedding areas, stopping occasionally to stick their noses in the air to check for the presence of an estrous doe. If the bucks detected some estrous odor, they'd charge into the bedding area and quickly sort out which deer was to be the object of their affections. And if they didn't detect a hot doe, the bucks would immediately head off to check some other promising spots.

I've seen the same type of behavior when hunting along parallel runways during the rut. I can almost always count on any big buck activity occurring during the midday hours. And if I do see a big buck, he's almost always doing the same thing. The searching deer will be in that familiar 'rut walk', stopping only long enough to scent-check any and all crossing runways he encounters. If the buck sniffs some estrous scent, he'll immediately jump on the trail of the hot doe. And if he doesn't, the buck will continue his search.

It wasn't until about 12 years ago that I finally figured out why mature bucks waited until later in the day to scent-check doe/fawn bedding areas. They know that waiting until that time will ensure that all the antlerless deer will be bedded down. It's the same reason why big bucks often wait until later in the morning to cruise parallel runways. By that time all the antlerless deer will have left nearby feeding areas—which means the bucks will be able to scent-check 100-percent of the antlerless deer that visited those feeding areas. Like I said, I don't believe it's learned behavior, but rather, something nature has endowed upon whitetail bucks.

Warm Weather Doesn't Totally Shut Down Activity

I'm sure that most deer hunters would agree that bouts of warmer than normal weather can dramatically suppress daytime rut activity. One only has to look at the slow ruts we've endured the last two years to appreciate what I'm saying. There's no doubt that the warm to downright hot temperatures we endured during the past two Novembers are responsible for the depressing ruts we've experienced in each of those years. But that doesn't mean midday activity during those years was non-existent. The big buck mentioned at the beginning of this article was out 'cruising', even though the temperature was in the 70's. And I had an encounter with another big buck just this past season that proves the previous experience wasn't a fluke.

It was 2 o'clock in the afternoon on the fourth of November when I climbed the 16 feet to my treestand in a mature red oak. I usually have no trouble keeping a positive outlook when the rut is in full swing, but things were different on this day. The temperature had eased into the lower 70's here in my home state of Wisconsin, and as a result, I was having a tough time remaining focused. Perhaps that's why the buck managed to approach so close before I realized he was there.

The rut-crazed deer was busily rubbing his antlers on a three-inch sapling just 50 yards from my stand site when I first spotted him. He soon finished his business and began walking slowly toward me. I let the buck get approximately 10-yards straight out in front of me before stopping him with a voice-grunt. I was already at full draw with the Mathew's MQ-32, and an instant later an ACC-340 was speeding toward the big deer's vitals. The buck kicked out his hind legs at the hit, but ran only about 30 yards before stopping. I watched as the deer tipped over for good several seconds later.

My brother Mike recently had an experience with a monster whitetail that further illustrates the benefits of hunting during the midday. Mike's encounter took place at 10:30 in the morning on a bluebird November day. As my brother told me later, "I could hardly believe it, I was sitting on my stand when I looked off to my right and saw this huge buck standing 75 yards away glaring at my decoy. The sun was shining directly on the buck, and it was fairly warm, but that didn't seem to bother him in the least. The next thing I knew, he was slowly walking my way."

The trophy whitetail continued to cut the distance until he was within 35 yards of Mike's stand site. But for some reason, the deer started acting hinky at that point. According to Mike's description of the ordeal, it was just one of those things that older whitetail bucks seem able to do; the monster 10-pointer had somehow sensed that something wasn't quite right. The buck hadn't pushed the panic button, but at the same time it was apparent he wasn't coming any closer. Unfortunately, my brother's arrow skimmed just under the buck's chest.

Water Is a Key to Success

There's one very important point that must be mentioned regarding rutting buck activity during bouts of warm weather. The closer you set-up to watering areas the more midday activity you're likely to see. It's a well-known fact that big buck can go for days during the rut without filling their bellies. But they can go only a short time without water. Here in the north rutting bucks must have water every day. What's more, antlerless deer tend to feed and bed closer to their water supplies during periods of warmer weather. So it only stands to reason that the bulk of rutting activity, especially during the midday hours, is going to occur relatively close to deer watering spots.

My friend Dan Perez from Missouri is one of the most accomplished trophy whitetail hunters I know. Dan has managed to arrow some very impressive bucks while hunting in Illinois during the rut the past few seasons. Every one of those deer was taken in very close proximity to water. Interestingly, the biggest buck, a 10-pointer that scored in the upper-140's, was shot at 3:30 in the afternoon. Dan was set-up within 20 yards of a water hole when the buck made its appearance. "The 10-pointer was trailing along behind two does, but instead of following them when they went to get a drink, he circled around the water hole," Dan told me. "That move eventually led him to within 10 yards of my stand site."

I can't say for sure that any of the theories I've cited in this article are justifiable explanations for why rutting bucks are so active at midday. But then I don't know if such an explanation even exists. I do know this, however. My hunting partners and me have had enough encounters with mature bucks at midday to know that it's a consistent form of behavior. And that's all the proof I need to justify spending a little more time on my rut stands during the middle part of the day.

14 Sunup to Sundown: The Rewards of All-Day Hunting

BY GARY CLANCY

Our hunting camp has averaged a 70% success ratio for 17 years! Why? Because every hunter stays in the woods all day, every day!

For the past 17 seasons, a group of us, with face changes brought about by the introduction of a young son, the death of a friend or the relocation of a member, have met on the south ridge of a sprawling hardwood valley on the eve of the opening of the deer season. We are a group of hunters much like your own I suspect. We are truckers, machinists, students, retirees, and businessmen. We hunt from three to seven days each, depending upon our individual schedules and the length of the season. To look at us, it would not be apparent that we differ in any way from other hunting camps, but we do. In an area where the success rate has fluctuated between 18 and 31 percent over the span of those 17 seasons, our group of hunters has compiled an outstanding 70% rate over the years.

Why? I've given that question serious thought. A couple of our hunters are better than average woodsmen. Two are crack shots. One is a student of whitetail behavior. A few insist on frequent scouting trips prior to the season. And although woodsmanship, familiarity with the area, a knowledge of whitetail habits and marksmanship come into play, the biggest reason our group consistently does so well is because each of us spends *all day, every day* in the woods.

Deer don't spend much time hanging around cabins, tents, campers and motels. Whitetails don't tend to frequent country cafes and roadside taverns. They don't often saunter by the strings of idling pickups and automobiles parked along country roads. No, deer spend their time in the woods, and so do our hunters. An hour or more before first light our hunters slip into the timber. Those who hunt farthest from camp will not be back until an hour after dark.

Whitetails do not do anything by the clock. Instead, they are creatures of instinct and habit. But for the sake of clarity, we can break the hunting day down into four periods to better illustrate how whitetail habits and hunter activity at the different times of the day interreact to create hunting opportunities all day long. The four periods are: first shooting light until mid-morning, mid-morning until noon, noon until mid-afternoon, and mid-afternoon until the end of hunting hours.

At no time during the entire deer season am I more confident, more keyed-up and charged with anticipation than during the season's first hours of daylight. Of course with nearly half of the total harvest in some states occurring during the first morning of hunting, it is hard not to be excited, confident, and bubbling with expectations. Even after the opener has passed, those first hours of the day are a favorite time for most hunters. Because most hunters consider these hours "prime time," all of us who hunt on either public or private land where hunting pressure is a factor, benefit from a combination of the whitetail's natural inclination to be on the move at this time of the day and increased activity due to hunting pressure. Any time you have that kind of "double whammy" working in your favor, the odds of your lining your sights up on a buck escalate.

The very best early morning stands are located where they take advantage of the whitetail's natural movements between feeding areas and bedding sites while at the same time allowing the hunter to cover the route a spooked deer will take to reach safety. Although you might expect that such stand locations are rare gems, fortunately, the opposite is true; these double duty stand sites abound.

The key to locating these prime early morning stand locations is to first pin-point the area where the deer are feeding and where they tend to bed down for the day. In farm country and fringeland habitat this process is simple. Any farm kid who rides the school bus morning and evening can tell you where he has seen deer feeding, or you can locate your own by taking a few "deer spotting" drives with the wife and kids in the evening. A little backtracking will lead you to the bedding areas. The heads of draws, south facing slopes and brushy flats are favored locations. Where timber is at a premium, whitetails often spend the day in sloughs and swales. In big timber this detective work is not so simple. But even here, the deer will often key on specific areas to feed. An oak ridge in a predominantly conifer forest is sure to attract attention from the acorn loving whitetail. Clear cuts and burns which have grown up to new grasses, forbs and seedlings are used heavily by foraging whitetails. So are the swaths created by powerlines and pipelines.

My favorite place for a stand along the route deer naturally travel, as they meander from breakfast to bed, is the thickest piece of cover I can locate along that often ill-defined passageway. The closer it is to the area the deer bed, the better I like it. My reasons are simple. Deer which are undisturbed tend to dilly-dally along the way as they leisurely move between feeding and bedding areas. At no point do they tarry as long as they do when in the security of thick cover along their chosen route. And, when these deer are pressured and hurrying from open feeding areas to the security of bedding sites, they invariably slow down when they slip into thick cover enroute.

Our natural inclination is to erect our stands where we have the greatest field of view. Although these stands are great for *seeing* deer, they are not conducive to clean, one-shot kills. Whitetails, even when not pressured, just naturally hurry through these areas which offer hunters panoramic views and unobstructed shooting. When pressured, they often *race* by these stands. Me, I would rather have one shot at a slow moving or stationary buck in cover, than to fling a clip full of lead at a whitetail racing across the open. At my favorite early-morning stand locations, a little judicious pruning has created fire lanes where I can take a clear shot as a buck steps across these narrow slots.

Mid-Morning to Noon

Natural movement is limited during these hours, but whitetail activity often peaks as hunters vacate stands and make their way to the warmth of car heaters, camps, or saunter over to visit hunting partners. Many hunters still-hunt during these hours, and even the best still-hunters move many deer which they never see. Some hunters meet at mid-morning to begin conducting drives. All of that hunter movement puts deer on the move, deer which can end up in your sights if you stay put on a good stand.

The number one location for a stand during the mid-morning until noon period is a funnel area. A funnel area is any man-made or natural constriction in the cover which will limit a whitetail's options when it's sneaking away from other hunters. Brushy fencelines connecting two woodlots; that place where the timber narrows along the creek; a narrow cedar swamp twisting between two ridges of mature pine; these are a few examples of funnel areas.

The hardest part about sticking it out on a stand during the mid-morning to noon period is that hunter traffic can become discouraging. Often, as hunters have trudged by within site of my stand I have had to fight with myself to stay put, to convince myself that hunter traffic is working in my favor, instead of against me. I have to constantly assure myself that whitetails are masters at slipping around, between and through hunters and that my best chance for a buck is to let those mobile hunters move a deer past my stand.

A couple of years ago, I climbed into my mid-morning stand about 9:00 o'clock. Above my stand an old logging road skirted the side of the hill. That logging road was a favored route for hunters entering and leaving the valley, but it also dissected two prime bedding areas, and I was betting that sooner or later one of the hunters using the trail would slip off into the brush and send a buck sneaking my way.

About a half hour later I had climbed into the stand, a group of three hunters tromped up the trail, guns over their shoulders, talking loudly and having a good old time. Barely were they out of sight when a lone hunter plodded up the old tote road behind the trio. Ten minutes later two more hunters made the climb and I began that old familiar tug-of-war within my gut. The "sitter" in me prevailed, and fifteen minutes later I heard a twig snap above the trail and turned slightly in my portable stand to get in a better position. The buck came sneaking down off of the brushy flat above the old logging road, stopping to look both ways before crossing that busy trail, reminding me of my children as they crossed the street in front of our house on the way to school. Satisfied that the coast was clear he effortlessly cleared the logging road, took three more bounds down the hill and then slipped into that familiar ground-eating fast walk which a whitetail most often uses when he wants to put some distance between himself and whatever disturbed him. At 30 yards the buck stopped, turned his swollen neck to study his backtrail, and I sent a 12-gauge slug through the 200-pound buck's lungs.

I was taking pictures a few minutes later when I heard voices above me and turned to see two young hunters crash down off of the flat and meet on the logging road. "See anything?" I heard the farther hunter ask. "Naw," answered the nearer hunter. "Let's go back to the truck and get a sandwich and come back later."

Hunter traffic is not a deterrent to success during this period, rather, it is the catalyst for fast action.

Noon Until Mid-Afternoon

Any time you have sufficient numbers of hunters in the woods to keep the deer on the move, the same funnel area stands used during the mid-morning to noon period are your best choice during this period. Often I move from one stand to another located in a different funnel area just for a change of scenery. Climbing into a new stand is often enough to recharge my sagging confidence cells. I don't go deer hunting to battle boredom, and making sure I have a number of stands from which to choose helps insure that I stay alert.

After the first few days of the season, however, hunters can be mighty scarce in the woods. Fewer hunters hunt after the first two or three days of the season, and those that do are rarely still in the woods at noon. Fortunately, for those of us who prefer to spend all day in the woods, when hunting pressure does not force a whitetail to "hole-up," he will be active for a short period around noon. This is when a buck will rise from his bed, stretch, urinate, defecate and browse for up to an hour before again lying down. Often a buck will lie back down on his old bed, or make a new depression very close to the one he vacated. All of this activity takes place within the confines of the bedding area, and rarely will a deer venture more than 100 yards from the place where he had bedded for the morning.

This is my favorite time to slowly prowl along the edges of known bedding areas. Most of the places whitetails bed, and especially the larger bucks, are so thick as to discourage still-hunting. But by s-l-o-w-l-y patrolling the edges of these thickets and using binoculars to pick apart the cover, I have often been afforded opportunities at whitetails as they enjoyed the mid-day stretch.

Without getting into the whole business of binoculars for the whitetail hunter I can tell you from my own experience that if you do not use good glasses to probe the places bucks bed, you will see only a fraction of the deer up and about during the mid-day stretch. When first attempting to peer into the thickets with binoculars, I could see only a wall of twigs and branches. But with practice, I learned to ignore the clutter and concentrate on the openings. I learned to detect the slightest motion. To pick up on the subtle color difference between a deer hide and the hide of an ash tree. If you insist upon relying upon the unaided eye for this type of hunting, you are in for a lesson in frustration.

As much as I love to prowl the edges of bedding areas, there are many times when such a tactic is useless. Anytime the footing is noisy due to either dry forest litter or crusted snow I opt for a stand overlooking bedding sites for my noon to mid-afternoon vigil. If I can locate a rise above a suspected bedding site, I often opt for a ground blind. I can move quietly into a ground blind and create less commotion than I can when climbing into a treestand. However, if a ground blind cannot afford me a peek into the buck's bedrooms, I will take my chances on being detected and get into a treestand as quietly as possible. Even if the buck does not show for the noon-time stretch, there is a good chance that hunters moving back into the woods later in the afternoon will disturb deer which will offer me a shot.

Mid-Afternoon Until the End of Hunting Hours

Archers know that the last minutes of light are often the best moments of the day for whitetail activity. Forced to choose one hour out of the day for bow hunting I would without hesitation select the last hour of legal hunting time. Maybe that is why it has always been a surprise to me that relatively few hunters are actually *hunting* right up to the last legal minute during the firearms deer season. There seems to be a tendency with firearms hunters to vacate the woods early, to return to the warmth of home or camp. Maybe it is an unconscious desire to be out of the woods before dark. Whatever the reason, few gun hunters are still seriously hunting during the hour of dusk, and that is a big mistake.

Whitetails are creatures of habit. They are accustomed to moving from daytime bedding areas to evening feeding areas late in the day. Hunting pressure will cause them to delay this normal cycle, but more often than not, I have found hunting pressure to be light during the last hour of light, even during the early days of the firearms deer season.

Many hunters opt to spend the evening hours looking over the open places deer feed during the evening. Again, it is a case of greater visibility attracting more hunters. However, deer which have been pressured during the day are reluctant to step into the open while shooting light remains. The bigger the buck, the less chance you have of finding him ambling into the open before full dark. That is why I prefer to hunt from a stand located nearer the bedding area during the evening. When that buck makes his move from his bed and begins the slow trip to chow, I want him to be where I can intercept him at the beginning of the trip.

In northwestern Wisconsin where I annually hunt during the week of Thanksgiving, the deer browse heavily on scattered clearcuts where forbs, grasses and shrubs abound. When not pressured, they often spend the entire day in some of the more mature clearcuts, but during the gun season they head for the security of heavy cover by day and feed in the clearcuts at night. Hunting in Wisconsin ends at 4:30 each day, which that far north is about the same time as the sun sets at this time of the year. I had put a portable stand up in a pine where I could overlook a 75-yard-wide swath cut through the forest of mostly mature pines. My scouting had shown that the deer were not using the narrow clearcut for feeding, but were crossing it as they moved between bedding sites and a larger older clearcut to the east.

A doe and fawn picked their way across the clearcut at 4:00 o'clock, and a few minutes later another doe, this one alone, did the same. When only minutes were left to hunt, another deer stepped from the now-black timber and with head held low slowly walked across the opening. I cranked the Bushnell scope up to 7 power and studied what I could see of the deer's head for any sign of antlers. I saw none. But then, just before slipping into the timber on the far side of the opening, the deer lifted its head and looked in my direction. A fat spike buck was just what Nancy Clancy had ordered when I had left home, and that was exactly what I was looking at. As the buck walked into the timber I put the crosshairs on his chest and touched the trigger. It was 4:29.

Hunting all day is not for everyone. Many hunters have no desire to spend all day in the woods. For many hunters, deer season is a time to get away from the city and spend some time in the woods with old friends. If they happen to get a buck, well, that is a nice bonus. More power to these folks. But if you are tired of coming home without a deer, if you really want to begin seeing more deer and having more opportunity to fill your tag, then I suggest you plan now to spend *all day, every day* in the woods.

Hanging in There: Tips for All-Day Hunting

Hunting all day can be torture if you are cold, wet, tired, hungry or thirsty. To make sure my all day hunts are pleasant affairs, I have learned to take a few precautions.

One is to get adequate rest. I enjoy a game of cards or an evening bull session as much as anyone, but at the risk of being labeled "an old party pooper" or worse, I turn in early when hunting. In the morning I am up early and on my stand in plenty of time without rushing.

Cold and wet hunters don't last the entire day in the woods. With today's fabrics and insulators there is really no reason to suffer from being cold or wet. I always carry a large fanny pack or day pack in which I have a light suit of rain gear and one extra layer of clothing (a down vest is my personal favorite) which I can put on as needed. When hiking into my stand in the morning I often carry a layer or two of clothing in the pack to avoid perspiring on the hike in.

Also in the pack is enough food and water to see me comfortably through the day. I have learned that I eat more during the day than I think I will while packing lunch in the morning, so I always throw in a little extra. When the weather is cold, I allow myself the luxury of a small fire on which I warm up sandwiches (wrap them in aluminum foil), a small can of beans and a cup of coffee or tea. Hot food in the belly makes the afternoon and evening hunts all the more enjoyable.

My fanny pack also contains a drag rope, tree steps, scents, a compass, matches, a couple of disposable hand-warmers, extra cartridges, dog whistle, T.P. in a plastic bag and a larger plastic bag in which I fully intend to place the heart and liver of a buck.

If the author can locate a site for a ground blind which affords him a peek into a buck's bedding area, he often opts to keep his feet on the ground for the noon- to mid-afternoon period.

The author's well traveled day pack holds everything he needs to spend a safe, comfortable and enjoyable day in the woods.

Without binoculars, the author claims that trying to still-hunt the edges of bedding areas is a waste of time.

Treestands in a variety of locations afford the author the opportunity to move as the time periods and hunter pressure dictate.

While other hunters are on the move, seeking companionship and milling about, the hunter still on stand reaps the rewards.

15   Beaver Bog Bucks

BY BOB MCNALLY

Sure they're tough to hunt, but that's why the bucks are there!

Ray McIntyre was out of his usual treestand element, but he knew he was in the right place at the right time. McIntyre is president of Warren & Sweat Tree Stands, in Grand Island, Florida, and as such, the bulk of his hunting is done from the treetops in prime whitetail regions throughout America. But McIntyre was in rubber wading boots, chest high in dark, tannin-stained beaver bog water, and he was looking through binoculars at one of the best bucks he'd seen in awhile.

McIntyre is a self-proclaimed "bog rat," because he knows the biggest, oldest and wisest whitetails invariably head to the thickest, nastiest, most impenetrable tangles they can find once hunting season gets underway. Those places often are ponds and swamps created by beaver dams—which take on different wetland forms throughout the whitetail range in America. But in McIntyre's home hunting turf of Florida, beaver swamps are big, mucky, palmetto-and-brier-infested spots full of mosquitoes, ticks, alligators, and cottonmouths. They're the kind of areas most sensible people avoid like an IRS audit. But McIntyre has killed dozens of deer—including many of his biggest bucks—from such places.

So on that particular cold December day, McIntyre was wading back into a boggy spot far from the nearest road. He was trying to locate an isolated high-and-dry place in the Upper St. Johns River basin of central Florida. He had been hunting uplands adjacent to the beaver swamp for several weeks, and with each passing day the deer—especially the good bucks—had become increasingly scarce. That's when he knew it was time to track into the cold water of the beaver bottom, just as the savvy bucks had.

Like he'd done so many times before, McIntyre got a topographic map of his hunt area, then an aerial photo of the region. By comparing the two maps and using knowledge he'd gained of hunting the upland territory earlier that year, McIntyre discovered that there were several small islands—just high spots, really—in the middle of a huge, nearly impenetrable beaver bottom in the heart of the area he'd been hunting. So early one morning McIntyre got his rifle, compass, binoculars, lightweight treestand and chest waders and headed for a Florida jungle that more hunters would call hell than heaven.

He drove to a savanna near the beaver pond bank, crossed it, then when he approached water he changed from knee-high rubber boots to chest-high rubber waders. (In winter, swamp water is cold, even in Florida, and waders afford some protection from snakes.) It took some time wandering around in the flooded cypress trees, briers and swamp water, but eventually McIntyre located what he had been looking for.

"A lot of times you can tell a high spot or island from surrounding beaver bog because some trees are just a bit taller than others nearby," he said. "I saw a pretty good group of tall trees in the area about where my maps showed there was an island. So I headed toward it, in about waist-deep water."

From years of hunting beaver bogs, McIntyre knew it was smart to check well ahead with binoculars in order to spot deer that might be unaware of his presence.

"Deer don't expect danger from water, especially older animals that have learned they're safe on islands surrounded by beaver ponds," McIntyre said. "If you wade quietly, keep the wind in your favor and take your time hunting, you can sneak right up on huge ol' mossy-horn swamp bucks hiding on islands. I've stalked close to bedded swamp bucks, and I've even shot some of them from just a few yards while they were sleeping. It's really exciting hunting, but you've got to do it right."

From about 75 yards, McIntyre scanned the beaver swamp island with binoculars. First he spotted a sow wild hog with several piglets. Then, some distance away, he saw a doe with two yearlings feeding on browse. He was just about to circle the island to check other areas from a distance when sunlight reflected off something near a big, fallen cypress tree.

"I had to move slightly to get a clearer view of the shiny object, but when I did, the deer turned, too, and I saw his seven-point rack glistening in the sun," McIntyre said. "The deer was bedded and turned slightly toward the sow hog and pigs, and I got a good look at his rack. It was an easy shot to the neck. The buck never got up from his bed."

McIntyre waded to the island, field-dressed his deer, then scouted the place. It was a whitetail haven, with trails, buck rubs and scrapes everywhere.

"It was a long, narrow island maybe two acres in size that necked-down in one place, and deer sign there was incredible," he said. "It was the perfect place to hang a treestand, which is what I did. I hunted that island off and on for a couple years, and I took a lot of good bucks and wild hogs there. There even were some black bears that occasionally moved onto that beaver pond island because it was remote and a real haven for animals trying to escape man."

McIntyre emphasizes that beaver bog islands don't have to be large to accommodate deer. In fact, he's taken a tremendous number of whitetails from mere "high spots," or "tussocks," as he calls them, that aren't much bigger than a small bedroom. All a deer wants from an island is a comparatively dry place to lie down that is remote and isolated enough to avoid the hunters, dogs and civilization of nearby uplands. Such beaver bog islands, says McIntyre, are "predator proof" for whitetails.

Deer become so habitual in their use of beaver ponds that McIntyre says whitetails—including huge bucks—use them even during dry spells when much of the sloughs evaporate. One reason for this is because an in-the-timber beaver pond has much more cover, such as briers and thickets, than nearby places that don't fill with water.

I hunted just such a "seasonally" dry beaver bayou with McIntyre one autumn at deer-rich Portland Landing Hunting Reserve, near Camden, Alabama. McIntyre has a favorite area in Portland Landing that he calls his "hole." It's a big, dark, imposing beaver swamp full of cat-claw briers, tangled thickets, inky boot-sucking mud and some of the best bucks the "black belt" region of west-central Alabama can produce.

I followed McIntyre into the place one morning before daybreak, and to me, in the dark, his "island" didn't look any different than the rest of the huge beaver swamp we were in. But when daylight came, it was easy to see that his island was just slightly above the high-water marks on nearby cypress trees.

Also on the island, where I hunted from a portable treestand, there was an abundance of low, thick cover that offered beaver bucks browse, as well as water oaks that were "raining" acorns. McIntyre showed me a trail deer used to access the island during high water near the oaks. The trail was still heavily used in the mostly dry wetland, even though animals could easily step onto the island from any direction. It was obvious that the bulk of the deer coming to the island were walking the same trail they used in wetter weather.

"Whitetails are creatures of habit," McIntyre said. "For years they use trails that lead to islands from beaver swamps, and when the water recedes they still use the trails. In fact, during periods of low water, looking around in dried beaver swamps is a great way to pinpoint high spots or islands where deer concentrate when the water rises.

"Sometimes in big beaver bottoms that are wet most of the time, I rent a small airplane and fly the place to learn where islands are located. I look for oak trees because they survive best on high ground, or trees taller than the rest of the swamp vegetation. In some areas it's easiest to find islands during winter when leaves have fallen from trees."

McIntyre has spent so many years walking and sloshing through beaver habitat that he has little trouble finding his way around—even in the dark—with a compass, flashlight and map. But if you're like me and can get lost on an interstate highway, that same equipment McIntyre uses plus a handheld GPS navigational unit can be a real asset. Such navigational aids are extremely accurate and easy to use for hunters traipsing through a big beaver bog for the first time. Once I've found a swamp island with plenty of deer sign, I simply mark a trail to the place with reflective tape and/or orange ribbon.

As noted earlier, often the best islands in beaver bottoms have an abundance of deer food, like browse or oak trees that drop acorns. In some big swamps, high water that washes up and out of a flood plain can pull huge quantities of acorns with it when the water recedes. This happens a lot in broad, lowland rivers where there are beaver bayous.

Once, while hunting with good friend Toxey Haas, owner of Mossy Oak Camouflage, I was shown such a remarkable spot in an isolated area of a then-dry beaver swamp. It was December, and the Mississippi bottomland had been flooded that fall. The water had washed out hundreds of acres of lowland hardwoods, mainly chestnut oaks, which bear massive acorns the size of golf balls.

When scouting the beaver pond edge, Haas had located several places where acorns had piled up in unbelievable concentrations as the swamp water receded. In a couple places, so many of the giant acorns littered the ground that walking on them was treacherous because they acted like massive ball bearings. In some spots the acorns were stacked several inches thick, and whitetails were flocking to those stockpiles like nobody's business. The tremendous abundance of food, plus the remoteness of the beaver swamp made for a hunting combination that proved to be the demise of more than one good buck that December.

Haas and friend Ronnie "Cuz" Strickland hunted near the edge of that Mississippi bayou late one afternoon. Strickland was running a video camera and got footage of Haas taking a huge seven-point buck. At the shot, the deer instantly headed into the beaver swamp—his long-time, natural haven and hiding area. The deer died in the water, just 30 yards from Strickland and Haas.

The most intriguing and telling part of that remarkable footage is that the buck immediately headed through three-foot-deep water when he was hit. There is no question that the animal was trying to escape to his secluded beaver pond home.

Some beaver habitats that attract and harbor tremendous numbers of deer are in lowland marsh areas. Some of the best whitetail beaver bayous I've ever hunted are choice duck and goose spots that I discovered held whitetails while hunting waterfowl. Successfully hunting such wetlands for whitetails presents special challenges, but they can be worked successfully.

Often such broad, muck-bottom beaver marshes have few trees large enough to accommodate stands. They typically have dense marsh grass, willows, alders and similar thick vegetation. Ground blinds can be very productive in these marshes. Also, large tripod, or "Texas tower," stands can work well when placed near trails and "runways" in willow-alder-marsh grass.

Some lowland beaver quagmires are bordered by ridges and high ground where tall trees grow. These peripheral areas are good spots from which to watch marshes with long-range rifles. Sometimes taking a stand in such an "overlook" is helpful in simply learning whether good bucks are using a broad beaver-built marsh.

I have a choice hunting spot in northern Illinois, for example, where a broad beaver-dammed duck marsh has virtually no trees for proper treestands. But several hundred yards away there is a hardwood ridge, and I place a tall stand in oaks there so that I can watch the bog. It's shotgun-only hunting, so I rarely get a shot at the bucks I see in the wetlands. But by carefully watching deer through binoculars and seeing where they bed in the marsh, I've successfully stalked, jumped and shot several of them.

Mentally marking the exact place where a buck beds in a marsh is vital, and it's important to stalk quietly to the spot with the wind in your face if you're to be successful. Proper use of a compass helps, too. Several years ago I spotted a heavy eight-pointer in that Illinois marsh, so I came down from my treestand and started a stalk. But once on the ground, sneaking low and quiet through the marsh, I got confused about the location of the small willow bush where I'd mentally "marked" the deer. The general area near where the deer was bedded was full of little willows, and when I flushed the deer from his hiding place, he unexpectedly got up behind me. Three snapshots from my 12-gauge Ithaca pump finally brought the buck down—with only the last slug hitting the deer.

That buck taught me to properly mark a spot before starting a stalk. The right way to "mark" a spot is to line up two or three easily identified objects, rather than just picking a single one. When you're on the ground stalking and trying to stay hidden, it's easy to get confused about the location of your mark. But by picking out several objects in a straight line and taking a compass bearing, the mark will be more definite, and you're more likely to be successful.

Big beaver marshes and bayous lend themselves to mini-drives, especially places where there are few trees. One key to successful drives is to have drivers with the wind at their backs, and they should slowly and quietly walk, almost like stillhunting, rather than yell, hoot and holler. Standers should be downwind, and if possible, they should get in portable treestands.

In the north, late-season hunting in big, tangled beaver pond draws can be remarkably productive because they freeze, making access much easier. One of the best spots I ever hunted was a cedar-tree swamp in central Wisconsin near the town of Black River Falls. It was impossible to work the place early in the year because tangled brush and sucking mud made it treacherous. But when the mud and swamp water froze solid, it was the first place I headed to for whitetails. Not many other hunters ventured into the frozen swamp because it still was a difficult place to get around in, due to its dense cedars, alders, briers and willows. But the place held a tremendous number of deer, and I took some nice bucks there.

Some of the best beaver bottoms for the biggest bucks also are among the most inaccessible and difficult to hunt. In fact, much of the time I gauge how good a beaver bog will be for hunting by how difficult it is to get into and out of. Hunting such spots is neither for overfed hunters, nor for those with physical limitations.

Even for healthy, fit sportsmen, beaver pond hunting can be taxing. For this reason, using the right hunting gear is important. Knee-high, hip-high or chest-high rubber boots have served my lowland hunting well. I carry a minimal amount of gear, using the smallest, lightest treestand possible. Any firearm capable of downing deer works okay in the beaver bottoms—so long as it's light, fast-handling and reliable. I also never venture into lowland tangles without plenty of insect repellent, a strong flashlight with extra batteries and plenty of trail-marking tape to find my way out again.

It may sound a little paranoid, but when I'm hunting alone, I always let someone know precisely where I am. This is especially important in beaver bog hell holes. Tell your wife or your hunting buddies, or leave a note in your car about where you are. Broad, wet and cold beaver bayous can be lonely, spooky places in the dark—which is precisely the reason they're so popular with wide-racked whitetails that have learned that these areas are rarely visited by man.

Part Three
The Rut

Whitetail Hunting's Big Show!

The rut . . . the whole rut . . . and nothing but the rut!

For some whitetail hunters, the rut is everything! It's now or never! Do or die! Bucks will be going bonkers pursuing does! Running right into our laps. Practically committing suicide.

Oh yeah? Well, if rut hunting is such a lay up, how come every hunter in the woods doesn't drag out a deer?

The truth, of course, is that while the rut can make your chances for bagging a buck considerably higher, rut hunting has its own disciplines and nuances that you must understand to hunt effectively. Hunting during the rut is not like collecting a paycheck or harvesting a crop. You have to hunt skillfully and know *the reason why* behind every move you make. Even during the rut, you have to *earn* your buck. Even then, you may not collect him!

16   Early Rubs—And How to Hunt Them

BY GREG MILLER

If you thought that scrapes were misunderstood, try asking hunters about rubs. Here, once and for all, are the facts about early antler rubs.

There was a time I absolutely hated the early part of the archery season—my hatred stemming from the fact that I had no clue how to figure out big bucks at this time of year. Oh sure, I knew all about doing the long-range observation thing in the weeks leading up to archery season. In fact, it was a rare occurrence when I hadn't spotted at least a half-dozen, shooter-size bucks prior to the opening of bow season. Figuring out where those bucks might be once opening day arrived, however, was another matter. I remained convinced for some time that I never would master the task.

But then I happened to witness an interesting and very informative occurrence while on one of my preseason observation trips. I had been watching a big buck as he grazed hungrily in a distant alfalfa field. After feeding for perhaps 15 minutes, the buck suddenly strolled over to the edge of a nearby woods. He first sniffed and then licked a stout, forearm-sized sapling. The buck then lowered his head and did his best to destroy the little tree. He was still grinding away on the sapling with his huge rack when darkness fell a half-hour later.

It was while I was closely inspecting the antler-scarred tree a few days later that it suddenly hit me: whitetail bucks did this sort of thing all the time! They made antler rubs all across their core areas throughout the entire pre-rut period. Further, from what I'd seen in the past, there usually was a spurt of rubbing activity just prior to opening day of our archery season. All I had to do was figure out a way I could use this particular buck behavioral trait to my advantage.

I've spent a great deal of time throughout the past 20 years increasing my base of knowledge about buck antler rubs. There's no doubt in my mind that this increase in knowledge has made me a more successful trophy whitetail hunter. But becoming more knowledgeable has also made me aware that some obvious fallacies concerning antler rubs are still making the rounds. One of the most oft-repeated of these fallacies has to do with early rubbing activity.

According to what some people would have you believe, the first bit of rub activity that occurs is an indication that the bucks are in the process of removing their antler velvet. In reality, however, early antler rubs have very little to do with actual velvet removal. In truth, the first real flurries of rub activity that occur are a signal that antler velvet has already been removed. (See "Smooth Transition," page 102.)

Interestingly, in most parts of North America, this first flurry of rubbing activity occurs in the days just prior to the opening of archery season for deer. Even more importantly, the vast majority of this rubbing activity occurs along those routes the bucks are currently using and will continue to use throughout the first few weeks of the archery season. This last bit of information can prove to be extremely beneficial to early season bowhunters.

Before continuing further, I think it's important to shed some light on several other key points regarding early antler rubs. To begin with, my research would indicate that the biggest bucks in a given area are usually the first animals to become rub-active. Also, big bucks usually make substantially more antler rubs during the early season than do immature bucks. And last, big bucks won't hesitate to take on some very large trees immediately after velvet removal. Smaller bucks just don't seem to possess this same aggressive attitude. At least not during early fall.

As stated, the majority of early antler rubs usually are found along the travel routes being used most by bucks at this time of year. However, bucks also display a real propensity for doing a lot of early rubbing around the outside perimeters of preferred feeding areas. Although it's always nice to see these first bits of buck sign suddenly appear, the importance of perimeter rubs as hunting aids is far too often overrated.

This is especially true when talking about mature bucks. Numerous past encounters with humans near food sources has resulted in big bucks everywhere developing mentalities that allow them to effectively deal with the situation. In most cases, they simply refuse to travel anywhere near a food source during daylight hours.

Still, those clusters of fresh rubs you find near food sources early in the season are proof positive that there are, indeed, some bucks nearby. Just keep in mind that, in most cases anyway, these bits of sign should be viewed as reference material only. You'll almost always realize a higher degree of early season success by setting up some distance away from the edges of feeding areas.

My good friend Doug Below has used his extensive knowledge of early antler rubs to ambush several large Wisconsin bucks. Doug agrees with me that big bucks usually become rub-active first. "I've actually seen a number of smaller bucks that were still in full velvet on opening day of the bow season. But I've never seen a mature buck in velvet at that time," he told me. "Obviously, if the bigger bucks are shedding their velvet first, then they must be responsible for the majority of early rubs. At least that seems to be the case in my hunting areas."

Doug also agrees with me that early rubs can play a huge role in hunter success rates. "Hunters need to realize that whitetail bucks relate very strongly to their rubs, even during the early part of the bow season," he stated. "But it's equally important to remember that your best chance of ambushing a big buck will come from stand sites located along active rub lines, some distance away from feeding areas."

Doug was quick to add that hunters should display extreme caution when scouting for rub-line stand sites during the early season. "I've noticed that big bucks have a tendency to bed somewhat closer to feeding areas at this time of year.

I believe that the thickness of underbrush and foliage has something to do with this behavior. But whatever the reason, I'd recommend that hunters limit their initial scouting and hunting efforts to about a 200-yard radius of feeding areas. If you haven't seen any buck activity after a couple hunts, then move your stands farther back into the woods."

According to Doug there is another definite "perk" to be realized by hunting along early rub lines.

"There have been numerous times when sitting along an early rub-line has provided me with an opportunity to see every buck that was living within a particular core area," he stated. "This is because the bucks are still pretty much in their bachelor groups at this time of year. And where one member of a bachelor group rubs, they all rub."

Doug cites the story about one of his best ever bow-killed whitetails, a massive 21-point, non-typical, as a perfect example of early season bachelor group behavior. "It was the third day of the season, and I was sitting on a portable treestand I'd placed along a very active and distinct rub-line," Doug told me. "Some time before dark, a small buck wandered by on the rub-line. He was soon followed by another buck. Behind that buck was another. All told, there were five bucks in the bachelor group. As is usually the case, the largest buck, which happened to be the non-typical I arrowed, was bringing up the rear."

Doug brought up an interesting point regarding the perimeter rubs I mentioned earlier. "There are those rare occasions when setting up near clusters of perimeter rubs could prove to be a productive tactic," he stated. "This usually happens only if hunting pressure in the immediate area is relatively light. And even if this is the case, you'll probably only have a few days at the very beginning of the bow season when you can expect to ambush a big buck near a feeding area. After that you're going to have to relocate back into the woods a ways."

There's another benefit to be realized from becoming at least somewhat "literate" about early antler rubs. Not all bowhunters are provided the luxury of getting out during the pre-season and watching the bucks they plan on hunting later on. Nor are they afforded the time to do anything even remotely resembling some intensive pre-season scouting. Believe me, acquiring a basic understanding of early rub behavior can provide bowhunters with a way to overcome these negatives.

The preseason scouting regime I've come up with could hardly be considered complicated. It does entail doing a bit of legwork though. What I do is walk around the entire outside perimeter of a suspected feeding area, all the while keeping my eyes peeled for fresh antler rubs. Although I make a mental note of the location of any perimeter rubs I find, the primary focus of my search lies in another direction. In most cases I'll turn my back on clusters of rubs I find right near a food source and instead search for a "line" of rubs. I'll then follow this line of rubs (which is an obvious preferred buck travel route) some distance away from the food source before selecting and preparing a stand site.

There are a couple important facts regarding early season rubs that hunters should know about. To begin with, antler rubs usually appear only in those places where bucks feel safe and secure letting down their guard for a brief time. Second, whitetail bucks display a real propensity for rubbing in the same general areas year after year. What this means is that, provided you continue to apply a cautious approach, it's entirely possible you could realize an impressive string of early season bowhunting successes.

The Drawbacks

Like all other potentially productive big buck hunting tactics, there are certain negatives associated with setting up along early rub lines. Perhaps most notable of these negatives is the fact that the tactic is a hit or miss proposition at best. The naturally reclusive behavior and rather restrictive travel patterns mature bucks often display at this time of year are most responsible for disturbingly low success rates. But there's another reason why bucks often show an obvious aversion to traveling along some of their initially established rub lines. And that reason has to do with human presence. More specifically, it has to do with your presence!

It's true that whitetail bucks can become somewhat preoccupied with rubbing during the early season. They might even do a bit of scraping at this time. However, they aren't doing these things to a degree where it could be considered a major distraction. What this means is that big bucks will still have nearly 100 percent of their survival instincts tuned to their surroundings. There's darn little that will escape detection by the bucks under such conditions.

Another negative associated with using early rubs as a hunting aid has to do with the thickness of underbrush and foliage at this time of year. Simply put, early rubs can be hard to spot. Because visibility is so restricted, it's entirely possible that you would walk within just a few feet of a fresh rub and not see it. These same thick conditions can also make it extremely difficult to ascertain if a rub you've found was made at random or is one of a "line" of rubs.

Because of these negatives and many more, trying to ambush a mature whitetail buck during the early part of the archery season will forever remain an extremely tough chore. Now, you'll notice that I used the word "tough" and not "impossible." This is because whitetail bucks will never abandon their habit of making antler rubs. Early season bowhunters would be well-advised to learn how to use this very predictable aspect of big buck behavior to their benefit.

Smooth Transition

Contrary to what some people believe, it takes very little time at all for bucks to remove the velvet from their antlers. In fact, the process sometimes can be completed in as little as 30 minutes, even by the largest-racked bucks. Another fact: In their attempts to remove antler velvet, bucks often will do a lot of brush rubbing. (They push their antlers into a clump of brush and rub furiously.) Once the velvet is removed, however, bucks will then direct their rubbing attentions to saplings and small to medium-sized trees. One last note: Even though it's still early in the fall, larger bucks often display very aggressive attitudes during these initial rubbing sessions, which means they will take on some fairly large trees.

17   Scrap the Scrapes?

BY GARY CLANCY

Studies show that scrape hunting may be highly overrated,
but it can still produce . . . if done right.

I t's time for me to come clean—to admit that as much as I hate to face the truth, it's clear that I'm hooked on scrape hunting. I mean, when I see a freshly pawed scrape, my heart starts racing, sweat begins to trickle down my back, and instinctively I begin searching the timber for the bruiser buck that left his calling card. If the scrape is really big, the symptoms are worse, and if I happen upon a whole line of scrapes, well, let's just say I carry a paper sack with me to control hyperventilation.

To those fortunate enough not to be as severely addicted, a scrape is just a bare patch of earth where a buck pawed and peed. But to me, a scrape is a vision! When I see a scrape I don't just see dirt, I see the buck that made it. In my mind, I watch him work the overhanging branch, licking, nipping, chewing, nuzzling, sometimes rubbing his face on it or hooking it with his antlers. I see the leaves and debris fly as he uses his front hoofs to paw out the scrape. I see him stepping up into the scrape, hunching slightly, squeezing his hind legs together and urinating so that his urine dribbles over his tarsal glands before soaking into the freshly turned earth. I smell the rankness of it all.

When I come upon a smoking-hot scrape, my first instinct is to find a tree and get a stand into that tree as quickly as possible. I've spent hundreds, maybe thousands, of hours sitting in stands over fresh, dark, reeking scrapes, watching them ever-so-slowly become old, dry, leaf-littered has-beens. On occasion, my vigilance has been rewarded. I've seen some very good bucks while hunting over scrapes; I've even killed a few. But my average, when comparing bucks seen to hours hunted, is dismal. That's why I'm trying to beat this addiction to scrape-hunting, because I'm finally convinced that after 30-plus years of hunting over them, most of my time would be better spent hunting somewhere else. Here's why.

What We Now Know About Scrapes

For most of my deer hunting career, what I've known about scrapes was what was passed down to me by other hunters or what I read in books and magazines. Unfortunately, much of that information was inaccurate. During the 1980s and '90s, however, there was a tremendous amount of research done on whitetail deer behavior. Because much of this research was inspired by hunters and directly or indirectly funded by hunters, scraping was one of the behaviors studied. So what I'm going to share here is not some backwoods lore that my Uncle Harry passed down to me like his Grandpa Joe did to him. You can take this information to the bank.

Scrapes serve two purposes in the whitetail world. One is for a buck to signal other bucks that he is a deer to be reckoned with. The other is for a doe to determine the social standing and overall health of the buck that made the scrape. One whiff of a buck's urine and the doe can determine whether the buck will make a suitable mate.

Scrapes originate with the scent-marking of an overhead branch. A buck will spend a lot of time chewing, nuzzling and rubbing his face and antlers on the overhanging branch. All of this activity deposits scent from the buck's preorbital, nasal, saliva and forehead glands. Because a buck licks himself, it is safe to assume that the scent of his urine and tarsal glands is also deposited on the overhanging branch.

Bucks use overhanging branches, or "licking sticks," year-round. When the scraping period commences, some of these overhanging branches will be scraped under and others will not.

Scraping is most intense during the 10- to 14-day period preceding actual breeding. Once does are in estrus, scraping comes to a near standstill. Studies have shown that a mature buck will make up to 80 percent of his scrapes prior to the breeding period.

Research has also confirmed what many serious whitetail hunters have suspected for years, which is that mature bucks are responsible for the earliest scrapes, often beginning in September. Mature bucks are also responsible for the most and largest scrapes. Immature bucks begin scraping later (mid-October), and tend to make fewer and smaller scrapes. If you have look diligently and are not finding scrapes until a couple of weeks before the breeding season, the sad truth is probably that you do not have any mature bucks in your hunting area.

Whereas a buck in the presence of a soon-to-be-hot doe or showing off for another buck will paw out a hasty scrape just about anywhere, most scrapes are made in specific locations. Remember that scrapes are a buck's billboards, and he wants his advertisements in places where they are going to be noticed by the maximum number of deer. Trails and travel routes are always good places to look. Along the edges of openings—be they fields, cutovers or natural openings—are other excellent places to look for scrapes. Remember that deer like to scrape on level ground, and they prefer not to scrape on rocky soil, where the grass is thick or where the ground is too wet.

A scrape is usually round or oval and starts out being two to three feet in diameter. However, as a scrape is reworked it becomes larger and larger. Also, the relatively few scrapes that are made after breeding commences tend to be significantly larger than scrapes made prior to breeding. Sometimes different bucks will scrape very near each other so that a cluster of scrapes appears. If this activity continues, these individual scrapes will eventually be transformed into one giant scrape. I've seen some that I could park my pickup in! Scrapes like this tend to appeal to every deer that passes, regardless of its sex or age.

Of special interest to me was the research that found that about half of the scrapes made last season will be opened again this season and that mature bucks, especially, were likely to open last year's scrapes. I have been hunting one particular place where I have found scrapes for each of the past 27 seasons. Through the years, the exact location of the scrapes has changed as overhead branches either died or grew too high for the bucks to reach, but the scrapes have appeared each fall around the edge of what had once been a homestead. This tells me that not only does a mature buck reopen many of his old scrapes, but when a mature buck dies, another takes his place. Prime scrape locations tend to have scrapes year after year.

So What's Not to Like?

With all of this information, you might ask: So what's not to like about scrape-hunting? The answer lies in the disturbing fact that research has again confirmed what all of us were dreading was true: namely, that a whopping 90 percent of all activity at scrapes takes place at night. I could live with 70 percent. I would be ecstatic if the magic number were 50. But 90 percent means that only 10 percent of the action is going to take place during shooting hours, and then there is no guarantee that I will be sitting over the right scrape. In fact, when you consider that a mature buck may paw out 100 or more scrapes, what are the odds that I will be sitting over the right one during that 10 percent time period? Not good is the only answer I can come up with.

What to Do?

So does all this mean that I'm going to give up hunting scrapes entirely and recommend that you do the same? No. But I am going to spend less time hunting over scrapes than I have in the past, and I'm going to be fussier about which scrapes I hunt over. The best scrapes to hunt over are not always going to be the biggest or most obvious. Sure, these scrapes are getting a lot of activity, but most of it probably occurs at night. The scrapes to concentrate on are not the giant scrapes found where deer congregate to feed at night or the string of scrapes along a cutover. I'm convinced that if you want to maximize your odds of catching a buck visiting a scrape during shooting hours, you need to be hunting scrapes that are located on the edge of, or within, that buck's bedding area. By doing this, you maximize your odds of catching the buck visiting the scrape during shooting hours for three good reasons. One is that you are more likely to catch him paying a visit during the early morning hours before bedding down for the day. The second is that deer tend to get up and move around a little at midday, and though a buck will probably not wander a half-mile down to a cutover to check his scrapes, he may well work the scrapes that are near or within his bedding area during this time. And the third is that the first scrapes the buck will check in the evening are those nearest his bedding area.

Another way to stack the odds in your favor is to hunt places where you have consistently found scrapes in the past. Big bucks, as mentioned, have a history of scraping the same places year after year. One of my favorite tricks is to beat the buck to the punch and lay down a mock scrape right smack in the middle of his previous year's scrape. Big bucks don't take kindly to that. The aggression this act ignites is sometimes enough to trigger the buck to check on the scrape at 3 p.m. instead of 3 a.m.

Scrape-hunting is not a waste of time. But neither is it the surefire tactic I had long believed it to be. For hunting over scrapes to be worth my time and effort, I need to fine-tune my methods. I'm in the process of doing just that, and from what I've seen so far, it's working. I'll keep you posted as things develop.

18   Moon Glow and Rut Timing

BY CHARLES J. ALSHEIMER

Along with writer Jeff Murray and whitetail researcher Wayne Laroche, Charles Alsheimer has produced some of the most interesting and thought-provoking theories ever on the moon's effect on rut timing. The first half in this two-part chapter was originally published in the 1996 edition of Remington Country *magazine. The second is from Alsheimer's landmark book,* HUNTING WHITETAILS BY THE MOON.

The pen can be a powerful instrument. If you don't think so, just stop for a second and think about how you've formulated many of your ideas about whitetail deer hunting through what you have read. As I reflect on my career in the out-of-doors, I can remember many papers and articles I've read that led me to believe a certain way about the white-tailed deer. Only later, through research, did I realize my initial reading was either not true or only partially accurate.

I can remember that the first articles I ever read on whitetail scraping behavior stated that each buck had its own individual scrapes. Of course, we now know that the best prime scrapes are visited by several bucks, and in some cases can resemble whitetail bus stations. Another interesting thing I was taught about the whitetail deer was that they could not see colors, only shades of black and white. This was a theory that I never quite bought into. Now, through research, we know that whitetails have the physical equipment to be able to detect a range of colors, though probably not in the same way we do.

Yet another example of what I bought into was that in the North, the majority of whitetail does come into estrus and are bred the same time year after year (Jackson-Hesselton, 68). During the period from 1961–1968, New York's Department of Environmental Conservation conducted a study headed by Lawrence Jackson and William Hesselton, both Senior Wildlife Biologists with the state. By using the embryos from 864 dog- and road-killed does of various ages, they were able to determine the breeding dates of the whitetails from various parts of New York State.

The whitetail's gestation period is roughly 200 days. Therefore once the age of the embryo was determined, the doe's breeding date could be pinpointed. According to Jackson and Hesselton, most female deer are bred during the 20-day period from November 10 to November 30.

Unfortunately for me, it was many years later that I came to realize that the accuracy of these dates was plus or minus seven days. Along with thousands of others, I didn't notice or understand this disclaimer and viewed the dates as gospel.

Regardless, the study intrigued me because it was done in New York State (where I live), and it was the first research I'd ever seen on the subject of the whitetail rut and breeding dates. Armed with this information, I was able to plan all aspects of my fall deer hunts. For the most part, I found it to be fairly accurate, at least during my early years of deer hunting.

★ ★ ★

Part One
Moon Glow: The Rut Trigger You Can Predict

In 1979 I left a sales and marketing career and devoted my life to wildlife photography and writing. Armed with a camera, I moved from a paneled wall office to a forest office. Since that time I've probably spent as much time pursuing whitetail deer as any person in North America. Over the years I've burned thousands of rolls of film on deer from Nova Scotia to Texas to Saskatchewan and hunted whitetails extensively across the continent.

The last 17 years have been both a blessing and an incredible education. The more I photographed and studied whitetails in the North, the more I began realizing that something wasn't quite right about the breeding date research I had learned about in my early 20's. Fortunately, I had the presence of mind to keep notes and document when all my photos were taken, right down to the day. Being able to draw upon this information has proven to be valuable beyond measure.

During the '80s America saw an explosion in whitetail interest. Not only was research offering new and intriguing insights into whitetail behavior, but also the relatively new phenomenon of deer hunting seminars burst onto the scene. Because of this, I began speaking on the whitetail throughout the country. Wherever I went, hunters were hungry for information on the whitetail rut. Though I was disseminating information through my seminars, I was also listening to what America's deer hunters had to say. One question I was frequently asked was, "Why does the rut seem early some years and late others?"

This was also a question I had begun asking myself. Though much of the research seemed consistent with what I was witnessing, there was a great deal of rutting behavior (chasing, scraping, etc.) that I was observing and photographing that was not occurring at the same time each year.

It was my feeling after ten years of intense whitetail photography and hunting throughout the North that the full moon around November 1st was having an influence on when the does were coming into estrus and being bred. I also realized that the rutting behavior of bucks was being triggered by the timing of the does' estrous cycle.

Some years I was seeing tremendous buck behavior in late October and early November, other years mid-November, and yet other years in late November. Also, contrary to what I had been taught early in life, I was seeing and taking my biggest bucks under late October's/November's full moon. My whole hunting philosophy had done a 180-degree turn in ten years.

Rather than being discouraged when the full moon arrived around November 1st, I found myself longing to hunt the period, because I knew my successes would soar I couldn't put my finger on why I had more success during a full-moon period. I just knew it was happening.

Exciting New Research

About three years ago I began hearing about the research Dr. James Kroll, Dr. Grant Woods and others were doing regarding how the moon was affecting whitetail behavior during the rut. Frankly it fascinated me, and little by little things began falling into place.

While doing a story on whitetail tracks, I came to know Vermont wildlife researcher Wayne Laroche. Though our initial contacts dealt only with his research on whitetail tracks, our ensuing conversations turned to his work on how the moon affects the breeding dates of whitetail does. Laroche, with the aid of sophisticated computers and light meters, was coming up with some very interesting hypotheses. What he was doing fascinated me, and I offered to provide him data I had collected over the years. I drew this information from several sources.

For ten years I had photographed extensively on large estates in New York and Pennsylvania. From notes, journals and slides of rutting behavior, I was able to piece together exactly when significant rutting events happened from 1985–1994. Next I was able to provide Laroche breeding data I had from different northern whitetail breeders. This was a key piece to the puzzle, because the data showed exactly when does were being bred and having their fawns. An added bonus was that in each case Laroche was able to know exactly how old each doe was.

Two other pieces of data I collected were random samples of New York State hunters' diaries, which showed deer sightings by date, and sheriff department information on deer/car collisions. The latter two information sources provided valuable data on deer movement around full moon periods and just prior to breeding dates.

New Breakthroughs

I became so intrigued with this research that after the 1994 deer season I made arrangements to monitor five deer in a 15-acre enclosure during the 1995 autumn months. There were two does, 1½ and 4½ years old, and a 1½-, 2½- and 3½-

year-old bucks. Though the deer were confined, the habitat was very natural, with mixed hardwoods and hay fields. In addition I made plans to keep close tabs on the breeding dates of some northern deer breeders' does.

Based on Laroche's moon findings, I knew the projected breeding window for 1995 would be November 15 through the 29th north of the 30th latitude, with the peak time being November 22nd. In 1995 the full moon occurred on November 7th. Therefore, Laroche's breeding window would be under the dark of the moon (last quarter, new and first quarter of the moon). After extensive conversations with Laroche prior to September, we both felt confident that the 14-day window prior to November 15th should see the best buck activity. With everything in place, we eagerly waited to see how things would unfold.

Late October arrived without much fanfare. The bucks and does on the New York and Pennsylvania estates, as well as here on our farm, were not overly active. However, on October 25th I saw a marked increase in buck movement (October 23rd was a new moon). On the night of October 28th, there was a dramatic increase in deer/car collisions in the county where I live.

The next day one official asked me, "What on earth happened last night? Our scanner went crazy with reports of motorists hitting deer."

My response was, "The rut has started, hold onto your hat."

On November 4th western New York received an inch of new snow during the day, with the skies clearing by nightfall. That night, with a near full moon and the temperature around 25 degrees, things went crazy in the woods. Tracks were everywhere in the fresh snow the next morning. The enclosure that housed the five research deer had seen all kinds of activity around the perimeter of the fence. In three different locations, the predator-proof electric wires were broken. At one location the 8-foot-high fence was dented from the outside, at about the 6½-foot mark. A deer had tried to jump from the outside to the inside of the enclosure.

Around the outside of the 3,000-foot fence perimeter, I counted nine paw beds. None had a licking branch over it and all were within ten feet of the fence. Though I saw none of them being made I know full well what was going on from photographing this type of behavior before. What had taken place was a buck on the outside of the fence showing his aggression to a buck on the inside of the fence. Had I been able to actually witness what had transpired, I'm sure I would have observed a lot of snort wheezing to go along with the ground being pawed clean.

From November 1 through the 14th, buck sightings were as high as I've ever seen on our farm. Part of this was due to the fact we were in the fourth year of a quality deer management program (during which no yearling bucks were allowed to be killed), and there was a fair number of mature bucks around. But the big reason was that the full moon had not only triggered an explosion in buck activity, but also set things in motion for the does to come into estrus.

In spite of all the chasing going on during the first part of November, I didn't notice any breeding. But then I didn't expect much, if any, until after the 14th. On November 16th the 1½-year-old doe's scent began attracting the three enclosure bucks. On the 17th the oldest buck bred her. On November 22nd the 4½-year-old doe was bred by the biggest buck. Also, four of five does I was monitoring at another whitetail breeding location were bred during Laroche's predicted breeding window. On both of the large estates I'm involved with the activity was very similar to what I've described here.

From a research standpoint, 1995 is only one data point, and to have anything conclusive '95 must be compared to prior years. At this point the data is not voluminous, but there is enough information from prior years to see that the moon has a definite impact on not only buck rutting activity but also in setting a doe's breeding clock, with the latter being the most significant. By being able to determine when the bulk of the does are going to be bred, the timing of buck activity in the form of scraping and chasing can be predicted with accuracy.

Based on Laroche's observations, decreasing day length at some point in the fall (in the north) resets the reproductive clock in whitetails, thus placing the breeding season in November, December and January in the northern hemisphere. The doe's estrous cycle is set at some point after day length falls below a critical duration by occurrence of the full moon, which provides a bright light stimulus to the pineal gland for several nights in a row each lunar month. Then a rapid decrease in lunar brightness at the third quarter triggers hormonal production by the pineal gland. Physiological changes prompted by the pineal gland culminate in ovulation and estrus coinciding with loss in light levels after the full moon.

To get a better grasp on why the moon affects the breeding dates of whitetail does think of this: Optimum fawn survival from many predators will occur when they are born under the dark of the moon (new moon). Knowing this and the fact that the gestation period (how long the fawn is carried by a doe) for a whitetail doe is roughly 200 days and that the lunar cycle is 29.5 days, one can quickly back the calendar up and see that if birth occurs under the dark of the moon breeding will also.

From a biological standpoint, a northern whitetail doe's estrogen level peaks around November 1st, as does a buck's sperm count. So, with both male and female whitetails poised to breed, it only stands to reason that there has to be some mechanism in place for the does to come into estrous and be bred under the dark of the moon. That mechanism is a full moon.

Solving the Puzzle

When the full moon occurs, bucks literally go bonkers, and the reproductive process within a doe is set to go off after the full moon ends. Therefore, the period just before, during and right after the full moon that triggers the breeding offers the potential for incredible rutting activity. I say potential because there are a few factors that can limit the amount of daytime activity during this time. Inclement weather, hunting pressure in a given area and, most importantly, how finely tuned the deer herd is can affect buck activity. An area with many mature bucks and a good buck-to-doe ratio will offer the best number of daytime deer sightings during this time. A finely tuned herd will also improve the accuracy of the moon's effect on doe breeding dates.

How far north one is also influences the accuracy of Laroche's hypothesis. South of the 40th latitude—roughly along the line separating Maryland from

Pennsylvania—the rate of day length change is slower, and the contrast between winter and summer is not as defined. Because of this and other factors, breeding dates can be later and more spread out than in the north.

At first glance it all seems too easy. Let me assure you it's more complicated than just looking for November's new moon and backing up 14 days to see when the peak buck activity will be. When a new moon occurs in mid-November, the whole process is fairly easy to predict, though it will vary because the lunar orbit is different from period to period. However, when the new moon falls on either end of the month of November (in the North), predicting peak buck activity and breeding times becomes more sophisticated.

Hunting Strategies

Once predictable breeding dates are known, coming up with a fine-tuned strategy is much easier. In most cases the 14-day period just prior to the beginning of the breeding period will offer the best hunting. And some of the most intense rutting activity will occur during the full moon period preceding the breeding.

On October 26th this year, there will be a full moon. Judging from past notes, journals, photos, etc., I'm confident the stage will be set for prime buck activity from the last week in October through the first week in November, north of the 40th latitude. And if the weather is cool and the days relatively windless, there should be good buck activity beginning around October 20th.

I've taken the biggest bucks of my life during the full moon period prior to the breeding, and most were taken between ten in the morning and two in the afternoon. (So, don't let the term "breeding moon" fool you into thinking it literally means the bucks will only move at night.)

During this time bucks will be on the move scraping, fighting, seeking and chasing does. If hunting pressure is low and weather conditions cool, it's not uncommon for a rut-crazed buck to be on the move for four to five hours just prior to the breeding period. In some cases a traveling buck will make between five and 12 scrapes per hour, if he lives in an area where there is a fine-tuned deer herd.

With scraping and chasing at their peak, the best strategy is to hunt near active scrapes that are close to (but not in) a known bedding area. If these scrapes are in funnel areas your chances will increase even more. The key is to try to catch the buck moving between the bedding and feeding area as it searches for does. By setting up close to the bedding area, you'll be able to intercept bucks that move out of the bedding area just before nightfall. Also, the chance of continuous action throughout a morning is better in such locations.

Just prior to the breeding period, antler rattling, calling and using decoys in and around scraping areas will work well. With bucks cruising in search of does, a bowhunter equipped with a good grunt tube has the potential for seeing a lot of action.

One strategy I've used with great success is doe bleating. If the action is slow, I'll give off two or three doe bleats every 20 to 30 minutes. Doing this will get the attention of any buck that may be cruising through the woods. If I see a buck that's out of range, I'll either doe bleat or grunt at him. If a buck is in an aggressive mood, he'll almost always respond to either of these vocalizations, especially the buck grunt.

Once the breeding begins, hunting becomes more difficult, especially if there is a poor buck-to-doe ratio. With a buck in every hot doe's thicket, scraping activity tends to drop off dramatically and nearly ceases. Because a doe will "smell right" for up to 72 hours, a buck will stay with her during this period and move only when she moves. Consequently, when the breeding starts, I change strategies and begin hunting the doe groups.

In reflecting on the events of the last 20 years, I can't help but be amazed by what has been learned about the whitetail. During this time hunters have been enlightened on everything from whitetail vocalizations to range movements to rutting behavior.

Though the current insights regarding the moon are nothing short of phenomenal, I firmly believe much more will be learned in the coming year as the research becomes more fine-tuned. When this happens, the hunter will surely reap the fruits of the researcher's labors.

★　★　★

Part Two
The Rut's Timing Is Everything

The day was Nov. 19, 1997, five days after the full moon. It was the third day of New York's shotgun season, and business had kept me from hunting earlier in the day. With three hours of daylight left, I headed to one of my favorite stands on our farm.

For nearly 300 yards, I crept through thick hardwoods and hemlocks. The day was clear and cold, and a foot of powder snow made for quiet walking. When I was within 100 yards of my tree stand, I slowed to a snail's pace. The woods were dead calm and I didn't want to ruin the evening's hunt by spooking deer. After reaching my tree, I took great pains to climb silently into the stand. Once on the permanent stand's platform, I rested my shotgun against the tree before scanning the woods in every direction.

Eye Catcher

Behind the stand and up a steep bank, a brown spot caught my eye. I had hunted here the night before and passed up a 4-pointer. I didn't recall seeing the dark spot in the snow and low hemlock growth. I fished my binoculars out of my hunting coat. I couldn't believe what I was looking at 60 yards away. A big buck was bedded, angling away. Only his hindquarters were in clear view. His ribs, front shoulders and head were obscured by thick saplings. All around him was thick brush and hemlocks. I'm sure he felt secure bedded in such tight quarters. Even so, I couldn't believe I had been able to climb into the stand undetected. For the next 45 minutes the buck and I played out the greatest drama I've encountered in the deer woods.

Because of my seat's location and where the buck was lying, I couldn't sit down and shoot. I had to stand to keep an eye on him. From years of photographing bedded whitetails, I knew of just two ways the buck would get up: He would bolt out of his bed and run, or he would stand and stretch before taking a step. Therefore, I kept the scope on him at all times. I didn't want to risk not being able to react fast enough if he jumped up and ran.

Even if he did get up, I wasn't sure I could get a shot because of the thick brush. Through my 7×scope I studied the saplings in front of him to see if I could find a shooting lane. It looked like I would have about a 6-inch opening if he stepped into it. If he moved in any other direction I wouldn't have a shot.

Study Time

I studied the buck for the next 15 minutes. His eyes were fixed on the hemlocks in front of his nose. This made me think a doe might be bedded in front of him, although I couldn't see anything. Despite resting the gun against a tree, my arm tired after the first 20 minutes and I had to bring it down to rest. About that time I realized I would have to take the initiative. Because the day was ending fast, if I didn't try to get him up, it would quickly be "O-dark-30."

With my shotgun shouldered and braced against the tree, I got out the grunt tube and blew softly. He didn't hear me. I gave two loud guttural grunts and the buck looked my way. I thought he would get up but he didn't. Instead, he looked back into the hemlocks. His behavior indicated a doe was with him, and I knew he wouldn't leave her for anything.

Forty minutes into the ordeal, the buck began to doze, resting his muzzle in the snow. While I contemplated my next move, I got a break. A flock of turkeys was moving off an oak flat atop the steep slope above him, heading for a roost. With my scope on the buck, I saw two long-beards walking straight at him. When one of the gobblers was 10 yards from the buck, I could see he was going to get up. I clicked the safety off and got ready. He stood, stretched and stepped into the narrow opening.

At the roar of the 12-gauge, the hard-hit buck lunged forward and the woods exploded. Turkeys flew everywhere and a doe ran through my scope picture. She stopped after about 20 yards and a second deer, a yearling 4-pointer, rose from his bed in the hemlocks. He walked up to the doe, licked her flanks, and bred her on the hillside within sight of me and the big buck I had just killed. I couldn't believe the scene.

In more than 40 years in the deer woods, I had never encountered anything like that 45-minute drama.

Timing the Moon and the Rut

I shared that 1997 hunting experience for two reasons. First, it points out how the rut makes a white-tailed buck more vulnerable. Second, and most importantly, it shows how predictable the rut can be when the rutting moon period is factored in. That's what this book is all about.

In 1997, the rutting moon was Nov. 14. I made the following prediction in the September 1997 issue of *Deer & Deer Hunting:* "If past patterns hold true this year, the first week of November doesn't look promising. However, my records show if the weather cooperates—meaning cool temperatures with at least some clear skies—and hunting pressure isn't high, buck activity should become very good around Nov. 11 or 12, just before the full moon. From Nov. 11 until the prime breeding begins around Nov. 20 and 21, bucks should be highly active if the region you hunt has a reasonable doe-to-buck ratio."

Anytime I stick my neck out with a prediction, part of me says, "Alsheimer, do you really want to do this?" Even though I believe more strongly each year in what Laroche and I are doing, the feeling is always there, though it is waning. Well, 1997 is history. The data collected in Fall 1997 and Spring '98 shows that more than 70 percent of the does in the research project were bred in or near the peak Nov. 20 to 27 window we had predicted.

They say repetition is the key to learning, so to better understand how the rutting moon affects the rut's timing, allow me to repeat how it works. Roughly five to seven days after the rutting moon, does begin coming into estrus. The full-blown 14-day breeding window follows. That means a number of things for hunters.

For starters, it's critical to know when the rut kicks in so you can take advantage of the best window of opportunity the rut can offer. Second, knowing that scraping and chasing are at a fever pitch for about 10 days just before breeding begins can greatly increase your chances. Third, it's important to know when scraping and other rutting behaviors start tapering off so you can anticipate shifts in hunting strategy.

At risk of sounding repetitive, many factors influence the rut's timing, but all things being equal, daytime activity normally picks up three to four days before the rutting moon shines full. To our eye, the moon appears full or nearly full two days before its full phase. I believe white-tailed bucks sense something significant is occurring in the doe population, and start becoming active on the eve of the rutting moon.

And They're Off!

I believe this "sense" has much to do with the amount of sex-related pheromones hovering in the air. The way bucks respond to these scents reminds me of race horses at the Kentucky Derby's starting gate. When those horses burst from the gates, they hit the track with a lot of pent up energy. It's only much later that they get the spoils, in this case the finish line. In between, they expend a tremendous amount of energy.

The same holds true for white-tailed bucks. With the smell of does every-where, bucks jump out of the gates a couple of days before the rutting moon shines full. If temperatures are cool and human pressure is minimal, they go ballis-tic for the next 10 days. During the early part of the race, bucks can stay on their hoofs for six hours at a clip and make six to 12 scrapes per hour. Such behavior can only be called chaos. But be warned: The chaos can end as quickly as it began, es-pecially if the doe-to-buck ratios exceed 4–1. Bonker bucks become breeding bucks in a heartbeat once does are in estrus. When that happens, things get signifi-cantly calmer in the woods.

Classifying the Rut

After six years of intense study, I believe the intensity of each year's rut is a little different because of when the rutting moon occurs. From journals and obser-vations I've made since beginning my study in 1993, we'll see a classic rut if the rutting moon occurs during the first eight days in November. I define a classic rut as one that resembles what most hunters envision the rut to be. For example, hunters in my region have long preached the best time to hunt deer in New York's Adirondack Mountains is always around Nov. 11. If you look at much of the old writings, you'll find hunters used to think the best time to be on the trail of a rut-crazed buck was Nov. 10 to 15. Also, most of the older breeding research said peak whitetail breeding occurs Nov. 15 to 30 in the North.

I believe the rut is most intense when the rutting moon occurs the first eight days of November. This belief stems from my years of observations, accurate breed-ing data, and the fact white-tailed bucks and does reach their hormonal peak around Nov. 1. When cool temperatures, the rutting moon and the deer's hor-monal peak occur in unison, the rut can be explosive. That mix shapes people's opinions about when the rut occurs. But ruts like that only occur about once every three years.

When the rutting moon does not occur the first eight days of November, at least two factors in the previous paragraph—moon and hormone peak—are not synchronized. And if warm temperatures settle in during the rutting moon, all three factors can be out of sync. That scenario can make things tough in the deer woods.

The data I've collected so far makes me think the chase phase is less intense when the rutting moon occurs outside the Nov. 1 to 8 window.

Timing Recap

Although there are parallels between the pre-rut, rutting and post-rut moons, each is significantly different. It's important to keep your eye on the calen-dar so you'll know what to expect.

In the case of the pre-rut moon, deer activity will be sporadic during this full-moon period. There will certainly be a little chasing, scraping and breeding.

It's just too early for bucks to be wound up and on the go like they'll be 30 days later.

About the time the rutting moon arrives, a buck has a fire in his belly and he's ready to go. Starting a few days before and ending about 10 days after the rutting moon, the woods will be humming. Whether you call the activity bonkers, ballistic or frenzied, this is when hunters dream of being in the woods. If you have a two-week period for vacation, this is when to take it. Write it down or etch it in stone, because you don't want to miss this handful of days.

By the time the post-rut moon inches over the horizon, the rutting game is about over. Any bucks left standing are worn out. And if these survivors live in "run-and-gun" and "brown-it's-down" country where gun-hunting pressure is intense, they will be so secretive that you'll need radar to find them.

19 Hunting Strategies for the Rutting Moon

BY CHARLES J. ALSHEIMER

In this chapter from HUNTING WHITETAILS BY THE MOON, Charles Alsheimer puts his theories into practice in the field. You can do the same.

Although white-tailed bucks scrape, rub and chase does, it's the does that create the rut. Therefore, my hunting strategy revolves around pursuing mature white-tailed bucks as they react and interact with doe groups.

As already mentioned, a whitetail's rutting switch is thrown from mid- to late October (in the North). For the next 30 days, a buck develops an ever-increasing case of "sexitis." During this time, bucks let their guard down and become vulnerable. Once the rut's breeding phase is full blown, a buck becomes harder to hunt because he's around does. So, the best window of opportunity for hunting the rutting moon, which is the second full moon after the fall equinox, is about three days before the full moon until about seven to 10 days afterward.

A whitetail's range can be broken into three zones: feeding, bedding and the area in between, which I call the transition zone. If pressure isn't severe, the transition zone is where I ambush the most bucks during the rut. Why? For five reasons:

Mature bucks seldom frequent feeding areas during daylight hours.

If they do, does are usually nearby and the scene can resemble a fire drill when chasing starts.

With several deer in the feeding area, you have all kinds of eyes to contend with before the moment of truth arrives.

You must stay out of the bedding area to keep a slammer buck from changing its habits.

The transition zone is where most rutting sign will be found and where a buck is most vulnerable.

Most of the time I hunt transition zones during the rutting moon period to kill a mature buck. Generally, a transition zone is anywhere from 50 yards to over a mile in length. It all depends on how far the bedding area is from the feeding area, or how far one bedding area is from another. If a transition zone is thick or happens to be a natural funnel, your chances for success increase.

If conditions and habitat are right, a number of trails will pass through a transition zone. It's along and near these trails that I look for key rutting sign in mid-

October. As with pre-rut scouting, I go into these areas between mid-morning and noon as inconspicuously as possible while searching for sign. Generally, I don't have to spend a lot of time in any one location because my off-season scouting has shown me where to look.

Scrapes: The Whitetail's Billboard

As the rutting moon arrives and the rut intensifies, three types of scrapes show up: boundary, secondary and primary. Boundary scrapes are made randomly as bucks travel through their territory. These scrapes often show up along the edges of fields, fence rows, old roadways and along creeks. Yearling bucks make many (but not all) boundary scrapes as they try to figure out their first rut. Therefore, I pay little attention to these scrapes except for checking the track sizes. If the track is more than 2¼ inches wide (with no more than a ¼-inch split in the toes) the buck probably is mature and weighs more than 175 pounds.

Secondary scrapes are generally found along well-used trails between bedding and feeding areas, and they can offer an excellent chance to kill bucks. In many instances, bucks make a line of these scrapes (20 to 50 yards apart) between the bedding and feeding areas. Because these scrapes are on trails, bucks frequently rework and freshen them. I've probably killed more bucks along secondary scrapes than at any other place.

The "mother lode" of scrapes is the primary scrape. Unfortunately, these scrapes are often few and far between because it takes a mature buck population for them to exist. The primary scrape is the true "bus station" for white-tailed bucks, and it is something all hunters yearn to find. Primary scrapes are normally found in strategic locations during the rut. You'll find well-worn trails to primary scrapes, and more often than not, these scrapes will be in thick cover where mature bucks feel secure.

Become a Scrape Doctor

I try to plan my scrape hunting around three or four good scrape locations, rotating between them so as not to over-hunt any one. Because I'll be rattling and calling from these ambush points, I look for hot scrapes with medium to heavy cover. If I find a highly used area that looks good for an ambush, I'll make a licking branch where I'd like a buck to stop. I do this by cutting a fresh branch from a tree and securing it about five feet off the ground. This works great along a trail where you know a buck must stop for you to get a clean, standing shot. If bucks like the licking branch, which is usually the case, a scrape will open under it.

Once I make a decision on a scrape location, I begin doctoring it. Not all scrapes are candidates for doctoring or for using lures around them. I've found that huntable scrapes need to be on flat or fairly flat ground in well-used travel corridors (funnels) that give bucks a sense of security.

To make lures shine, find a primary or secondary scrape to hunt over. The most critical aspect of scrape hunting is to make sure there is a good licking branch above the scrape. Remember, whitetails work the licking branch far more than they paw the ground.

Using lures to attract bucks was in part an outgrowth of my days as a fox trapper. Through experiences as a trapper, I realized my chances of trapping a fox increased according to the amount of fox scent I had around the set. Because of this, I felt confident that deer could be lured into bow, gun and camera range in much the same way. By using the premise that a whitetail scrape resembled a fox set, I've been successful at making certain scraping locations into whitetail magnets by using lures and attractive licking branches.

When I trapped fox I used to make the set hotter by applying liberal amounts of red fox urine around the bait and set. Also, if I caught a fox I'd try not to disturb the set because I knew the fox's odor would enhance the set, making it more attractive to other foxes in the area. I'd also make a scent post near the set so a roving fox could smell the locations from a distance. In all cases, I made sure I left no human odor behind.

I share this fox trapping scenario because I use the same principle when using deer lures around scrapes and when making scent trails. I begin by making sure I leave no human odor around the scrape I intend to doctor. I use 35 mm film canisters with the tops half perforated, and I then boil the canisters in water to kill human odors. I place three cotton balls inside each canister to prepare them for hanging above the licking branch.

I also wear rubber boots when hunting around doctored scrapes and when going to and from the area I intend to hunt. To eliminate human scent on my boots, I periodically wash them with soap and warm water, then rise them with boiling hot water. I also use latex gloves when tying scent canisters above the scrape.

Concocting Lures

Since the late 1980s, I've used two lures to hunt whitetails. I make one from pure whitetail urine and vaginal discharge from Holstein cows. Using the vaginal discharge of dairy cows probably comes as a shock to some. I began using it in 1982 (I gave it the name *white lightning*) when I heard of a dairy farmer from a neighboring state who had bow-killed some impressive whitetails while using it. He had collected and used only the discharge from cows in the peak of their estrous cycle. If I cannot get fresh whitetail urine to mix with the discharge, I use fresh Holstein urine.

A key aspect of using lures successfully is to keep them fresh. Regardless of what lure is used, freshness is essential because pheromones in the lure dissipate rapidly. Because of this, I refrigerate my lures and try to use them within a week to 10 days. I never carry them over to the next year.

To doctor the scrape, I tie one or two scent-laden canisters on the licking branch, at least six feet off the ground. Then, I fill the canister with lure. I do this with an eyedropper, inserting the lure through the large hole in the side of the canister. This can be expensive because it takes about one ounce of lure to fill the film canister.

Many will wonder why I use vaginal discharge lure above the scrape. After all, does and bucks urinate on the ground, not in the tree branches, right? Well, I used to think this way but after a good deal of experimenting I've found that bucks aren't concerned about where the smell is coming from. Having the canister in the air allows bucks to smell the lure from farther away.

Lastly, I do one rather radical thing at the scrape site during the doctoring process. When I'm hunting over a particular scrape I'll urinate onto it after my morning sit. The tactic might be a surprise to some, but I've used it for nearly 15 years, and like many hunters, I've found it works well. However, if you are on medication, don't use your own urine because medication can foul the urine and spook nearby deer.

Using Human Urine

Fox trapping taught me that I was more successful when I made a set as powerful smelling as possible. By urinating into a scrape, I'm able to put more than 10 ounces of "lure" onto the fresh earth. If I were to place commercial lure on the scrape, it would cost roughly $75 ($7 per ounce) every time I doctored it. However, this isn't the only reason I do it. I do it because it works.

Both human and whitetail urine are animal urine by nature. Each gives off the same ammonia smell after being exposed to dirt and air for a while. I've doctored scrapes in this fashion all across North America, and never once have I seen a buck become alarmed. In all cases, bucks smelled the ground and worked the scrape before moving on. Using your own urine is a way to make a scrape hotter without killing your pocketbook.

I never use human urine to doctor scrapes at the end of the day. Whitetails are on the prowl at dusk, and I don't want to risk spooking them before the urine breaks down. Also, I never use human urine in scent canisters that are for vaginal discharge lures.

To keep the scrapes as hot as possible I replenish the lure in the canisters every other day. The important thing is to keep the odor strong. Also, fresh earth under the scrape seems to be an attractant, so I make sure that the scrape beneath the licking branch is kept roughed up and free of debris.

Build a Better Mouse Trap with a Scent Trail

I also use lures to make scent trails in and out of the woods I'm hunting. This tactic is used by deer hunters across America, and there are a number of ways to lay a good scent trail. Some hunters drag a scent-laden rag behind them as they walk into the woods, while others use scent pads on the bottoms of their boots. I periodically squirt estrous lure on the bottoms of my rubber boots as I walk into my stand, starting the process when I'm within 100 to 150 yards of where I intend to hunt. I walk past the stand to make the trail where I would like a buck to follow, then backtrack and get into the stand.

The Stand Location

Setting up the ambush over a hot scrape or scrape line can be tricky. First, try to find a hot scrape as close to a bedding area as possible, or in a funnel that has a lot of use. By doing so, you'll be in better position to intercept a buck visiting his scrape during daylight hours. Remember, nearly 65 percent to 70 percent of scraping is done under the cover of darkness, so by being close to the bedding area, you can intercept a mature buck when he leaves his bedroom at the end of the day. If you set up too far from a bedding area, the buck won't reach you before quitting time. The same holds true in the morning, though it is not as critical because during the chase phase of the rut, bucks are on the prowl until midday. By being close to the bedding area, you will catch a buck returning to his bedroom.

Stand placement in relation to the scrape is critical when bow-hunting. Terrain often dictates where this will be. I set up 20 to 30 yards downwind from the scrape rather than right on top of it. Of course, gun hunting over scrapes is a whole different ball game that doesn't require detailed preparation because distance isn't a factor.

As I mentioned before, I like to hang a stand in fairly thick cover so I can incorporate calling techniques with the scraping process. When rattling, you need to obstruct a buck's view when he looks for the two combatants. Because I'm usually set up in thick cover, I don't go past 15 to 18 feet high with my stands. Any higher, and tree branches and other foliage will be in your way. Also, few people feel comfortable in a stand that's 20 feet high or more. When bow-hunting in close quarters near scrapes, I seldom sit when on stand because I've learned deer can surprise you at any time. Standing also gives me more shooting angles. The moment of truth can be a bang-bang affair, and by standing, you're better prepared for the magic moment.

Importance of Hunting Rubs and Rub Lines

Often, where you find scraping you'll find rubbing. They go hand in hand, so when you find heavy rubbing in an area of heavy scraping your chances of success increase greatly. I always look for traditional signpost rubs wherever I hunt. Unfortunately it takes a good population of mature bucks for a true traditional signpost rub to exist, so, in most of the whitetail's range, where 80 percent of the buck kill is yearlings, there are no signpost rubs. But if you find one, it's a real hotspot and a prime hunting location.

If a signpost rub cannot be found, look for big rubs, rub lines and clusters of rubs in the transition zone. Rub lines often reveal the way a buck was traveling. If the scarred side of the tree faces the feeding area, the rub was probably made in the morning when the buck returned to his bedding area. If the scar faces the bedding area, the rubs were undoubtedly made when the buck exited in the evening.

If there is a definite line of big rubs in an area, a stand should be hung downwind of it. Such a rub line is a visual aid showing the area where a buck likes to travel.

One piece of rubbing sign that gets my attention in a scraping area is a cluster of rubs. When you find a cluster of rubs in a prime scraping area or an active funnel, you know there are a lot of bucks around. And if there is a good population of does, there's even more reason to be excited. Heavy rubbing by bucks leaves pheromones that induce does to come into estrus. With doe groups in the area, the chance of killing a buck increases dramatically as the rut moves through the chase phase and then climaxes with the breeding phase.

Calling All Bucks

Whitetails are no different from other animals in that they are curious creatures. Throughout their lives they communicate with each other using a variety of bleats, grunts and snorts. For the first six months of life, fawns bleat and mew to their mothers. Adult bucks and does also communicate with each other by grunting and bleating. And, of course, whitetails use the snort to alert other deer of danger. During the rutting moon, when the rut is blooming, bucks also respond to the sound of two bucks fighting. Using antlers, grunt tubes and other calls to communicate with whitetails at this time can be challenging, exciting, and on occasion, very productive.

Calling

When I began calling deer, I only used antlers. Though there were successes, it wasn't until I began using a grunt tube, alone and in conjunction with antlers, that my success at luring deer close increased significantly. During the last 14 years, I've discovered that deer are more responsive to a call than anything else. For this reason my grunt tube goes with me whether I'm hunting with gun, bow or camera. Regardless of where I hunt in North America, I find that for every buck I rattle in, 10 to 15 will come to grunting and bleating.

Whether you are a novice or seasoned veteran, it's important to realize that you don't need to know how to make every vocalization of a whitetail. As a seminar speaker, I urge hunters to keep calling simple. Commercial deer calls that are capable of making a whole range of calls have not been around very long. Though researchers isolated about 400 different sounds of a whitetail when a vocalization study was done in 1984, it isn't necessary for you to know every one. The key is to be able to master two or three and know how and when to use them.

My favorite calls are the bleat, trailing grunt and tending grunt. I find the bleat to be a good locater call, much like a turkey yelp. I often use the bleat a couple of times just before and after I do a rattling sequence. I'll also use it when the action is slow and I haven't seen deer in a while. Basically it sounds like *neeeaah*.

The trailing grunt is a short grunt that bucks make when traveling through the woods or when around other deer. It's not uncommon for a rut-crazed buck to make a short grunt every one to 10 steps if he's in the right mood. If I see a buck walking through the woods, I'll use this grunt to stop him and to coax him in my direction. This is also a call that I use when no deer are in sight. If a buck is sexually active but not with a doe, there is a good chance he'll respond to a grunt.

The tending grunt can be a lethal weapon if used properly. When a buck is with a hot doe and is either frustrated by her rejections or is interrupted by another buck, he'll make a grunt that has a ticking cadence. If I'm hunting in thick cover and a buck walks through, I'll use a tending grunt to bring him to my stand. This is a great call to use when bucks are on the move and the rut is boiling over.

Rattling

During the rutting moon, bucks are very aggressive. Often, all it takes for a fight to occur is for one buck to look at another buck the wrong way. Over the years I've found that the best time to use antlers to bring a buck close to my stand is from about a week before the rutting moon until the third phase of the moon, which is seven days after the full moon. The seven days that follow the rutting moon are the best time during the period.

When I rattle, I do it aggressively with a sequence that seldom lasts longer than five minutes. Few fights I've witnessed have ever lasted longer, so I keep it short and loud and make it as aggressive sounding as possible. Generally, I rattle for a minute and half, pause for 30 seconds, rattle for a minute and a half, pause for 30 seconds then end the sequence by rattling for a minute and a half. I also found that rattling two hours before or after daylight works best. But don't rule out midday, because I've rattled in some nice bucks when the rutting moon is full.

When rattling, do it in the thickest cover possible, especially if you're bow-hunting. When a buck responds to antlers he will come in cautious, looking for the combatants. If he can't see them, he'll usually hang up. Thick cover forces him to come closer. Though you can't make as many natural sounds, like breaking branches and raking the ground, rattling from a tree stand gives greater concealment, allows you to see the buck coming, and keeps the incoming buck from spotting you.

Tease with a "Deke"

A great way to attract wary bucks during the rutting moon is with decoys. I began extensively using decoys shortly after Flambeau developed its 3-D doe decoy in 1989. Since then, I've hunted and photographed over decoys from New York to Texas to Saskatchewan. In the beginning I thought, "This is too easy." I quickly learned that there were many do's and don'ts in using decoys. I've found the rutting moon period, when bucks go bonkers, to be the best time for decoys, be it buck or doe.

Because incoming whitetail bucks almost always circle the decoy, I prefer 3-D units over silhouettes. As good as today's decoys appear to be, their most common shortcoming is a lack of motion. Without some kind of motion, decoys, at best, work only about 50 percent of the time. From early on, I realized that to be more successful I'd have to make approaching bucks more curious and less cautious about the decoy I was using for bow-hunting.

Though it took a little effort, I remedied the situation by attaching a paper clamp to the rump of the decoy. I use the clamp to hold a white handkerchief, and I tie monofilament fishing line to the handkerchief and run the line to my tree stand. Then, after attaching the line to my boot I'm able to add just enough tail flickering to the decoy for a buck to think the decoy is real.

Deer do not pick up a decoy's presence easily if the decoy is in thick brush. So for best results, decoys should be placed at the edge of a field or in a well traveled funnel where deer can easily see them.

Because 3-D decoys can be cumbersome and noisy to assemble, think through how you're going to get them to your hunting position. If you must assemble them every time you use them, do the assembly at least 100 yards from where you intend to hunt. Nothing will ruin a set-up quicker than plastic parts banging together. Also, never leave a decoy set up when you are not hunting over it. Once a deer has been fooled by a decoy, your chances of fooling him again are almost zero.

Three things are important when readying a decoy for hunting:

Get rid of any human odor by spraying the decoy liberally with scent eliminator.

Make sure the decoy is anchored to the ground. The last thing you want is for it to fall over in the wind or from the soft touch of a deer.

Never carry a decoy without wearing blaze orange. Today's decoys are authentic looking and for this reason safety is paramount while moving them around.

Buck or Doe Decoy?

Whitetails will respond to buck and doe decoys. If you want to use a doe decoy, the best time is from about one week before the rutting moon until the end of the breeding period. Buck decoys work better if there is high aggression in the population, which happens when there is an abundance of mature bucks in the herd. If this is the case, a buck decoy will work well during the pre-rut and rut periods. If the area you hunt has too many does and a lot of yearling bucks, a buck decoy will not work as well as a doe decoy.

When bow-hunting with a doe decoy, avoid placing it less than 15 yards from your stand. It's far better to place the decoy 20 to 25 yards upwind of your stand, with the decoy facing or quartering away from you. In most cases, a buck will circle a doe decoy, rather than coming straight to it. Also, if a buck suspects something is odd about the scene (which can often happen) it will hang up within 20 to 30 yards from the decoy. By placing the decoy about 25 yards from your stand, you will be able to get a shot when the buck hangs up. This will often be at point blank range. If a buck comes all the way to the decoy it will give you many opportunities for a broadside shot while it explores the backside of the doe decoy.

When bow-hunting with a buck decoy, I plan my strategy differently. I place the decoy about 20 yards upwind of my stand with it facing or quartering toward me. Unlike the doe decoy, where the buck approaches from the rear, a buck will usually approach a buck decoy from the front. So, it's best to have the buck decoy facing you. The antlers I use on the decoy are always representative of the area I'm hunting. In high-pressure areas where there are few mature bucks this means nothing larger than 100-class Boone-and-Crockett antlers. Always remember that bucks size each other up by body, antler size or a combination of both. This sets the tone for their aggression toward each other. Using only one antler on a buck decoy will suggest that the decoy is a fighter, thus stimulating aggression.

If you bow-hunt over a buck decoy and the approaching buck is one you want to take (and shows an aggressive "attitude") you'll have to shoot him before he reaches the decoy. If you wait for him to get to the decoy, the speed of a frenzied fight will make it impossible for a shot.

Part Four
Tactical Whitetail Hunting

Using the Strategies That Consistently Bag Bucks

Don't just sit there. Do something!

We've been hearing advice like that all our lives, and sometimes it pays off. Then again, sometimes it doesn't.

For many whitetail hunters, there is no choice. The grounds you can legally hunt over, the sites where you can take a stand, are few and far between. A shot at a buck will be about as rare as four aces in hunting-camp poker.

Others are more fortunate: They have room to put a variety of game plans into motion. If that's the case in your hunting, you could do a lot worse than paying attention to the advice which follows. Do these maneuvers always work? Of course not. Nothing does. But they have worked so consistently in the past that there's every reason to believe that they can help you fill your tag.

20   Stalk or Sit? Whitetail Hunting's Toughest Call

BY BOB McNALLY

*Smart, successful whitetail hunters adapt their tactics
to conditions and terrain to take buster bucks.*

It was a cold and rainy December dawn in central Georgia—a miserable, clammy, horrible day to hunt whitetail deer, at least in the minds of most sportsmen. But for Stacer Helton and Kenny Driggers it was perfect weather for hunting their favorite way—stillhunting in the tangled creek draws and drainages that lace their Washington County hunt property.

Dressed in head-to-foot Cabela's camouflage Gortex rain gear (with large, hunter-orange, outer-vests for safety), caps, gloves and rubberized boots, the duo headed into one of the thickest, most tangled and impenetrable spots they knew. It was a place they hunted around frequently from perimeter treestands, and it was a spot they knew held some gigantic bucks. But from long experience they also realized the biggest racks that resided there rarely left the safety of the tangles. Moreover, it was virtually impossible to get into the large bottom to hunt it without spooking or alerting bucks that lived there—at least until conditions were ideal for stalking.

The Georgia deer season had been open for nearly two months, making every buck with decent head gear more than wary of humans. But that was all the more reason why the pair of hunters was anxious about their drizzly day deer hunt. The tangled lowland they targeted harbored an even larger number of good bucks late in the season than it did early in the year. Big, though wary, bucks in good numbers slipped into the spot from surrounding property to avoid hunting pressure. In dry conditions it was virtually impossible for any predator, particularly humans, to approach bucks living in the dense, noisy cover without putting them on alert.

The only way to effectively hunt the long, irregularly-shaped creek bottom (that included a series of beaver ponds) was in rainy or windy weather when bucks were bedded, and stalking conditions were best.

Shortly after dawn, with rain coming down at a steady rate, Stacer and Kenny parked their truck and planned their soggy hunt. They knew the place well, so didn't need maps, compass or GPS. The creek draw forked near the road where

they parked, and each man would slowly, quietly and carefully stillhunt up a separate draw, *into the wind*. They'd each cover a couple miles, and would take the
whole morning to hunt. This wasn't a "push" or drive; but a planned, carefully ex-
ecuted stalk or "stillhunt" for Washington County monster bucks they knew lived
there. It was a hunt they'd waited weeks to make, hoping, praying for the right
weather to execute correctly.

By working up separate creek draws that angled away from each other in a
"Y" shape, the hunters also helped one another. Any deer inadvertently alerted
might be pushed to their hunting partner. The key was to move quietly, slowly,
watching and waiting for long minutes before moving carefully another few yards
into the wind. Deer would be "laid up" in the rain, often under large-leaf magnolia trees or tight-limb cedars, or in dense brier thickets or blowdown tree tops.
Binoculars and predator patience were vital allies for each man.

Not long into the hunt both men encountered deer. Does, yearlings and
small bucks were regularly spotted, though carefully avoided to prevent spooking.
Each hunter stalked a creek hillside, rather than right in the boggy beaver bottom.
They didn't walk ridge crests, but worked well down the incline, wind-blown rain
in their faces, just on the edges of the thickest cover. Silent stalking was best on the
low, soggy, leaf-strewn slopes. They also used stream-side cover to their advantage,
thereby avoiding being detected easily by deer in winter hardwoods devoid of
green underbrush.

About mid-morning, Stacer spotted a decent eight-pointer, placed the
crosshairs of his variable Zeiss scope on the buck's shoulder and considered touching off the Remington 7mm STW. The buck was bedded in the tangles of a huge
oak crown that had fallen from creek-side up a hill. The leaves were gone, but oak
limbs and twigs were a perfect backdrop to conceal the buck. Stacer had scanned
the area ahead of him for 10 minutes before he saw the deer turn its head and look
into the wind, away from the hunter at about 80 yards. He figured the buck at 2 ½
years old, a nice whitetail, but not the sort of animal he wanted on that perfect
rainy, windy stillhunting day.

When he was certain no other deer were bedded nearby, Stacer crossed the
creek silently away from the deer, looped far around the eight-pointer, and continued his stalk into the wind on the opposite stream ridge without spooking the
buck. An hour later he heard a distant shot, and figured Kenny had tagged a deer.
Stacer moved on, along the creek edge, carefully scanning cover far ahead with his
Burris binocular, while rain increased to a steady, drenching downpour that covered his scent and steps to even the most wary of whitetails.

Late that morning, near the end of the stalk, Stacer sat down on a log, while
the storm reached its zenith. There was no lightning, it was too cold. But the wind
was howling, rain coming in sheets and nearly sideways. Stacer had seen plenty of
deer, nearly two dozen, all of them bedded in the thick draw. Many were bucks, including a couple marginal "shooters." But he didn't see anything worth disturbing
the creek bottom for until he happened to notice something move far upwind. He
spotted a pair of does through his binocular, bedded under a giant magnolia. He
carefully scanned the area, about 150 yards away, but saw no bucks.

About that time the rain turned to a light drizzle, a good time to head out of the woods toward home and some hot food, he thought. He checked the does one last time, but they were gone. Somehow they'd gotten up and moved off without him seeing them. He quickly scanned the thicket along the creek closer to him. Nothing. Through binoculars he looked along the hillside, and 50 yards up a ridge, under some white oaks, stood the doe duo, quietly feeding. Suddenly they looked up alertly. Stacer turned the binocular that way, and there stood the buck he was looking for. Heavily muscled, his rack was tall and stark white in the gloomy, wet woods. Though the rut was a memory, the buck still was doe curious, and stood watching the other deer intently as Stacer touched the trigger of his Remington, anchoring the 208-pound, nine-pointer.

Kenny Driggers had collected a buck, too, a dandy eight point, though he saw an even bigger buck for a fleeting moment but couldn't get a sure shot through creek-bottom tangles.

"I think stalking is the best way to shoot a trophy buck, especially in areas having heavy hunting pressure," says Stacer in a thick Georgia accent, reminiscent of president Jimmy Carter, a fellow Peach State resident. "But it's only effective some of the time, and conditions have got to be *absolutely perfect* or you'll do nothing but spook bucks and ruin a great hunting area—maybe for a whole season."

"It's important to know your hunting area well before stillhunting," concurs Kenny Driggers. "Scouting in the off-season is a good way to learn terrain, especially if you carry a good topo map and a compass or GPS. Once you find thick, 'core' bedding areas—especially brier patches along creeks, in draws, and near beaver ponds—you've found the ideal place to stalk. But never go in there looking for deer until the weather cooperates. Rain is best, and I like it *pouring* because deer are bedded, so can't hear or scent a hunter as well as they normally can. Sometimes deer move around a lot in a light rain, and while you can stalk effectively, you can spook more whitetails than if they're holding tight in bad weather. Heavy snowstorms and strong wind are good stalking conditions for the same reasons.

"Naturally, wind must be used as your friend, and you've got to stalk quietly into it to keep from being detected. Deer know they're vulnerable in unsettled weather, so you've got to be super wind-conscious. Swirling or changing wind is a hunt killer. If the breeze switches to an unfavorable direction, get out of the stalk area fast, or you'll blow the opportunity of slipping in on a buck that's learned to live peacefully in a place he has confidence people stay away from.

"It's important to use quiet clothing for stalking. In rainy weather, Gortex is vital, but use only material that's completely quiet, like that made by Cabela's, 10× and Browning."

Stacer says field edges are choice places to stillhunt, too. He stays well inside the woods, about 50 or 100 yards, watching carefully with binoculars far ahead of him, both in the woods and out in the field.

During midday scouting trips, Stacer carries a rifle, and makes certain he always uses prevailing wind in his favor—because *scouting* deer can suddenly become *stalking* deer.

"A lot of whitetails move around and feed in the middle of the day, especially during the late rifle season, and particularly during the full moon," explains Stacer, owner of Skinner's Guide Service in the town of Sandersville. "Midday hunting can be good then, and often the wind is up so stalking can be very effective. It's a good time to scout areas for placing stands, but you might as well have a rifle with you because you never know when a big buck might appear."

While Stacer is an expert at stalking, he spends plenty of time in treestands and ground blinds, especially during calm, stable weather. When he's hunting hot deer feeding areas or buck sign during the rut, he'll most of the time be found sitting in a stand covering such areas. Last year in Alberta, Stacer took a 10-point, 300-pound buck that gross-scored 172⅞ Boone and Crockett points. Taken from a ground blind, the deer dropped at a measured 350 yards. Two days later, in a Saskatchewan stand, he downed a 171⅝ net B&C buck at 145 yards. Back home in Georgia, just before the state season ended in January, Stacer shot yet another dandy 200-pound buck from a stand at 175 yards that scored 140 B&C points.

Although most hunters know that where they place a stand is vital to success, Alex Rutledge, a well-traveled hunter from Missouri, says most sportsmen don't know that different stands perform better at certain times of day.

"In most regions, there are 'morning stands' and 'evening stands' that produce best for whitetails," explained Rutledge, a pro staffer for Hunter's Specialties products. "The very best hunters I know move their stands frequently, and they often employ two stands—using one location at dawn, another at dusk.

"In 'fringe country' where woodlots are surrounded by farms, fields and grain crops, the best evening stands are often stationed along wooded trails leading to the fields, since bucks often feed late in the day or even at night. The only chance a hunter has for them in legal shooting hours is when they're moving down trails to the feed areas.

"Morning stands should be located along trails in areas *near* where deer bed during the day. The edge of a creek bottom, swamp or dense stand of pines would be good to check for a morning-stand site.

"A lot of inexperienced hunters don't know how long they may have to spend sitting—quiet and motionless—in a treestand to finally get a chance at a big buck. It's not unusual to spend four hours or more in a stand 20 feet off the ground. So make the best of it from the beginning by placing a comfortable stand that allows you to relax while sitting and standing. I carry a small backpack with lots of items that allow all-day stand hunting if I choose to do that. I have a lunch, coffee or canteen, candy bars, knife, flashlight, insect repellent—anything that makes life on stand easier. A hunter who is comfortable and relaxed is most likely to spot game and then make a killing shot."

David Cummings of Green Bay, Wisconsin, is an inveterate dairy farmer. All his life he's seen how animals react to their environment, and he believes whitetail deer do likewise.

"I really studied the solunar tables when I run my farm," says the 57-year-old hunter who has about 50 deer to his credit. "Livestock can be resting through the day, but during a minor or major feed period they'll be on their feet and eating—unless, of course, the weather is bad.

"Heavy rain with lightning is therefore terrible for stand deer hunting. But right after a rain, or a snowstorm, is the best time for a deer hunter to go on stand. A cold, still morning is prime, too, especially if there's a major or minor feed period going on at the same time.

"Moon phase means a lot, but the only time it keeps me from stand hunting is during the week of the full moon. I know deer feed at night during the full moon and are not likely to feed during the day, so I stalk during that time. When the moon is dark, I hunt from stands as much as possible because deer move around so much. If you have to hunt during the full moon, silent stalking is most productive."

The important thing to remember is to be adaptable. Don't be "married" to stand hunting, and never hunt a single stand too much. Try different places, always with favorable wind. And when stand hunting conditions are terrible, and you're not seeing bucks like you should, make a silent stalk. You'll likely be surprised at what you'll find.

21 Deadly Deer Drives: The 'Nudge' Beats the 'Push'!

*These fine-tuned strategies can put new life in your gang's deer drives—
especially if you've been moving too loud and too fast!*

Driving deer is an art form, practiced by many, perfected by few. When done correctly, it's one of the deadliest methods for collecting venison, but conducted otherwise a deer drive is good exercise and little else. Does, fawns, and young foolish bucks are often pushovers for a good deer drive; but old mossy-horned bucks seldom fall for any but the most fine-tuned of drives, and good old-fashioned luck helps.

The best deer drives are pulled off by small groups of good hunters who know the country and each other. The most fun are probably those organized, disorganized affairs at Camp; where Joe takes the standers in one direction and Harry leads the drivers off in the other. The standers seldom take the right stands, but the drivers seldom get it quite right anyway so it doesn't make much difference. While the hunters try to sort the blame, the bucks run over the hill wondering what all the ruckus was about. The worst are those big neighborhood campaigns, which can, if you don't watch it, get ugly.

The bucks lived on an off-limits-to-hunting mountain and sneaked down, under cover of darkness, to the cornfields on the fringe of a growing city. The corn lay between a busy highway and the mountain. A few houses and an automobile graveyard were scattered among the cornfields, and the bucks were perfectly comfortable among either. At the far end of the fields was a busy industrial complex. There was thick brush further separating the fields from the mountain, traversed by a relatively open power line right of way, which made a perfect spot to ambush the bucks at daylight as they made their way back to the mountain.

Each morning our small group took stands on the power line in the predawn darkness. When it got light enough to see well, the end two or three standers would drop off and slowly drive the fields and brushy edge, parallel to the highway and the power line, toward the busy industrial complex into which the deer seldom, if ever, ventured. Apparently, even deer have their limits as to how much land development they'll tolerate.

As the deer sneaked ahead of the pushers, they stopped to watch and wait among the junked cars or beneath the picture window of a house (a highlight, or lowlight, depending, was catching sight of the lady of the house in her nightgown framed by the antlers of a nice buck). Admittedly, we were treading a fine line here when it came to strict interpretation of the safety zone law, to say nothing of historic societal bias toward peeping Toms in general. But the homeowners were tolerant and the junkyard operator appeared only mildly curious of our early morning shenanigans.

Of course, the drivers couldn't shoot, but sooner or later the bucks would break for the mountain rather than enter the industrial war zone. Though once in awhile they panicked and ran toward the highway. Then we got a good chuckle as irate commuters screeched their brakes and laid on their horns. Still, most of the bucks ran for the mountain.

They usually crossed the power line in an all-ahead-full mode and then the fun really began. But the hunters in the group were good shots, and many a buck met his maker on these early morning deer drives.

How Most Drives Go Wrong!

Off and on for 40 seasons now I've hunted out of a deer camp that is a good example of the flip side of deer driving as art form. We drive deer relentlessly, though with little organization and even less success. While we generally do the same drives year after year, we only very seldom get them done the same two times in a row. It seems our camp is a nest for freelancers, each hunter having his own idea of just how it should be done. Thus, it isn't much of a surprise to come upon a stander in the middle of the drive. This sort of disruption tends to have unsettling effects on the deer and an even bigger negative impact on a drive's success.

Likewise, with our drivers. Many in our gang are notorious for skirting the tough places, leaving gaping holes in the drive. And, in the opinion of many, deer are quick to pick up on such weaknesses and find the holes in the attacking line. The result: many of these abortive attempts produce ample exercise and laughs, but very little meat.

Deer drives fall into three general categories: noisy, silent and a variation in which the drivers beat on trees with sticks. Noisy drives were once traditional around here. For a time I thought all deer drivers danced to the same fiddle: take a few steps and yell like hell. The progress of the drive was easily followed, even from the next mountain, by simply listening to the "Yo's, yeehah's," and "get on there's," three popular cries of the typical yelling deer driver. I grew up a yelling deer driver. So did my dad and his.

The "Silent" Drive

But by the time my sons began hunting, the noisy drive had pretty much given way to the silent drive—with or without the stick drill (although I've participated in drives where there was both yelling and stick pounding). Lately I only very rarely, maybe once this past season, heard the familiar cries of a noisy drive. I kind of miss them, but I still wonder what the deer think when they hear a bunch of guys advancing on their day beds, yelling like crazed banshees and/or beating on trees. Innocent bystanders, who might think hunters are a little odd to begin with, are probably at least mildly puzzled when a full-fledged noisy drive comes through the neighborhood.

I wasn't a very old buck hunter before I began to question just what all that noise did for our success. I harbored suspicions that any deer not give to flat-out flight at the first "yeehah" might just figure out where the holes were and exit through them. This theory gained plausibility when I noticed that many bucks were shot, or shot at, by drivers as they tried to break or sneak back through our noisy line. But I had also learned at a tender age that young buck hunters don't question, at least not out loud, the traditions of old buck hunters. So I remained mum. Eventually the silent drive thing shook itself out, thus saving grace on my part.

As far back as I can remember there were some local groups who drove deer silently—at least making as little noise as possible. It didn't take a great deal of investigation to learn that they were among the most successful gangs each season. When a line of men moves through the woods, making only the subtle sounds of quiet walking, apparently it makes the deer nervous, but often fails to trigger their flight alarms. In the ideal world of deer drives, the deer shuttle ahead a little and watch their back trail, then they move a little more and wait some more. Pretty soon they find themselves standing where a poster can see them. More often than not the poster is offered a good shot at a standing or slow moving buck. That is the way it's supposed to work.

When Bucks Wise Up!

Of course, where deer are constantly harassed it makes little difference if the drive is silent or noisy, because such bucks immediately switch to the evasive mode at the first whiff of scent or hint of man sound. Whether or not anyone sees them feeling then becomes largely a matter of luck. Bucks which have learned through bad experiences just what a drive is all about can be very slick when it comes to defensive maneuvers. And I admit that of late, at least around here, such deer are becoming way more common than they used to be.

We once cornered a big buck we'd been chasing hard all season in a small thicket with only two good avenues of escape. We cut off both and I took up the track in fresh snow. It seemed the buck was doomed. The track wound around the thicket and then broke out along a thick multiflora rose hedge, one of the two escape routes where a hunter waited.

Elated at this turn of events, I hurried along, paying little attention to the track, more listening for the expected shot than anything. A light came on that perhaps I should look down at my feet, when suddenly the hunter loomed ahead and I hadn't heard a shot. Feeling stupid, I was not all that surprised that there was no buck track anymore. After all, this was a buck which had repeatedly given us the slip for nearly two weeks.

Wheeling about and hurrying along my back trail, it wasn't far until I realized that he just might do it again. The doomed buck had jumped into the multiflora rose hedge, stood there as I hurried blindly past, then jumped out and raced back to the thicket.

Worse, he then exited by the other route we had cut off: But the stander had decided the chase was going the other way and left. I could only laugh when I saw the wide splayed hoof prints overlaying the boot tracks of the departed hunter.

Strategies for Winning Drives

I've noticed that deer push best in the direction they'd most like to go. A deer's best defense is his nose, so they naturally prefer to move with their noses into the wind. Jump deer and it is only a few hops before they try to turn into the wind. I also suspect they are most comfortable moving toward heavy cover rather than away from it. When deer drives move away from fields, rather than toward them, deer are often more cooperative.

You don't need a large group to pull off a good drive. A few, even two or three, good hunters who know the lay of the land can move a bunch. Of course, like all worthwhile endeavors, it pays to pick and choose whom you hunt with, where you drive and to remember that carefully planned drives usually pay the biggest dividends.

On the mountain behind my house, naturally the one I hunt most, we drive deer often. One of our favorite, though certainly not the easiest, methods is to drive off the points guarding the water gaps or deep hollows. It may surprise you to learn that those points can be successfully driven by one hunter, if he knows his business. Although it's probably a stretch to say that one or two hunters can cover all the possible escape routes. However, we've learned through trial and error that each point has one or two preferred escape routes. So we cut off the best with what we have and hope for the best. Sometimes you get the buck and sometimes he gets you. But that's deer hunting and we've learned also that persistence usually pays off.

I should probably mention that the toughest thing about driving the points, which are often the steepest and roughest places, is that once the driver reaches the bottom, someone must climb back up to do the next one. It's sort of a given that a day of this will make you sleep well the night after. But, while not guaranteed, the exertion could also fill your tag.

The most unique deer drive which I've ever participated in was called, for want of a better label, the V Drive. Because I had acquired the blueprint for this drive in a rather questionable atmosphere (an old-timer in a severely whisky-altered state had hastily drawn out the details on a napkin in a dark, smoke-filled barroom) our gang entered into the operation somewhat skeptical.

As near as I could follow, given the circumstances, the V-Drive had the hunters spread out along the arms of the V, with the leader at the apex. The drive proceeded in the direction of the open end. After everyone had slipped quietly into position, the leader was supposed to blow a loud whistle, whereupon the drive crept forward five steps and stopped until the next whistle. Obviously this was a different deer drive, if for no other reason than the fact that there were no standers.

Despite the fact that this was one of those infamous hot tips which all bar-rooms in deer country are famous for—and in spite of the persistent nagging feeling that we'd been had—early next morning found us, presumably, in position at one end of the long mountain with only the vaguest idea of what might happen next. It still wasn't entirely clear where the deer would, or more to the point, might, go once the drive began. But we knew they would go somewhere and, what the heck, we'd done dumber things.

However, when I blew the whistle and crept forward the requisite five steps, the thought did cross my mind that an old man might be, at that very moment, perched on the same bar stool, hung over from the night before, but, nonetheless, having the time of his life. By the time I had blown the whistle the 5th or 6th time and had sneaked forward the compulsory 25 or 30 steps I was laughing myself.

But when a shot rang out from somewhere up ahead and then another, I got very serious about where I put my feet following the next tweet. One day in flint-lock season our usual group of about a dozen suddenly swelled to more than twice that number—too many, as far as some of us were concerned. But we had all come to drive deer, and we were already up, so we went along. It was one of those things you know you shouldn't get into, but you do anyway.

Everything went okay until the last drive before lunch. I think each drive had produced a shot or two, but nothing to get nervous about. Then we decided to push a rocky, steep face of the mountain which we normally left alone due to a lack of manpower to do it right. That day we had the manpower—in spades!

The standers headed off a deep hollow and the drive began. It wasn't long until white tails were dancing everywhere ahead of the drive. Soon it seemed like everyone was shooting, reloading and shooting again—some even again—awesome when you consider the time it takes most of us to recharge a discharged flinter.

When, finally, the shooting stopped, I cautiously peeked out from behind the big oak I had been hugging, wondering if we'd tagged any hunters along with the deer. Blue smoke still hung in the air and the stench of burning sulfur was strong. I looked up the hill at J.B., our leader, still hugging a big rock, and down the hill at my buddy, Bill, still backed up against a big tree. The look on their faces said pretty much what I felt: Some deer drives can be too good!

22　Profile of a Tracker

BY JEROME B. ROBINSON

Deer hunters with great tracking skills are universally envied and respected by their peers. This one is no exception.

Country wisdom says that if you put a boy on a stump and tell him to stay there until a buck comes along, and one does come along and he shoots it, he will be a patient stump-sitter all his life.

But if the boy gets bored and leaves the stump to have a look around, and subsequently shoots his first buck while he is sneaking through the woods, you have the makings of a stillhunter: a tracker who hunts for deer rather than relying on the deer to come to him.

My New Hampshire neighbor and frequent hunting partner, Alfred Balch, was never a patient stump-sitter.

"I get curious about what's happening over the hills," he admits. "I figure you are only going to see deer if you or the deer are moving. One of us has to move or there's not going to be an encounter."

Alfred was taught about the ways of wild things by his father back when it was expected that a man would teach his son to hunt. He shot his first buck when he was 10.

"Dad was following a fresh track up on Bear Hill and I was tagging along behind him," Alfred recalls.

"Suddenly Dad stopped and whispered, 'Do you see him?'

"I couldn't see the deer, so Dad lifted me up on a stump. I could see it then. Dad handed me his rifle and whispered, 'Shoot him like I showed you how.'

"I aimed that big gun and let roar and the deer went down. I dropped the rifle in the snow and ran to the deer. It was dead. A 6-pointer. When Dad came up I said, 'Isn't he a beauty?'

" 'He's a beauty a'right,' Dad said. 'But next time don't throw my rifle in the snow.' "

For five more years, until he was old enough to draw a hunting license and hunt alone, Alfred shared his father's rifle and got a deer each year.

"We always got our deer by going out and looking for them," Alfred recalls. "Dad taught me that if you want to learn about deer, you've got to track them. See where they're feeding, what they're eating; find out where they bed in different kinds of weather and at different times of year."

Forty years later, Alfred still goes out tracking deer the year around, roaming the nearby mountains whenever he gets a chance, gathering knowledge about the deer so that when he goes out to hunt, with a bow in September, a muzzleloader in October, or a high-powered rifle in November, he knows where a particular buck is most likely to be.

"A deer track always leads to more deer tracks," Alfred says. "Following tracks teaches you the patterns deer follow. Tracking teaches you about their habits. You won't learn those things sitting on a stand.

"Tracking gets you in shape, too," he adds. "You hitch onto the track of a rutting buck and you're going to cover some country. If you do a lot of tracking you get conditioned to moving in the woods and balancing yourself so you're not so awkward and noisy."

Hunting with Alfred, I am often struck by the way he moves, for I rarely see him move at all. I see him stopped beside a tree someplace, and later I see him stopped beside another tree, but I seldom see him in motion.

When I mentioned the mystery of how he gets from place to place, he said, "Walk for one minute, stop for three."

But I think he meant that he stops three times as much as he walks, for if he really moved for a minute at a time, I'd see him more than I do, and so would the deer.

He stops and studies the woods around him for a long, long time. He looks for a piece of a deer, not a whole deer. The crooked line of a deer's hind leg sticking out from behind a tree, the straight line of a deer's back: these are the kinds of pieces he searches for. "I know I'm going to see a moving deer—it's the one that is standing still or bedded that I'm looking for," he says.

Before he moves, Alfred plans his next few steps so that he can take them without looking down at the ground.

"Know where you're going to step before you start walking so that you don't have to look at the ground when you're moving," he told me once. "Keep your eyes open and watch for deer, not your feet. If you have to look at your feet, you're moving too fast.

"If you're seeing deer's flags, that's another indication that you're moving too fast," he adds. "Those are deer that saw you first. You can't go too slow."

Alfred's way of hunting is to find a good track and work it. Before the snow comes, when tracks sometimes appear to be nothing more than obscure disturbances in the frozen leaves, he reads them with his fingers.

"Press your two fingers right down into this track, right to the bottom," he commands. "Feel it?"

When you do it, the track becomes alive to your touch. A mere hole in the leaves until you touched it, the track now takes form. You can feel the length and breadth of the long cloven hoof, can feel whether the points on the bottom of the track are sharp or rounded.

"Now pull the leaves out of that track and you can see it," Alfred adds.

I once told Alfred about a study I had read in which biologists had measured the hooves of 2,500 deer and determined it is impossible to tell the sex of a deer by its tracks alone.

"That's because they measured the feet on dead deer," Alfred shot right back. "It's not just how big a track is that tells you if it was made by a buck or doe, it's the way they put their weight on their feet.

"In the fall when a buck's neck is swollen, a buck carries his weight on his heels," he explained. "That tends to make his toes spread apart when he is walking and brings his dewclaws in contact with the ground more often. A doe generally holds her toes together when she's walking and makes more of a heart-shaped track. Her dewclaws only show when she's moving fast.

"In shallow snow a buck drags his toes so it's plain to see even if the snow is only an inch deep. Does pick their feet up and set them down clean," Alfred continued.

"Where the tracks go tells you something, too," he added. "A buck in the rut will generally be moving alone, striding right out through the woods, not on any particular trail, really covering the country.

"Droppings tell you some more," Alfred said. "A buck dribbles his droppings as he moves along. A doe tends to drop them in a clump.

"A buck's track will lead to his scrapes, hooking around bushes and trees he has rubbed. You put all these factors together and you know damn well when you're on a buck track."

Why do bucks put their weight on their heels?

"Just look at a buck in fall," Alfred says. "His neck is swollen up twice its normal size and, as the rut wears on, he loses weight on his back and loins. He's carrying most of his weight up front, so he balances it by setting back on his feet."

Alfred locates big buck tracks by hiking a wide route around the edge of country where he expects deer to be moving, looking for the freshest signs of an extra big one.

Before taking a track and following, he often makes a swing around the outside of the country the track leads into, to see if it comes out the other side.

"No use following a track into a place when you can check to see if the deer stopped in there or moved through," he says. "Of course, lots of times you can't check the far side, so then you have no choice, you have to follow the track from where you found it."

Identifying the freshness of a track depends on accurate observation of weather conditions. "You have to pay attention to when things happen to know when a track was made," Alfred explains. "For example, if you know it stopped raining at 3 o'clock and you find a track that hasn't been rained on, you know it was made after 3 o'clock. It helps to remember what time frost came and what time the ground thawed and when snow started or stopped. These things tell you how fresh a track is."

When there is no snow on the ground deer tracks in leaves are more noticeable if you look ahead, rather than looking down at them. The tracks show up as a visible line of disturbance. When the line of tracks is obscure, getting your eye down close to the ground makes them show up distinctly.

"Crouch down and squint out there along the ground," Alfred told me one day when we were hunting on loose, newly fallen leaves. "See that line of tracks? Now stand up. You can hardly see them at all."

When you encounter a bunch of similar deer tracks going both into and out of a certain section of woods, it can be difficult to know which way the deer went last. "The best bet is to go in the direction that most of the tracks go," Alfred advises. "If a deer goes into a piece of woods and then comes back out and finally goes back in again, most of the tracks will be headed in the direction the deer went last."

Tracks tell you a lot about the deer and show you where they have been, but you have to rely on your wits to figure out where they are going.

When Alfred works a track, he doesn't just walk along following it. He'll follow the track a bit to get a sense of where it is going, then he swings out on the downwind side and hunts on a course that is parallel to the track. Every so often he loops back to the track to keep alert to its general direction.

When a buck stops to rest, he will often turn and walk straight downwind for 50 to 100 yards, then travel back parallel to its track for a little way before bedding down below the top of a rise of ground. This puts the deer in a position to overlook its backtrack so it can see, smell, and hear anything that may be following.

"By hunting parallel to a track on the downwind side, you have a chance of coming up on the buck without being seen or scented," Alfred explains.

When he hunts with a partner, Alfred likes to have one man follow the track while the other moves parallel on the downwind side as far out as he can be and still keep the track-follower in sight.

"That's a deadly method," he declares. "It's how Dad and I always hunted. It requires two people who hunt at the same slow pace, can move quietly, and have sharp eyes. By keeping an eye on the tracker, the wing man knows he's staying in line with the track."

Moving quietly takes practice and requires learning a different way of shifting your weight.

"Hold your weight back on the foot that's under you while you place your front foot and then roll your weight forward," Alfred instructed me one day when the leaves were frozen and it sounded as if I were walking on corn flakes. "If you feel a twig or something that is going to make noise under your foot, shift your weight back to your rear foot while you make a correction. Move slowly and don't just fall forward onto your front foot."

No one can move in complete silence, even in the best of conditions, but there are a few things you can do to limit the noise you make.

"The loudest sounds are those you make above the ground," Alfred notes. "The snap of a branch that catches on your coat carries farther than the crunch of a twig beneath your foot. Dry stubs that stick up from logs are particularly noisy—catch your foot on one of them and it makes a snap like a rifle shot.

"You're always going to make some noise, but you can try to make noises that sound like a moving deer rather than a man," Alfred instructs. "A deer takes a few steps and then stops for a long period—men tend to clump along with steady footfalls that warn wildlife from long distance."

Alfred moves in the shadows, avoiding open places as much as possible. He stops beside a tree and waits in the shadow of that tree, studying what's ahead until he is ready to move to the shadow of another tree.

"Stopping beside a tree breaks up your silhouette, and it also gives you something solid to lean on if you need to take a long shot," he reasons. "Staying in the shadows is just common sense; it makes you harder to see."

The sight of any deer stops Alfred in his tracks. "Whenever you have a deer in view, stop and watch," he advises. "A doe is often followed by a buck that may be moving 10 or even 15 minutes behind her. Her attitude will often tell you if there are other deer around. If she stares in one direction frequently, chances are good another deer is there."

Being alert to sounds is another important aspect of stillhunting.

A few years ago I was hunting caribou with Pat Cleary, a Montagnais Indian from central Quebec who was a fine tracker. Pat had been making slow but sure progress in following a single caribou bull across a long expanse of broken granite when he suddenly raised his head and listened.

Canada geese were clamoring in the distance.

"Those geese see the caribou," Pat said. "C'mon, we'll go over there."

We trotted for nearly a mile to a little lake surrounded by low willows. A big flock of geese sat on the water, still talking. Near them, on the wet, sandy shore, was the fresh track of the caribou bull we were after.

"We just gained a couple of hours on him," Pat said with satisfaction. An hour later we caught up with the bull; his double-shoveled rack now hangs in my cabin.

Sounds made by birds and squirrels can often tip you off to movement in the forest. When blue jays call excitedly or red squirrels begin to chatter, ask yourself what they could be talking about. Such sounds are often worth investigating.

For the past three years, Alfred has been carrying a thin stick in his pocket. It is exactly the width of the biggest walking buck track Alfred has seen passing through his hunting territory in recent years. Whenever he comes across a large track, Alfred pulls the stick out of his pocket and checks to see if it was made by The Big Guy.

One day Alfred took me high up on a hardwood ridge to show me The Big Guy's track.

"When he's in this country, this is one of the places he travels," Alfred said.

"A big buck has his own runways that are separate from the more noticeable trails the other deer travel," he continued. "When you are tracking a big buck it's important to remember exactly where it comes from and where it goes." Gradually, Alfred has put together a mental map of The Big Guy's travel pattern.

"One of these days we're both going to come to the same place at the same time," he declares. "Then it'll be up to me to see him before he sees me."

Each year Alfred is restless until he finds The Big Guy's track after hunting season has ended. Last year he didn't find the track he wanted until long after Christmas, and he worried that The Big Guy had died. Then one bright January day he stopped me on the road. He reached in his pocket and pulled out his measuring stick and held it up to me.

"He's still up there," he said. "I found his track crossing the ridge this morning."

23   How to Use Deer
Calls Effectively

BY PETER FIDUCCIA

Peter Fiduccia's book WHITETAIL STRATEGIES *is packed with tips and observations that will literally change the way you hunt. This chapter is one of the strongest ever written on the fascinating subject of calling.*

The rhythmic sounds of the buck moving steadily through fallen leaves were only overshadowed by the noise of snapping branches as he trotted along the river bed. Now the big buck was in sight and I could plainly hear the guttural grunts he was making every few seconds. His big white rack glistened as he trotted toward my stand. He was moving so quickly that I thought he would trot right by me without offering me a good shot. I took out my grunt call and blew an extended, soft doe grunt. The buck skidded to a halt and glanced up at me as I pulled the trigger.

Thirty years ago, this chapter probably would not have caught your attention and for a very good reason—you probably would not have believed deer calls worked. Using calls to attract deer back in the 60s was a well-kept secret used only by the old, savvy woodsmen who hunted the remote wilderness areas of the country. These old timers rarely talked about the effectiveness of using doe bleats. But, quietly and consistently, they used these rudimentary calls made of rubber bands and balsa wood to regularly attract whitetails.

It was just such an "old timer" who first introduced me to deer calls. During my second deer season, I was hunting in Childwold, NY (the Adirondack Mts.). I was sitting on a stand overlooking a swamp. Every so often, I heard a soft lamb-like sound. I honestly did not know what the sound was or what was making it. But, I did know that about every 15 minutes, the sound emanated a hundred yards or so from a dip below the ledge I was sitting on. Since this was only my second year of deer hunting, my patience level wasn't fine tuned. If I didn't see a deer within the first hour or two, I usually got up and skulked around hoping to jump a buck. To this day, I often smile when I think about those "patience-less" days. It never seemed to fail, no sooner did I get up and start walking around then I would hear a gun shot ring out close by me. I must have unknowingly driven a lot of bucks to many hunters in those days.

In any event, by 7:30 that morning, my patience was gone and I was determined to go check out what was making this lamb-like noise. Just as I stood up to gather my gear, I heard the noise again. This time, I also heard a similar noise coming from the swamp. I thought to myself, "What the hell did I do? Did I unsuspectingly post on the border of lamb farm on the other side of the swamp?" Just then, a big doe emerged from the swamp and trotted toward the ledge below me. Never swerving, she was determined to reach the source of the noise. I watched as she stopped and then began pacing nervously back and forth. Then, the excitement started. Right behind her, from the swamp, ran two bucks. I started shaking and tried to decide which one to shoot, when a gun shot rang out. The bigger of the two bucks dropped in its tracks. I threw my .30-30 to my shoulder and tried to draw a bead on the second buck as it and the doe weaved and darted through the surrounding mature hardwoods. I never pulled the trigger. Naturally, I was pretty shocked at what had just happened.

As I sat there disgusted, I saw a hunter who was posted well below me, stand and approach the downed buck. I grabbed my gear and went down to talk to him. This old gentleman was the source of the doe blat I was hearing all that morning. He told me how he used doe blats for years to attract whitetails, especially from heavy cover like the swamp we were overlooking. He busted out into laughter with tears in his eyes, when I told him I thought I posted near a sheep farm. "Boy, there ain't a sheep or a farm between Childwold and Tupper Lake and they're 30 miles apart," he laughed as he held his belly.

While the old-timer field dressed the eight-point buck, I stood there in amazement as he told story after story of how successful he had been over the years using a blat call. "Hell, boy, if you wanna kill bucks like this, learn to blow one of these here doe calls," he said. And the old gent placed an Olt der call in my hand. "Your friends will think you're crazy for using it," he said, "but, I can betcha it'll work."

That was my introduction to deer calling. I bought an Olt call that afternoon in a tiny general store in Tupper Lake during a heavy snow fall. I blew it on almost every hunting trip that season without success! However, I didn't give up. The memory of that morning's hunt and the old gent's stories remained vivid within me, so I continued to use and practice the doe blat call.

By 1970, I was a much better deer caller, having learned to use a variety of calls other than the blat and even called in and shot a few bucks. I knew I was on to something and promised myself that, through trial and error, I would gain experience and confidence and become an accomplished caller.

Hunters have long benefited from knowing how to use artificial calls to attract wildlife. A good example is elk hunters who have enjoyed the success of rattling, bugling or "mewing" bulls and cows for many years. Moose, duck, wild turkey, coyote and many other game animals have also been successfully "enticed-in" by sportsmen who made it their business to learn effective calling techniques to attract a variety of wildlife.

But deer hunters still are reluctant to try calls to attract whitetails. Unfortunately, these outdoorsmen are missing out on one of Mother Nature's natural seductions. By learning how, why, where, and when to use deer calls you will increase your success ratio.

All thirty species and subspecies of deer in the Americas are vocal animals. Whitetail, mule, and blacktail deer, for example, which cover a broad range on the continent, respond readily to calling. Biologists have confirmed and categorized thirteen different types of vocalizations made by whitetails.

Since I began deer hunting in 1965, I have taken 113 white-tailed bucks. Approximately half of these bucks were shot after I imitated deer sounds. Calling to deer has been one of the easiest methods I have ever used to trick white-tailed deer to my stand.

The secret to being a successful caller is the same as I have discussed in earlier chapters—confidence. Knowing your call sounds authentic and believing in its effectiveness is critical to your success. Confidence can mean the difference between seeing and actually bagging game. A few years ago, I received a letter from a *Woods N' Water TV Show* viewer who also read many of my articles. An avid deer hunter, Chuck Jermyn, first decided to use deer calls after reading an article I wrote. In his letter, he told me he "was skeptical," as most novice callers are, and how in his first year of calling he "didn't harvest a deer." In his second season, however, after spending the summer and spring practicing, Jermyn called in several good bucks! By practicing, he gained confidence and it paid big dividends for him.

Practice is the name of the game when it comes to deer calling. A good caller carries several different types of calls and uses them throughout the year. Whenever you see deer, no matter what time of the year it is, call to them. Learn what type of calls make them curious, alarmed, relaxed or nervous. The best time to test the effectiveness of calls is in the spring and summer when deer are vocal and are not harassed by hunting pressure.

In the spring, does are vocal when they give birth to fawns. These vocalizations are crucial to the fawn's survival and include feeding, alarm, locating and other types of calls to help the fawn in its day-to-day survival.

You can effectively replicate several types of deer vocalizations. Snorts, blats, bleats, grunts, whistles, and barks can all be used to lure deer to your stand, just like rattling. The four calls that will bring you the most success, however, are also the easiest to learn: the alarm snort; the burp grunt (doe and buck); the loud blat; and the social bleat.

There are several keys to successful calling. First, an experienced deer caller learns to blow all calls softly. Occasionally, a louder, more aggressive call may be necessary. But, overall, louder aggressive sounding calls will scare away more deer (including big bucks) than they will attract. Although you have read and heard to the contrary, common sense applies here.

Many of you have told me repeatedly that while using grunt calls, you have had varied success. Sometimes they attract bucks and sometimes they don't. Invariably, the next question is, "Why?" There are many reasons why grunts and other calls work well sometimes and not others. Most times, however, negative response is generated after a grunt is blown too loudly and aggressively.

Let's take an average size eight-pointer walking up a trail with his nose held to the ground. Suddenly, he hears your loud, aggressive grunt. Basically, what you've just done is yelled at the top of your lungs, "HEY YOU!" You just scared the crap out of the poor buck. What happens next is automatic. Out of instinct, he glances in your direction and then realizes he made a critical mistake by attempting to make eye contact with a more aggressive animal. Immediately, he avoids a confrontation by looking away and continuing to walk without looking back. No matter how long or hard you grunt at a buck under these conditions, he will not respond. Why should he? Through your loud and aggressive call, you just announced that you're unquestionably the biggest, "baddest" buck in the woods. If he has any sense at all, even if he is a big buck, he'll avoid the fight and walk off. If, by now, you doubt that, go back and reread the chapter on rattling and fighting behavior. Make your calls softly and you'll be more successful.

The next most common reason for lack of success when calling is calling too much. When you're calling, you're no longer hunting the buck, he is hunting you. So, it's important that while you are trying to gain his attention by vocalizing, you don't want to talk so much that he pinpoints your location or becomes wary due to the unnatural frequency of your numerous calls. Limit the number of calls you make to within common sense parameters.

Another reason for unsuccessful calling is calling to an animal that has responded to the call and is walking toward you. Once a buck responds and walks to you—stop calling. Let his curiosity work for instead of against you. With that said, there are many cadences to each of the primary vocalizations. Learn and practice them and you will add another potent weapon to your deer hunting arsenal.

Snort

Because the snort call represents, to most hunters, a deer fleeing, it is the most misunderstood and hardly ever used call. The snort vocalization has several meanings to deer. When you can decipher what each call means, you'll be very surprised at how effective each snort cadence is.

There are four cadences to the Primary Snort—the Alarm Call, the Alarm Distress, the Social snort and the Aggressive snort. Each of these calls has a specific meaning and is used during certain situations. When you use a snort at the right time and under the correct set of circumstances, you can trick your quarry into thinking you are another deer. Use the wrong snort cadence under the wrong circumstances, however, and the deer you are snorting to will turn itself inside out trying to avoid you.

Alarm Snort

The alarm snort is frequently heard by most hunters. I could even tell you when and where you probably encountered a deer making this cadence of the alarm snort. Often, a hunter walking along a logging road or making his way through the woods to his stand jumps a deer. Because the deer does not wind the hunter first, it only reacts to the hunter's noise. I know you've heard this snort often. This deer, buck or doe, can be called back if you know what to do.

When you encounter a deer unexpectedly, the deer may respond by blowing a single snort, then run several yards, stop and blow a second single snort. *"Whew . . . Whew."* It is alarmed, but has not been able to pinpoint why. The deer is trying to locate and isolate the danger. By blowing back at the deer with an alarm/snort call, you will stimulate the deer's curiosity. Often, it decides to slowly make its way back toward the location where it first encountered the perceived danger.

When you jump a deer that blows the alarm snort, wait until the deer has blown the second snort. Then, place the call in your mouth and blow hard once, hesitate about two seconds, and blow the call again. Do not blow the call a third time until the deer snorts back. Once the deer answers you, respond to it with two more snorts. Keep doing this as long as you hear the deer approaching and snorting.

Several years ago, I snorted at a buck 57 times. Each time, the buck answered with a snort of his own. I was convinced I was calling to a wise old buck. As the tension mounted, I became more and more convinced that this was a really big buck. Finally, the buck emerged from the pines and I was surprised to see he was a small six point buck. I shot him anyway.

Years ago, my wife Kate shot her first buck while still hunting toward her tree stand. As she approached the stand, she saw a deer. She tried to position herself for a shot and she stepped on a branch. The deer heard the snap and blew an alarm snort. It ran off several yards, then blew a second snort. Kate blew back at the deer, and the buck answered. Each time the deer blew two snorts, Kate blew back two snorts. The buck, curious to see what had frightened it, kept coming closer to her with each series of alarm snorts. Finally, after several minutes of exchanging snorts to one another, the spike buck made its last move when it stepped out from behind the cedars and Kate dispatched him with one clean shot. Kate would have never had the opportunity to shoot that buck if she didn't know enough to call back to the snorting buck.

All variations of the snort work well. You will find, however, the alarm snort to be the easiest snort to learn and use. However, the critical aspect when using a snort call is to not blow an alarm snort to a deer who is vocalizing an alarm-distress. You must know the different cadences of each call for them to be effective.

I often use the alarm snort when bow hunting. Intentionally, I walk through heavy cover with the wind in my face. Every few steps, I snap a twig or kick some leaves. I do this with the hopes of alarming a buck with the noise I am making. (Note: I have taken thirteen Pope & Young bucks. Half of them have been taken from the ground; and half of those have been taken while using this strategy.) Once I alarm a buck and he makes the alarm snort cadence of the primary snort, I know I have a better than average chance to call the buck back. I call this cadence of the primary snort, my "Too Late" call. As the buck and I exchange calls, he usually approaches without knowing I am hidden in heavy brush or pines and he continues to walk by me in search of "the other deer." I shot a few nice bucks at distances less than ten yards while using this tactic. The trick here is as the buck gets closer, you should blow the call more softly and in the opposite direction of the approaching deer. This makes the buck think the "other deer" is walking away and it often concentrates on nothing else other than trying to locate the "other deer."

Alarm Distress

Another effective snort cadence is the alarm–distress call. THIS IS MY FA-VORITE SNORT CADENCE. Here's how to use the Alarm-Distress call when hunting with companions. Locate thick cover like a cedar patch or a swamp and then post hunters along the networks of trails that are known deer escape routes. The trick here is to set hunters up on the outer fringes of the cover along escape routes. Don't be tempted to have them penetrate too deeply into the center of the cover. After all the standers are posted, wait a good half-hour for things to settle down. Then, walk into the middle of the thickest part of the cover without trying to be too quiet. When you have reached where you to be—take out interdigital scent and lay down several drops. Then, stomp your foot several times while blowing the alarm-distress cadence of the primary snort. The call sounds like this, *"Whew—whew—whew—whew, whew, whew, whew."* Make the first three snorts loud and hesitate about a second between each sound. Then, make the next four snorts without any hesitation.

As you have read throughout this book, always try to create as natural a display as possible when calling or rattling. I know this is repetitive, but drilling it into your head is crucial to your success. Try to duplicate the complete illusion of what deer would do when they are vocalizing or fighting. Make an all-out effort to create all the sounds, smells (like using interdigital scent when blowing the alarm–distress) and motions (shaking brush or saplings) that deer make when they are vocalizing or fighting. By doing this, it helps to put the deer at ease when it responds. Inevitably, the deer thinks it is hearing, smelling and, sometimes, seeing another deer. Therefore, it responds more enthusiastically and with less caution.

The Alarm-Distress is also used when you are hunting alone. I have had the most success with this cadence of the snort when I use it hunting by myself. I use it to roust deer from cattails, ledges, brush piles, small woodlots, laurels and from standing agricultural fields. For instance, when hunting a farm with a field of standing corn, most hunters instinctively feel or, perhaps, even "know" there is a buck hiding within the standing crop. Here is how to convince the buck it's time to leave the security of his hideout. Pick a corner of the cornfield where the last two rows of corn meet. Find some cover. With the wind blowing toward you, put out extra amounts (several drops) of interdigital scent. Then, make the same scenario of calls and stomps I described above.

Often, only minutes after making the first call, you'll hear deer stalking through the corn looking for a safe exit point. Once they have found what they believe is a good escape route, they traditionally poke their heads out of the corn, glance back and forth (as if looking for traffic) and make a determined effort to the nearest cover. Usually, it is an adjoining woodlot. When the buck leaves the corn and carefully picks its way along the edges before going into the woodlot, is when you'll get your best shot. For me, carrying the snort call has created numerous hunting opportunities. Without it, many deer would still be safely hidden within the sanctuaries of cover I regularly come across while hunting.

The Social Snort

The social snort vocalization is from a reaction from a nervous deer. I am sure you have seen and heard a deer make this call. It is usually made by a deer nervously feeding at the edge of a field or in a woodlot. The deer puts its head down to feed, focuses its ears in a particular direction and then lifts its head up quickly, looking in the direction its ears were just pointed. Reluctantly, the deer lowers its head to begin feeding again, only to repeat the process. This nervous feeding and looking behavior goes on for several minutes before the deer decides to blow a non-aggressive, single snort. By blowing the snort, the deer tries to encourage whatever is making it nervous to reveal itself by either approaching the deer or at least **answering** it. Often, if it is another deer that the first deer was reacting to, it will answer the single snort with a single snort of its own. This "return" call immediately relaxes the first deer and it begins to feed more contently without lifting its head every few seconds. Often, the deer will feed in the direction of the other deer that answered it—safety in numbers. If it doesn't hear a return social snort after making one, the deer usually stops feeding and retreats from the area.

When I see a deer acting like this, I know I can relax it and, sometimes, even attract it to me by using the social cadence of the primary snort. But, it's important to remember that the Social Snort only works on deer that are exhibiting the type of behavior described above. Never make the call until the deer has made a single quick snort **first**. Then, when it puts its head down to feed, make one, soft snort to the deer. Try to blow the call in the opposite direction of the deer. If the call is made correctly, the deer typically lifts its head, cups its ears toward you and then begins to feed again often heading in your direction. However, should the deer lift its head and become more nervous, you probably blew the call too loudly. Don't try to make another call until the deer starts to feed again.

I used the social snort last fall to attract a good eight-point buck while bow hunting in New Jersey. The buck was nervously feeding on acorns in a small woodlot that bordered an agricultural field. Every few seconds the buck perked up its ears and looked off behind him. Then, it put its nose into the leaves and resumed its search for more acorns. Before long, its ears started playing the radar game again. It lifted up its head, stared off into a thicket and walked off a short distance in the opposite direction of the bushes. I noticed it was getting more and more spooked each passing minute and that it was moving away from my stand. After watching his actions for a few minutes, I waited until the buck put its head down to feed again. I turned away from him and blew a single soft snort. The buck lifted its head, stared in my direction, and then began to feed again. Only this time, it moved purposefully and steadily toward me as it continued to feed. I didn't have to make another call. Within two minutes of making my first snort the buck was under my treestand. I released my arrow as the buck's nose was busily buried in the leaves looking for acorns. The buck never expected anything as the arrow found its mark. I don't think I would have had an opportunity to take a shot at that buck if I didn't try to relax it with a social snort. I think the buck would have eventually gotten so nervous from the original noise, it would have moved out of bow range and maybe even out of the area entirely, had I not relaxed it by making a social snort.

Over the years, carrying a snort call while deer hunting has helped me score on many deer—some of which I know I would never have an opportunity to harvest if I didn't use it. Most important, however, knowing when, how, why and where to use all cadences of the snort call has been most crucial to my success.

Aggressive Snort

The fourth cadence of the primary snort is the aggressive snort. The aggressive snort is difficult to learn and could cause more problems unless you are a very experienced deer caller. Because it is complex to learn when and how to use, I won't attempt to touch base with it here; but, if we meet at a trade show, or at one of my seminars, ask me about this snort cadence and I will gladly demonstrate and explain it in detail to you.

Blats and Bleats

Other primary calls include the blat and the bleat. Blats are made by all adult deer. Bleats are generally made by yearlings and fawns. Although, on occasion, a yearling musters up the vocal ability to make a blat. In any event, the two calls are distinctly different and should not be confused or you could get negative results. Remember, a bleat is much higher pitched than a blat.

Fawn Distress Bleat

Fawn bleats, used during the right time of year (usually the archery season), can be lethal. Fawns make several variations of a bleat. Fawns bleat when they're lost, hungry, hurt or in danger. For instance, a fawn separated from the group, lost, or is in danger bleats repeatedly for the doe. When the doe hears the distress call, it only takes her minutes to respond. Often, as she urgently responds to the call, the rest of the herd instinctively follows her. Frequently, this group includes a yearling buck. Occasionally, a mature buck may respond to the call knowing he will locate a doe near the source of the distress call.

A distress bleat must be blown aggressively. It sounds much like a rabbit in distress. *"Baa-AAA . . . Baa-AAA . . . Baa-AAA."* The pitch should be higher as you end the call. The more intensely you blow the call, the quicker a doe will respond. Blow the call in three successions only every half hour or so. By blowing it more frequently you will probably attract predators like coyote and fox rather than deer.

To imitate a hungry fawn, simply blow several very soft whiny bleats, "Baaaa . . . Baaaa . . ." every ten minutes or so. You must keep them nonaggressive to separate them from the alarm bleat. Many bucks have walked in to investigate this cadence of the bleat.

Adult Blat

All adult and yearling deer make the loud blat. It is the most social call made in the deer woods. The blat is used by deer via different cadences to locate, warn, fend off, attract, and generally communicate with each other. It is meant to sound social and will arouse the curiosity of both bucks and does. This call—"Baa-Baaaaaa . . . Baa-baaaaaa"—should be blown gently. Stretch it out to a whine at the end of the call and do not blow the call often! Once every 30 to 45 minutes is enough. If a deer approaches, stop calling. By eliminating the calling, you'll intrigue the deer to intensify its search for the source of the call.

Frank Brzozowski, an avid hunter, knows how well this call works. Frank, who hunted with me, never used a deer call while hunting. After seeing my success with deer calls, he decided to give calling a try on his next deer hunt. The following week, he left for a deer hunt in Alabama and brought a blat call with him. He attracted and shot an eight-point buck on that hunt using the blat.

"It took the buck only several minutes to respond," said Brzozowski. "I blew the call gently. Remembering I should wait a half-hour between calls, I put it away and began to watch the swamp. Several minutes later, I heard a twig snap and a low blat. I turned and saw the buck. Surprised that he answered me, I almost forgot to shoot. Luckily, I shot the buck before he could react to my presence."

One of my favorite calls from mid-December through late January is the estrus doe blat. Find an area that does use frequently. Make several long winy-sounding doe blats over a few hours. This time of year, an estrus doe walks through the woods emitting winy blats trying to attract bucks who have not yet picked up her estrus scent. The call can be made once every 15 minutes or so. Blow the call with reasonable volume (but, not too loud) creating a drawn-out winy blat. Like this *Baaaaaaaah . . . Baaaaaaaah.* You can repeat this call two to three times each hour. It's a terrific late season deer vocalization that has attracted big bucks for me over the years in many different states.

Because November through January can be cold, especially in the northern states, I protect the call from freezing by placing it inside the breast pocket of my shirt, underneath my jacket. In addition, knowing that deer move about much more during the midday hours late in the season, I either hunt all day or between 9:00 a.m. and 3:00 p.m. In either case, I dress in layers to protect myself from the elements to keep me comfortable enough to remain outdoors for a long time that naturally allows me to see more deer.

Grunt

Along with the snort, the buck grunt is probably the most common vocalization hunters hear in the woods. Though it is not commonly known, both does and bucks grunt. Does grunt most of the year, while bucks grunt mostly during the rut. Grunting occurs throughout the year. You will have optimum success, however, when you imitate the grunt of a buck in rut or a doe in estrus. The best response to grunting comes between late October and mid-November, and again in mid-December. Grunting reaches its peak when both bucks and does are chasing each other or freshening scrapes during the peak rut.

For a grunt call to work effectively, it should be blown *gently*. If it is not, you'll scare off more bucks than you'll attract. Even trophy-sized bucks sometimes avoid a conflict when hot on the trail of a doe. Smaller bucks are definitely intimidated by deeper guttural grunts. Most hunters describe the grunts they have heard to sounds made by a domestic pig. Others describe it as sounding like a burp. Both are correct.

Other cadences or categories of grunts include the tending grunt, social grunt, submissive grunt, and trail grunt. Still, other grunts are combined with snorts and wheezes and are antagonistic to other deer, especially one buck to another. Deer combine these aggressive grunts with postural threats. Keep in mind, however, most sexual grunts are short, have a low pitch and intensity, and are repetitive only when the deer feels totally secure.

As most of us know, the grunt call is most effective during the rut. However, don't confuse actual mating with chasing. Once a buck is paired up with a doe, it's difficult, as it is with any male animal that you are trying to call away from a female, to make the buck respond. Yet, when bucks are chasing after does, grunting can lead to more action than you can ever imagine and, sometimes, handle.

Facts About Grunting During the Pre-Rut

The most overlooked stage, and least exploited, is the productive pre-rut stage. The false rut typically occurs in early October. Archers and firearm sportsmen who hunt during this most beautiful month of the year, confirm to seeing a yearly event where, straightaway, within a 24-hour period they find a mass of fresh scrapes throughout their hunting grounds. What happens to cause this obvious intense breeding change in bucks? The onset of the pre-rut.

Grunt calling tactics for the pre-rut are wide and varied. Bucks and does are sexually excited for the first time in many months. They are enthusiastic to respond to anything that remotely suggests a sexual encounter. It is why false scrapes work so well during the pre-rut and why non-aggressive rattling techniques also get results.

One of the best grunt calls to make during the pre-rut is sometimes called a *trail grunt*. I have nicknamed it the *burp-o-matic* or *burp grunt*. It is a series (usually several in a row) of very soft, short, burp-like sounds made by a buck. Usually, his nose is held to the ground and he is zigzagging along searching out the scent of a doe. This scent doesn't necessarily have to be that of an estrus doe. Believe it or not, most bucks on these trails are chasing does who are about to enter estrus and are not in estrus, yet. It is why they are so excited. Bucks sense that if they can catch up with the doe, they can stay with her until she comes into estrus and will accept his amorous overtures.

The *burp grunt* sounds like this, *"Brp, brp, brp, brp, brp."* There are only a few silent seconds between each "brp." The key to this cadence is to keep it low. To judge what low means, you should blow it loud enough so a person could hear it 100 yards away (which really doesn't take much). Yet, not so loud that it sounds aggressive. I usually make the call every 30 minutes or so. If nothing responds, I repeat the sequence over and over again until I leave the woods. If something does respond, I immediately stop calling. Response does not only mean seeing a deer. A good caller learns to LISTEN as intently as he looks. Remember, almost 60 percent of any game hunters call, responds without the hunter ever knowing it was there. Keep a sharp lookout. More important, listen for response.

Last year, I was grunting for more than three hours and, to be frank, I became a little lackadaisical, from not seeing or hearing anything for quite some

time. During the next grunting sequence, I heard what I thought were antlers rubbing against a tree. Because I wasn't paying attention like I should have been, I
wasn't sure. The rubbing sound was close. It was just below the ledge I was grunting from. Trying to confirm what I heard, I stretched over the ledge to look and
there, ten feet below and twenty yards in front of me, was a dandy buck standing
by a sapling staring up at me. My heart sank as the buck whirled and ran off.

Sounds are as important as sights when calling deer. Listen for the snapping
of a single twig, the rustling of a leaf, the sound of a buck's antlers being rubbed on
a tree, the sound of urine hitting the forest floor and, to state the obvious, deer
grunting back at you. These are all pertinent signs of response and should be
treated accordingly.

While hunting with my wife, Kate, and my son, Cody (who was four years
old at the time), at Robert Bracken's Lazy Fork Ranch in Texas a few years ago, all
three of us were crowded in a tower stand meant for one adult. I was grunting repeatedly every 20 or 30 minutes. Because we were crowded, it was difficult for us
to turn and look out the back window of the blind. So, we watched the front and
sides. About an hour had passed when Kate whispered, "Oh no! Cody, are you
having an accident?" "No, Mom," the poor guy answered. Kate and I stared at each
other for a split second and then simultaneously realized what we were hearing!
We turned and looked out the back window, and there, directly under the stand,
was a big 8-point buck urinating onto the sunbaked earth. The buck paced back
and forth for several minutes, grunting and pawing where he had urinated before
walking back into the sacawista grass. Again, here's a great example of how important it is to listen for a response.

Remember, and this is the most crucial factor about calling, when a deer responds it is zeroing in directly on the location from where the sound is emanat
ing—that's YOU. All the deer's senses are focused on the noise. By continuing to
call as the deer approaches, you almost guarantee that the deer will "make" you.
And, he will either walk by like you weren't even there or he will bolt and run.
Sometimes, he will "make" you from cover, some distance away and you will never
even know he was there.

Primary Rut

The primary rut encompasses most of the serious, aggressive behavior of
deer during the breeding season. Therefore, I like to use two different cadences of
the grunt during this period. The first is the grunt-snort-wheeze. The second is a
variation of the burp-grunt I used during the pre-rut except the number of burps
is reduced and prolonged.

Grunt-Snort-Wheeze

The grunt-snort-wheeze is an antagonistic, aggressive call. Of the grunt call
cadences, it is the most difficult to master. This call is made by bucks of a higher
position in the herd. The sound made by these bucks is meant to get the attention
of subordinate bucks. It basically says, "Hey, you. Do you see this head gear? Are

you ready and able to take me on? If not, beat it." That's exactly what most bucks will do when they hear this call made by a hunter—they will leave the area. Interestingly, however, if there is an aggressive buck who holds a high position within the herd, he almost inevitably is motivated to respond. I use the grunt-snort-wheeze mostly with aggressive rattling and grunting tactics—which I use infrequently.

Begin the call by making a long, guttural, deep grunt, "Eeeerrrrrp." Follow this with a short snort, "Whew." For the sake of clarity, although it has always been called a snort, it's more of a nostril-clearing sound, than a "certified" snort. Imagine it sounding as if you had a runny nose that was not full of mucus. Although you blew your nose hard, you would only hear a quick "Whew" sound rather than a long and voluminous mucus-clearing type noise. This is followed by a short wheezing sound. The wheezing can best be described as a short cough from deep within the lungs. However, keep it short. Cough as softly as you can while expelling all the air from your lungs. Combine these three sounds, to create the grunt-snort-wheeze. Don't become disappointed if you don't have a buck respond right away—or at all. Again, this is a call designed to be used by trophy hunters.

The second cadence I use during the primary rut is the *Extended Burp Grunt.* Some call it the tending grunt. It is usually made by a buck with an estrus doe close at hand feeding or bedded down near him or, in some instances, has momentarily walked out of his sight. Every so often, the buck grunts to keep himself on the does' mind until she's actually ready to breed. He'll also make an extended burp grunt to warn off other bucks.

It is a highly effective call during the primary rut and is used from November 1 until late December. The trick to this call is that while it's a pitch higher than the pre-rut burp-grunt it is still not made loudly. Every 20 minutes or so, take the call and cup the end of the tube in your palm (the palm should be half-open and not tightly closed) and blow two or three short burps. They sound like this, *"Burp, burp, burp."* Each "burp" is slightly longer than the pre-rut "brp." When you get a response, whether it is by sight or sound, IMMEDIATELY STOP CALLING. Deer are edgy after several weeks of hunting pressure and react more cautiously to everything, including other deer vocalizations. Often, they hesitate in the cover, listening and looking before showing up or coming out. So, let the deer's curiosity work for you instead of against you. Let his inquisitiveness build to a fever pitch, until he can't stand it anymore and brazenly walks out trying to locate the source of the grunt. You can make this call throughout the day. During firearms season, don't grunt during prime times (i.e., when a majority of other hunters are in the woods—dawn to 9:00 a.m. and 2:00 p.m. to dusk); instead, grunt between 10:00 a.m. and 2:00 p.m. and look for considerable success with this strategy.

Late or Post Rut

During the late rut, most of the immature (or latest born) does, and any other doe that was not successfully bred yet, comes into estrus. Many hunters have conveyed stories to me, that during the late rut, they have had much success with grunting. This doesn't surprise me. Grunting can even be effective into January and February. Some does are still experiencing estrus cycles in December, January and even into early February. The post-rut is a period overlooked by many hunters who are sure that the rut is long over and have already put away their grunt calls.

One sign to look for during this phase is a quick and dramatic increase in deer activity. Does coming into estrus during this period are BUCK MAGNETS because there are not many of them and they tend to have an intensity about their odor and body language. Curiously, they are as "bent" about finding bucks as the bucks are about finding them. They will trot along depositing estrus urine and make a series of soft, prolonged grunts, too. Although it's the same grunt they make beginning in October, does are more vocal with it during the post-rut. It's worthwhile to note here that this doe-grunt can be used in any of the above periods mentioned and is a highly effective grunt call for attracting bucks. This is especially true during slow periods of the rut when bucks are not enthusiastic about responding to the grunts of other bucks, but will respond quite readily to a doe grunt. Remember, does grunt all year and are the major users of a grunt called a Cohesive grunt, which I think is better stated as a Social Grunt. Does grunt to reprimand fawns, to call fawns and yearlings and to warn off young immature bucks. These non-sexual vocalizations can range from a squeal to a deep, guttural sound.

The post-rut doe grunt is a prolonged winy type grunt. The doe wants attention and she wants it fast. She walks through the woods making this guttural sound until she gets some attention. It sounds like this, *"Buuurrrrp."* She makes this sound without any continuity. Sometimes, two or three burps in a short period; or even several minutes will pass between her calls. In any event, it's an excellent call to imitate as long as you do not make it loudly.

The post-rut buck-grunt is an excited sound. It's a buck in a rush to find the season's final does in estrus. His intensity is dramatic. This is where many bucks create their undoing, as they ignore anything in their paths in order to get the brass ring. It is a time when all bucks have an equal opportunity to breed. They know it and react accordingly. Many larger, more aggressive bucks are physically worn to a frazzle by now. Younger bucks know they have a better chance of chasing off a buck that, until now, was more dominant during the other two phases of the rut.

When grunting during the post-rut, you'll have more opportunities to see many more bucks than expected. This is the most forgiving period when it comes to grunting. If you are going to get away with making a mistake, it will usually be during this time frame as the bucks responding are in a frenzy. Sometimes, as the old saying goes, rules are meant to be broken. This is applicable here. Although I am a major proponent of calling and rattling softly, this is one time you can call a little more loudly and aggressively and get away with it. Sometimes, to get through to a buck passing by during the post-rut, you have to elevate the volume of your call almost twice as loud as the soft calls you have been making all season. The post-rut buck-grunt is strikingly similar to the primary cadence, except it is made repeatedly and a bit more loudly. It goes like this, *"Eeeerp, Eeeeerp, Eeeeerp."* A few second pause and then, *"Eeeerp, Eeeerp, Eeeerp."* Again, a few seconds pause and three more "Erps." If you see a buck, stop calling and let him dictate what your next move is. If he moves away from you without ever looking, call again and stop when he reacts. If you don't see a buck, you can make the call every 15 minutes.

Doe Grunt

A doe grunt is longer and sounds like, *"Aaaaaahhhhhhhhh."* The grunt of a buck on the trail of a doe in estrus sounds like a short burp, *"Erp-Erp . . . Erp-Erp . . . Erp-Erp."* If you hear and see a buck making this grunt, blow two short burp-grunts back. Usually, the buck lifts his head and walks straight toward what he believes is another buck on the trail of "his" doe. When you do not see or hear a buck, and want to attract one, extend the length of the call, *"Eeeeer-rrrp . . . Eeeeeerrrrrp."* You'll know immediately if you are blowing the call wrong if it sounds like a duck call. You will find the grunt easy to use and one of the best calls for attracting bucks to your stand.

Leo Somma, from Long Island, New York, started using a grunt call during the '93 deer season. While bow hunting the first week of December—the late rut—in an area that receives a lot of pressure, Somma began using his grunt call at around 3:15 p.m. He blew two long burps, waited several minutes, and repeated the call. He was going to wait another several minutes and blow the call again—when it dropped to the ground!

"I was just about to climb down from my tree stand to get the call," Somma told me, "when I heard a deer approaching. Within moments, a buck stopped 50 yards from my stand. He was on a well-used deer trail, apparently searching for the source of the call. He began rubbing his eyes and forehead on an overhanging branch. After several minutes, he went back exactly the way he came. In desperation, I tried to imitate a call by cupping my hand and calling to the buck. The buck didn't hear me and continued off. I have no doubt, had I not dropped my grunt, I would have had a shot at the buck."

Paul Butski is an expert wildlife caller. He has won several national turkey calling championships and now manufactures his own line of game calls. His favorite and most successful deer call is the grunt. "Before I began using the grunt call, I knew bucks were slipping by me undetected. Now, since I've been using the grunt, bucks are coming in and looking for me," said Butski.

To help increase your success when grunting, create more of an illusion by combining your grunt with intermittent antler rattling. Also, shake a sapling or the branch of a tree a few times when you are grunting. These effects add to the realism of your grunting.

The most important advice I can give you about calling is to practice each call long BEFORE THE SEASON. Practice not only makes you a better caller, but it also enhances your confidence level tremendously. Remember the principle: Concentration + Positive Thinking × Confidence = Consistent Success. Being confident in your ability to imitate different deer sounds and knowing when ot use an alarm-snort as opposed to a social snort, will put antlers on your wall and venison in your freezer. I'll close with this. When you think you've practiced your calling techniques enough, practice, practice and practice some more.

24 Track Him Down!

BY BILL VAZNIS

Tracking bucks in the snow and shooting them mid-stride is the ultimate challenge.

The trail led back and forth through the slash and then up the hill before disappearing near the crest. I rested for a moment prior to circling downwind, then eased myself over the top for a quick look. At first all I could see was snow and tree trunks, but then something caught my eye. It was a buck, although only a spike, moving slowly along the trail I'd been following for the past several hours. He was oblivious to my presence and looking straight ahead.

In hindsight, I should have waited to see what the other two bucks looked like, but this was the last day of the Pennsylvania deer season and time was running out. Since early morning I had been trailing the three bucks as they bird-dogged a doe and twin fawns, and I wasn't about to be choosy.

I immediately knelt down next to a small oak, and using the trunk as a rest, squeezed the trigger on my Ithaca Deerslayer. The 12-gauge barked, and the buck bolted for a few yards before toppling over.

That's when the other two bucks popped into view. One was a beautiful racked buck, and he high-tailed it up over the ridge and back into the slash. The other was a nice eight-pointer, and he ran downhill away from me and disappeared into the laurel.

I have certainly shot bigger bucks by tracking, but this one was special because as I was hunting out of state in unfamiliar territory. Tagging a buck on the last day under these circumstances made the hunt all the more memorable.

Each season hundreds of whitetail bucks are tagged by hunters who quietly track them down in the snow and shoot them, often in mid-stride. It is a tough way to bag a buck, clearly taking more skill and woodsmanship than driving with gangs or ambushing from an elevated stand.

Now it is one thing to sneak up on an unsuspecting buck as he goes about his daily business, but quite another to put the sneak on a buck who knows you are after him. Indeed, once a buck knows you are hot on his trail, he'll do anything and everything to shake you off. Most hunters have no idea how smart a whitetail buck really is until they pick up his trail and chase him.

163

When to Go

You can follow deer tracks anytime there's snow on the ground, but you generally won't be able to catch up to the deer that made them unless the snow is fresh. All too often the tracks you're following get mixed in with those of other deer, and unless the deer you're pursuing has a specific destination in mind or a distinctive gait or hoofprint, you'll undoubtedly lose the trail. There is an exception, however, and that is when you're following the tracks of a mature trophy buck. That deer's trail will stand out even if there are lots of other fresh tracks to look at!

Now the longer you can stay on the trail, the better your chances are of catching up to the buck, especially if the trail is smoking hot. After an hour or so you often get a general feel for what the deer is doing and where he is going. I once followed a 140-class buck in Idaho all day as he trotted from one bedding area to the next in search of an estrous doe. He even stopped several times to freshen scrapes and make new rubs. Unfortunately, he caught me flat-footed and bolted when I stepped into an overgrown field. I put the crosshairs on him but decided to pass on the iffy shot.

In any given season there are really only a handful of days when tracking conditions are ideal. A soaking rain followed by four to six inches of wet snow makes for great conditions. The rain softens forest debris, helping to quiet your approach, and the fresh snow covers old tracks and highlights new ones. The next-best time is the tail end of any storm that drops two to four inches of snow, unless the snow base is crusty or granular (which makes a quiet approach difficult).

Sexing Deer Tracks

The easiest way to learn how to differentiate between a buck track and a doe track is to catch a glimpse of a buck in the snow and then follow him. The more tracks you follow, the more second nature it becomes.

Generally, however, it is just common sense. Here are a few clues to look for. Because a mature buck is 25 to 50 percent bigger than a mature doe, expect his hoof to be longer and wider and his tracks to be splayed and deeper, if there is soft earth underneath. A buck often drags his feet in the snow, too, but when the snow depth approaches six inches, both bucks and does drag their feet.

Look for a buck's stride to be longer and the width of his trail wider than that of an average doe; after all, a buck's chest is wider and more robust. Finally, if you can find a clear impression in the snow, a buck's front hoofs will often show more wear and tear on the edges due to scraping activity.

James Massett, former president of the New York State Big Buck Club, is one of the Northeast's premier deer hunters. For more than 50 years he has tracked down deer in the snow in such wild places as the mixed spruce/fir forests of New Brunswick, New York's "forever wild" Adirondack Mountains and the big-buck province of Saskatchewan. He has bagged several bucks in this manner, including three that made the state record book—the largest scoring 152.

"If you still aren't sure what made the tracks in front of you, follow them for a quarter-mile or so and study the pattern in the snow," Massett said. "For example, sooner or later that deer will have to urinate. The position of the urine stain is positive identification—even if you are looking at a fawn track—as to the sex of that animal!

"A doe's urine stain will be in the middle and just behind the horizontal line between the rear hoofprints. The only exception is when a deer urinates on its hocks; both bucks and does do this on occasion.

"Quite often, however, a buck's urine stain is a little bit different. Sometimes the stain is to the left, sometimes to the right and sometimes in front of that dead-center mark. And sometimes bucks just dribble as they walk.

"In addition, when I'm following a big track I can often tell, before I ever see him, whether the buck is big enough to shoot. Let's say there are three inches of snow on the ground. When that buck drops his head to the ground to feed or sniff out a deer track, his rack, if it is of trophy quality, will leave impressions in the snow. These impressions will allow me to gauge the beam length, the mass, the inside spread and the number of points with one quick glance."

On the Trail

Now that you've picked out a buck's track, the trick is to get close enough for a shot. One of the more common mistakes made by trackers is weaving back and forth across the deer's trail, which generally destroys the tracks. You'll need to look back over the tracks from time to time to confirm that you are still on the right trail. Why? Because bucks have a habit of walking in other deer's tracks, or if you've jumped them, some bucks will even walk back on their own tracks in an effort to lose you.

Several years ago I picked up a hot buck track at first light. I followed the track for a mile or so as the buck headed toward an overgrown abandoned apple orchard—a perfect bedding area. I circled the acre or so of orchard to make sure the buck was still in there before going after him. I eventually found his empty bed, but he had not bolted out of there. Instead he'd simply circled around, keeping plenty of distance between himself and me without leaving the relative safety of the orchard. A team of blue jays kept tabs on him for me by squawking his whereabouts.

The more I circled around with him, the more tracks we left in the snow. He soon tired of the game, however, and unbeknownst to me, exited the orchard. When the jays stopped squawking I realized the buck was no longer nearby, but I could not find his exit trail. I circled the orchard two more times to no avail, until finally taking a closer look at the buck's entrance trail. That clever deer had left the orchard by walking exactly in the tracks he'd made when entering the orchard. He'd backtracked himself!

Finally unraveling the mystery, I found where he'd jumped off that trail and struck out in a new direction. I looked up just in time to glimpse his monster rack crashing through the trees! From a safe distance, he'd been watching me walk back and forth trying to sort things out. Once he knew I was on him again, he high-tailed it, and although I followed him for the rest of the day, I never got close enough for a shot. As I said earlier, it's one thing to sneak up on an unsuspecting buck, quite another to catch up to a buck that knows you're after him.

Tracking Speed

How fast should you track? That depends. Too fast, and you'll spook the buck into the next valley. Too slow, and you'll never catch up to him, especially if he's trolling for does. The rule of thumb is to keep pace with the buck. That is, trot when he trots, walk when he walks, inch ahead when he's lollygagging, and go for the gusto when he's running flat out.

The first buck I tracked down and shot is a case in point. I had picked up three sets of tracks during the tail end of a snowstorm, and after following them for a short distance jumped two does. The buck, however, stayed put until he couldn't take it anymore, then fled at full speed, never offering me a clean shot. I waited for about 20 minutes to let him calm down, then took chase. I ran when he ran and trotted when he trotted. I caught up to him in midafternoon and dropped him with my '06 at about 80 yards as he strolled through a section of pines. He never knew what hit him.

If I had simply plodded along behind him, I never would have caught up. And if I had rushed ahead when he had obviously slowed down, I would have pushed him farther into the wilderness.

The Last 10 Minutes

The last minutes before dropping the hammer are the most exciting. This is where your stillhunting skills really pay off. When the tracks indicate that the buck has slowed down and maybe changed direction a couple of times, you can bet that he is just up ahead. What you do next could spell the difference between venison steak—and track soup!

First, unsling your rifle and move ahead at port arms. You'll only get one op-portunity before he bolts. Don't blow it! Next, move forward only after you're sure the buck is not in sight. But be careful. He could be bedded just up ahead or stand-ing behind a blowdown, checking his backtrail. Glance at his trail only briefly to get a sense of direction, then sneak forward keeping your eyes trained ahead and to both sides. If you spend more than a few seconds out of each minute staring at his trail, your chances of seeing the buck drop considerably.

If I can't see the buck, I like to leave the trail at this point and loop uphill for a short distance. If he is not in sight, I'll drop back down to the trail for 50 to 100 yards before looping up or downhill again. If it appears the buck is circling a hill-top, I may try to cut him off by circling around myself. The point is that the buck is close by, so find him!

One year I stumbled upon the trail of a fine eight-pointer during the tail end of a snowstorm and followed it into an overgrown farm field. In no time it was obvious that the buck was looking for an estrous doe. I found where he had gone from one bedding area to another, rousting does from their beds. He'd follow each doe for a short distance to determine her breeding status before zigzagging toward the next likely bedding site.

That's how I caught up to him. When he zigged, I zagged, and I caught him flat-footed crossing through the goldenrod at 25 yards. I took this buck with my bow and a kidney shot—and he, too, never knew what hit him.

I don't want to make any of this sound easy. Tracking down a buck and shooting him under any circumstances is never simple. You're going to hear a lot of snorts and see many flags before you ever taste success. When you do finally succeed, however, no matter what size rack the buck sports, he will undoubtedly be your buck of a lifetime.

25 Tracking Snow!

BY CHUCK ROBBINS

Follow a buck long enough and soon you'll see
all the country the buck knows and maybe even get a shot.

I was still a wet-behind-the-ears buck hunter when Dad knelt in fresh snow, pointed to a track and whispered, "There, that's him. See the broken toe?" Sure, I saw it, I wasn't blind, but I wasn't sure I bought the idea.

"How do you know it's his track, couldn't other deer have a broken toe?"

"Yeah, but look how his dew claws sink in, see how he's dragging his feet and the track toes-in, not out like a doe's might. That's him, all right," he said, the tone of his voice spread his excitement through me as surely as a flu spreads through a school room. For a moment we stood there staring down as the falling snow slowly filled the track. Then somehow I knew that he knew the buck we were looking for had indeed just walked—right there. As my young grandson recently exclaimed when I confounded him about the same way: Awesome!

Other than tracking snow, I know of only one other pair of words in the English language that brings the hunter's blood to a boil so quickly—those would be big buck. And of course, adrenaline levels go off the charts when the two are combined. Given a tracking snow and the certainty those foot prints were stamped there by a big buck on the prod well, you know the feeling. It just doesn't get any better.

"C'mon, if we're gonna catch up to him before dark, we better get movin'," Dad said as he started off, his big boot tracks parallel and mimicking the buck's every move. Over the snow-covered fallen log, around the big rock, up through the opening in the ledge to the ridgetop. There the track abruptly turned left and circled back a few yards. We could see where the buck had pranced about nervously watching his backtrack, until he heard or even saw us coming.

Tracking deer in the snow is like reading an open book—tracks take the place of words—see the deer walking, running, feeding, bedding, etc. And just like reading a book and guessing its ending, as the track unfolds the hunter guesses what the deer will do next, where he is headed, etc.—but here the two (books and bucks) diverge slightly, because the more you know about deer and the country the more educated will be your guesses. Okay, I suppose the same could be said about a book's author and the subject, but you get the point—right?

Whatever the stimulus, the buck hightailed it out of there, over the ridgetop—running at first in great bounds, all four feet showing in a bunch tearing up black soil and leaves and scattering it on top of the fresh white mantle—the tracks far apart as he lined out at top speed. Dad stopped briefly where the buck had first landed after taking flight. "He knows we're on him, he's runnin' hard now," he said, red-faced—a mixture of exertion, excitement and the cold. "Get out the ridge to the Skidway, wait there until you see me. Keep your eyes open 'cause that's a good place for him to cut back over into the hemlocks," he warned, heading off. He reminded me of the neighbor's beagles the way he went: nose down, stuck to the track almost like he was following a real scent trail instead of a fresh track in the snow.

This was a classic way to track a buck: one hunter on the track and the other circling ahead through the woods to a predetermined ambush spot. I didn't know it then but in later years it would work often enough to become a favorite ploy.

I recall a buck that Mike Ondik and I jumped on a snowy day. He took the track while I circled ahead. We were hunting a piece of deer country that was as familiar to us as our own living rooms—we almost knew where the buck would cross. However, he was moving fast. The chase went much as we figured, but by the time I arrived at an ambush spot, his splayed tracks told me he'd already passed by. But then, it seemed the buck was starting to circle. "He's turning," Mike said, excitedly. "Head for the Big Saddle. If he goes back home he'll cross there." An hour later, as I sat quietly watching and waiting for Mike or the buck to appear in the Saddle, I spotted movement below among the dark shadows on sun-dappled snow. The five-point came on at a slow trot and the rest was, as they say, history. Knowing deer habits and familiarization with the hunting territory put him in the bag, so to speak—without the tracking snow the rest was a moot point.

I was young and in pretty good shape, so it didn't take me long to hurry the half mile to the Skidway. And it was a good thing, because just as I finished kicking away the snow and leaves at the base of a tree, up the ridge toward me came a deer and she was in a hurry. I put the crosshairs on it—a doe. I started to lower the rifle, but spied movement below, and there was the buck following in her tracks. Just then, both stopped as if they'd hit a wall—the doe in plain view but the buck hidden behind a tree—all I could see were his back quarters. The doe snorted loudly, wheeled about and raced back down the hill. The buck right on her heels—disappeared too quickly to get a shot off. Not long after Dad came panting up the steep hill, "What happened? He was right here. Why didn't you shoot?"

Well, what could I say? Sometimes you get the buck, sometimes . . .

In season, a fresh snow is often all it takes to make a big difference in attitude. I can't count the number of times during snowless periods when the hunters in camp were sulking, downtrodden at what seemed to be a paucity of deer. However, comes the snow and wonder of wonders—deer tracks everywhere! Spirits soar. We all act like we've been handed a new lease on life—the life of the hunt goes from dead slow to all-ahead full. Sometimes, if the Red Gods are in a good mood, too, we might even get a buck or two. But regardless of just seeing all those tracks in are enough—hopes rise, pulses race, it's the real deal once more.

Tracks in new snow not only build hope, they raise the odds—show where the deer are—at least where they've been quite recently—where they've fed, traveled, bedded, etc. It's difficult for deer to hide their activities or whereabouts in new snow. Old snow can tell the same story but encoding the message is made more difficult with time—through the added confusion of yesterday's tracks—more so when the snow is several days or even weeks old. But new fallen snow is like wiping a slate clean or turning a new page—what's happening is once again right there.

After nearly 40 seasons of following deer tracks in fresh snow, I'm still not always 100 percent sure if the track was made by a buck or a doe. But there are clues to help erase the doubt, or put another way, to raise the hopes. Bucks are generally bigger boned than does, so a larger track is a good place to start. There are, however, big does, so big tracks don't always compute. Usually, bucks are heavier, the foot sinks deeper, drag their feet and swagger about, instead of prancing straight line like a pretty-eyed doe. They urinate like we men do, sort of splash it all over rather than in a neat puddle. And often, especially after the shooting starts, travel alone. However, be aware of the qualifiers in the above statements—there are exceptions. But there are obvious signs, too, such as if the track you are following leads up to a freshly rubbed sapling, the bark peelings scattered atop the snow—not much doubt. There are subtleties, too, like more rounded hooves, toe-in, instead of toe-out, but you'd better look at a lot of deer tracks often before you rely on these as for-sure buck/doe criteria. My friend, Mike Ondik, has studied and worked with deer for more than 35 years. He raises deer and has looked at deer tracks on a daily basis for most of his adult life. Says Ondik, "Sometimes I'm still not sure, sometimes a big solitary doe can leave sign that looks awful good."

A sure way is to jump a deer, see the rack, then study the resulting track for individual characteristics—an odd-shape, like a broken toe or the like. But don't count on the Hunting Gods to provide such very often. Look at it this way—if it were easy and a sure thing it wouldn't be half as much fun as following a track all day to the point of near exhaustion, freezing your butt, and at dark, 20 miles from camp, find a big old doe standing in the track. Do that enough and sometimes you're bound to get lucky—and look at the bright side—it's not like hitting the lottery or anything so remote as that.

My son, Wade, then 12, his very first buck hunting day, found out real quick what effect a fresh deer track and the possibility that a buck might have laid it down has on the Old Man. Early in the morning, we crossed a large deer track that had a very small spot of blood showing in it (heaven sent?)—probably not from a gunshot but still it made the track distinctive and easy to recognize among the many other tracks we'd see that day. The deer that made it was alone too—a buck? Could be.

The snow was pretty deep—about a foot had fallen the night before. So after following the track all the rest of the day and into the late afternoon, Wade, traveling on short legs, was pretty tired and, from the look on his face, none too thrilled with the entire scene—hours of tramping through knee-deep snow; no shots; we hadn't even seen the deer leaving the track so who knew for sure whether it was a buck anyway—for all he knew it might well have been a ghost buck leaving the track? And it was getting dark fast and he had little idea where we were, but he was probably pretty sure that camp, and a warm place to rest, was a long way off.

On the other hand, when upon reaching the edge of the mountain for the umpteenth time, with darkness falling fast, I finally called a halt to the chase—I knew where we were, how far we'd come and how far in the dark back to camp. But that wasn't what was bothering me. What made me want to kick myself was dragging Wade, his first buck hunt and all, through an ordeal that realistically had no happy ending. I mean, what chance would a 12 year old have making a shot at a fleeing buck even if we did catch up to him? What was I thinking? Not much, I guess.

Following a track all day is exciting for a seasoned buck hunter, it's amazing sometimes what the hassled buck will do to shake his pursuer. Once a buck knows he's being followed, get set to travel through the roughest country around; through nearly impenetrable thickets; up steep ridges and down—follow a buck long enough and eventually you'll see all the country the buck knows. Every once in a while you can push a buck off his home territory, but it takes luck and a lot of walking to do so and most bucks will only go so far before they begin to circle back. Often that's their downfall—where persistence finally pays off for the hunter. I've chased many bucks from daylight to dark, finally getting my only chance in the last light of a long day.

We sat there in the snow, he dejected, me frustrated, staring down into the dark hemlocks below. When suddenly I spied movement, a deer was moving. At first all I could see were its feet and legs, then the powerful striding body appeared in the open hardwoods—high white-polished antlers glowing like scimitars in the fading light. "There, there he is. Wade! Shoot!" And he did. And the buck fell instantly.

Lucky? Yes. Justice? You bet. But the best thing: after the memory of the miraculous shot and unlikely ending fades; after the mixed feelings of pain and joy melt like old snow in the spring thaw; after everything—there was still the drama laid out there in the fresh snow that day just waiting for someone to come along and play it out. Wade probably didn't realize how lucky he was to have been a player. Not only did it place his first buck right up there among the all-time best memories of his hunting life—he found out first hand just how wild his Old Man can get given tracking snow and a likely looking track. By knowing little snips of inside information like that, next time he can choose his hunting companions more wisely.

Big Buck Sign!

Heart-pounding excitement is just one of the bonuses to taking a buck in good tracking snow. Another is that it offers unmistakable clues to the buck you're chasing, if you know how to interpret them.

Once there's close to a foot of snow on the ground, walk well-used runways to look for spots where a buck has put his head down to smell something in the trail. If the snow is deep enough, the whitetail should leave clear impressions of its antlers in the snow on both sides of the trail.

In some cases, tines might leave imprints, but, if nothing else, an outline of the beams should show. By using a tape measure or ruler, it's then possible to determine how wide a rack that particular buck has.

A friend of mine in Michigan's Upper Peninsula stumbled upon this technique by accident last winter. As a serious whitetail hunter who prefers to bowhunt, he does a lot of scouting, both before and after hunting seasons. In this case, he was scouting during mid-January (the season ended January 3) and was walking along a heavily used deer trail when he spotted odd-shaped impressions on both sides of the trail. The snow was almost knee deep at the time.

He had to study the marks for a few minutes before he realized they had been made by a buck's antlers as it puts its head down to smell the trail. Upon closer inspection, he noticed drops of urine along the trail near the antler impressions. While snow tracking bucks previously, he observed that they frequently dribble urine along their trail.

The spots of urine might have been deposited by the whitetail that left the antler impressions, but they could have also come from another buck that walked the trail ahead of him and that's what the trailing buck put his head down to smell. Or the buck could have put his head down to check the scent of a doe that he was following. Whatever the reason, my buddy found the antler impression and he was impressed by their spread.

He went home and got a yardstick to measure the rack's outside spread and came up with 30 1/2 inches. The accompanying photograph shows what my friend saw. The double marks on the right side of the trail (the deer's left side) indicate the deer either has two beams on that side or it moved its head. Most likely, it moved its head to make the double mark.

The whitetail that left those prints is definitely of trophy proportions and my friend hopes to get a look at the deer with an even wider set of antlers this fall. He was amazed such a big buck survived since there's a lot of hunting pressure in the area he hunts. He doesn't want me to mention his name so he won't have any more competition than he already does in his efforts to bag that buck.

Many hunters might be surprised at the caliber of bucks that escape hunters every year. One way to find out is to look for impressions in the snow. To have the best chance of being successful at finding this type of sign, get out as soon as possible after hunting season is over and the proper snow depth has arrived, to ensure some bucks still have their antlers.

26 Seven Stillhunting Myths

BY BILL VAZNIS

Who says that the only way to take a good buck is from a treestand? The author stillhunts all day, every day, even during the peak of hunting pressure.

The tempest had intensified overnight, and by dawn the streams and feeder creeks of the Moose River were overflowing their banks. The rain also fell heavily on the alder, mountain laurel and witch hazel that flourished up and down the valley, making any land travel a soaking-wet proposition. Nonetheless, as soon as the storm abated, I slipped into my rubber boots and wool trousers, and then headed toward a far-away ridge known to harbor bumper crops of sweet acorns.

I moved at a steady rate, but as soon as I reached the plateau, I slowed down to a snail's pace. The tracks, rubs and fresh deer pellets present indicated that deer were feeding here on a regular basis. I unslung my rifle, and began stillhunting through the underbrush searching for a racked buck.

I didn't have long to wait. A slight movement off to my left soon caught my eye, and when I cranked my head around for a better look-see, a yearling eight-point buck stepped into view. The buck was working the oak ridge feeding on the fallen mast, and was oblivious to my presence. When he dropped down behind a rock formation, I raised my Remington pump and placed the crosshairs on the near side of that boulder. When the eight-pointer stepped out from behind, however, I noticed his rack was broken and badly askew. I lowered my '06, and snapped the safety back in place. I still had nine days to hunt, and there were plenty of better bucks prowling around.

Stillhunting whitetails is an electrifying tactic. It is not a "gimme," however, whether you hunt deer on farmland or in the big woods. In fact, "sneaking and peaking," even with a rifle, is about the toughest way to punch a tag. You don't need to make it any more difficult, however, by listening to these half-truths and old wives' tales.

MYTH 1: You can't really expect to stillhunt a buck in the big woods. Deer are just too few and far between!

FACT: While it is true that deer are generally scarce in the big woods, you will see more deer by stillhunting than by trail-sitting.

The trick is to first find those wilderness pockets that attract deer, and then work the area methodically taking the prevailing winds into consideration. In the early season, set your sights on food sources such as beaver meadows, abandoned apple orchards, river beds and hardwood ridges laden with mast. Food is the key.

As the rut unfolds, old logging roads, plateaus above clear-cuts and that fine line that separates hardwoods from softwoods are excellent places to find scrapes and scrape lines, and rubs and rub lines—all excellent places to pussyfoot about undetected. If you examine the sign carefully, you should be able to determine when and from what direction the buck will likely return.

Once the rut is in full swing, you'll want to stillhunt natural bottlenecks, such as gentle slopes that lead to river crossings, and those low saddles between ridges in the hope of intercepting a buck as he travels from one concentration of does to another.

Keep in mind, too, those areas where you found buck and buck sign in the past. Except during the rut, wilderness bucks rarely travel far from these strongholds. You should thus be able to return year after year, unless there has been some natural catastrophe, and find deer.

The point is there is no need to stillhunt the big woods for days on end without spotting a buck. Rather, you want to hoof it right along until you come upon fresh deer sign, like I did to that Adirondack buck I mentioned at the opening. Then keep your eyes peeled—the fun is about to begin!

MYTH 2: You can't stillhunt active farmland when the woods are filled with hunters. All you'll manage to do is push a buck into someone else.

FACT: Stillhunting may be the very best tactic when the woods are filled with hunters!

Once the season has been underway, farm land bucks and suburban bucks move to safe zones that the average hunter prefers to avoid. Sometimes these are thick swamps. Other times they are steep hillsides, while at other times they are small strips of brush and grass growing near a residential dwelling or even alongside a busy parking lot.

A few years ago, I located one such brush strip in upstate New York. A logging road skirted the edge of the strip that was bordered to the east by an abandoned hay field and on the west by a large cut cornlot. Most of the hunters parked at the bottom of the hill in the corner of the cornfield and hiked up the road to a large woodlot atop the field. Then, at day's end, they would hike back down the same road not bothering to check out the 60-yard-wide strip of brush that bordered the dirt road.

After a week of hunters traipsing up and down the road, a few local deer figured out that that strip of brush was safe. The small herd of does and fawns I kicked out that morning still surprised me, but not as much as the racked buck did a few moments later as he escaped unscathed into the adjacent hay lot. Since then, I have located several shell-shocked bucks during the gun season by slowly stillhunting through those places lazy hunters avoid.

MYTH 3: Stillhunting is often a game of who sees who first. Wearing fluorescent orange makes the art of stillhunting a buck an even more difficult task.

FACT: You can still walk up on a buck while wearing fluorescent orange. You just have to be extra careful.

It is a proven fact that fluorescent or hunter orange saves lives, especially in those regions where deer hunters are as thick as mosquitoes after a summer rain. I wouldn't dream of hunting near my home in western New York without some hunter orange, even though it is not mandatory.

You can, however, minimize any potential adverse effects, and still remain safe and legal, by first learning to take advantage of all available cover. You want to move through the forest like you are trying to sneak up on a bedded buck. Brush piles, stone walls, creek beds and uneven terrain can help you conceal unwanted movements—movements that will alert a wary buck to your presence.

Secondly, avoid wearing fluorescent orange gloves, pants and long sleeve shirts or jackets. Movements from your legs, arms and hands are a big give-a-way in deer country. Try this demonstration, and you'll see exactly what I mean. Have a friend stand just within sight of you on the edge of cover, and wave first a bare hand, a dark-gloved hand and then a hand fitted with the fluorescent orange glove. The dark-gloved hand is the most difficult to see—even in motion—while the hand fitted with the fluorescent orange glove is spotted immediately.

Thirdly, consider wearing camo orange, where legal, to minimize the "large solid block" effect. And wear outer clothing that does not contrast sharply with your background, such as the new 3-D camo from Leafy-wear. The point is you can safely sneak about the deer woods, and remain relatively undetected, if you first think about what you are doing. Over the years I have taken several nice bucks while wearing solid orange, and one of those was a 220-pound, field-dressed 10-pointer at 21 feet!

MYTH 4: The best time to stillhunt is in the middle of the day when the action has slowed.

FACT: The best time to stillhunt is when the deer are moving: early in the morning, late in the evening and all day during the rut.

One of the secrets to increased deer sightings is to plan a strategy for each day's hunt according to the various stages of rut. For example, to intercept a buck early in the season, try stillhunting along a ridge or plateau that lies just above a known food source, like a clear-cut or beaver meadow, beginning at first light. When the rut starts, try slipping slowly downwind along fresh scrape lines. Later, when the rut peaks, sneak in and around those bedding areas preferred by does for the most action.

And no matter what the stage of the rut, check out the lee side of hills, thickly overgrown fields, uncut corn lots and protected valleys during severe and prolonged inclement weather. Catching a buck napping then is always a possibility.

MYTH 5: You must always stillhunt with the wind to your face, or rely on a good cover scent.

FACT: No and no. First of all, a whitetail's sniffer is 300 to 1,000 times better than a human's, and all the cover-up scents I've tried can't hold a candle to a whitetail's incredible sense of smell. They will pick you out every time, often without you even knowing it.

Secondly, who says you have to always hunt upwind? Most bucks travel cross-wind to some degree when they are in search of an estrous doe during the rut, and to see a buck first you can do no wrong by sneaking along cross-wind yourself.

Stillhunting cross-wind is also the BEST angle on the wind to catch a buck in his bed. Whitetails generally bed on the edge of thick cover facing downwind. A buck will quickly see you if you are trying to slip up on him from the upwind side. Your chances are better if you can work your way slowly through the bedding area cross-wind. Each fall I catch deer napping by working my way in such a matter along the edges of mountain laurel patches, brush-choked ravines and overgrown fields.

What about downwind? This tactic actually worked for me a few years back. One morning, during the middle of the firearms season, I spied a young buck sneaking into a thick patch of dogwood 200 yards long by 50 yards wide. I couldn't get a shot at him, so I decided to let my scent waft downwind towards him in the hopes of pushing him into an adjacent alder jungle. Sure enough, when the nine-pointer reached the end of the dogwood patch, he tried to hi-tail it over to the alders. My slug caught him before he had gone half-way.

MYTH 6: Any good deer rifle is good enough for stillhunting.

FACT: The best stillhunting rifles are quick to point, easy to carry and come either scoped or fitted with open sights. Traditionalists in New York and New England prefer the Winchester, Marlin, and Savage lever-actions fitted with low-power scopes, peep sights or see-through mounts. The most popular calibers, according to local gun shops, include the venerable 30-30, .32 Special, .35 Remington, and .300 Savage. My Winchester is chambered for the .356 Win.; my Marlin 1859SS for the 45/70. Both have open sights.

The number-one rifle for the modern stillhunter, whether he hunts New Brunswick or Montana, is undoubtedly Remington's Model 7600 pump. Mine is chambered for the 30.06, and fitted with a 1.55 variable. Remington's companion autoloader is a good second choice in either 30.06 or .270. Bolt-action magnums fitted with high-power variables, however, should be shunned. They just don't get the job done.

MYTH 7: You don't need any special equipment to stillhunt effectively.

FACT: When you are trying to get the drop on a racked buck, you need all the help you can get. Besides a short-barreled rifle, that help often comes in three forms: Binoculars, boots, and outerwear.

You rarely catch a mature buck in the open. To see him first, you often have to probe the shadows and brush lines for an exposed ear or antler tip. That's why I'd rather leave my lunch home than forget my Swarovski 8230's. They are waterproof, shock proof, light in weight, and offer clear, sharp images under low-light conditions. They are also somewhat moderately priced. I can't say enough good about these glasses for stillhunting.

Quality footwear is equally important. Although canvas sneakers and low-cut leather moccasins may be fine for any afternoon stroll over level farm land, they are actually the worst possible choice for extended stillhunting. In the big woods, you'll need rugged boots that support and protect your ankle from sticks and sharp rocks. They should also be waterproof, insulated enough for seasonal temperatures, and have an air-bob or modified air-bob sole for increased traction over uneven or slippery terrain. I like LaCross, Irish Setter, Danner's and Rocky's. For warm and dry feet, pick a pair lined with Gore-Tex.

Finally, as far as outwear goes, cotton can kill you if you are wet and miles from camp when the temperatures plummet. You'll travel quieter and stay warm, even when wet, if you choose wool, although Gore-Tex is working on some fabrics I hope to field test later this year that appear to hold some promise under wilderness conditions.

As you can see, with the right gun and the right gear, you can stillhunt effectively in the big woods as well as on crowded open farm land. You can wear hunter orange, hunt upwind, cross-wind and sometimes even downwind. But best of all, you can hunt all day, every day of the season. And that's no old wives' tale!

Part Five
Coping with Conditions

How to Succeed When All Bets Are Off!

Weather • Hunting Pressure • Late Season

Like most folks, I'm going whitetail hunting whenever I can. That means when I can get off work. It's that simple. Weather or not!

Not being able to cherry-pick my days in the whitetail woods, I have to play the cards I'm dealt. That sometimes means coping with a variety of unfavorable conditions, ranging from excessive Indian Summer heat; frigid arctic temperatures; high winds; rain that belongs in a monsoon; drought; and blizzards.

Also mix into this stew of woes those times of hunting in late season when every self-respecting buck in the country seems to have found some hidden sanctuary to ride out the season. Color them *Gone. Vanished. Disappeared.* It's *Mission: Impossible* out there!

Though the temptation is to linger in my bed at home or bunk in camp, I'll usually try to suck it up and get out there, despite wanting to shout at the heavens the way the erratic golfer Tommy Bolt was famous for doing. After narrowly missing a key putt, he would grimace at the sky and snarl, "Me again, huh?"

Even though the odds are against us, we're going hunting. And there are, after all, some things we can keep in mind to put some hope back into our hearts.

27   When the Pressure's On

BY JEFF MURRAY

When bucks feel the heat, you need to anticipate instead of react.

If pursing pressured whitetails isn't big-game hunting's greatest challenge, I don't know what is. I still wince when I recall a mid-November Wisconsin hunt that started on a high note and ended flatter than a Firestone ATX re- call. Though deer were plentiful within the state forest, I was new to the area and failed to incorporate the movement of other hunters. As a result, I was always one step behind. Put another way, I was constantly reacting instead of anticipating. That's no way to hunt whitetails.

Sine then I've managed to master a few principles of hunting pressured deer. It's not mission impossible if you bone up on three key facets of the game. The are, in order of importance: 1) learning where deer vacate and relocate, 2) modifying calling and scent tactics, and 3) identifying traditional escape routes. To hunt pressured deer effectively, you need all three. Here's the scoop.

Deer on Vacation

It may not be your fault that deer are spooky when you hit the woods. For example, other hunters might have passed through your hunting territory, bumping deer along the way. Or you just might be dealing with deer that are more wired than others. But the fact remains that any game plan predicated on locating deer that are on red alert needs to be totally revamped.

So exactly where does a buck go when he encounters the alarming stink of human odor? Usually not very far. Study after study proves conclusively that, contrary to popular belief, deer don't relocate in far-off places when they're spooked. Quite the contrary, once deer settle in on a comfortable territory they call home, whitetails don't spend much time outside it. And it's typically a square mile and often less, especially during the rut.

Consider a Missouri study conducted on a popular tract of public land. Even though the hunters sampled in this research project overwhelmingly believed that the deer had vacated the immediate area, radio-tagged whitetails proved otherwise. They were essentially just out of reach of rank-and-file hunters. I liken pressured deer on the move to a savvy National Football League receiver who knows how to exploit the "seams" of a good zone defense. You know, just beyond the linebackers but in front of the safeties, with the cornerbacks to one side or another.

There's no question that mature bucks wise to the traipsing of two-legged predators make easy work of evading hunters by simply filtering into hunter-unfriendly "pockets." Most such pockets fall into one of two general categories: where lazy hunters won't go, and where not-so-lazy hunters can't go. Examples of the former range the gamut, from a distant ridge surrounded by a swamp to a depression in a roadside cornfield.

Overlooked nooks and crannies rate especially high marks from whitetails these days. Indeed, they seem to have torn a page from the muley's Manual of Safe Bedding as they rely on a strategic vantage point rather than protective layers of vegetative cover. Today's deer, faced with ever-encroaching development and gradual deforestation, have evolved into excellent hiders. Plum thickets on the prairies and drainage ditches and CRP patches in farm country readily come to mind. Meanwhile, few modern hunters waste much time in "naked" spots like these. We're slow to catching on that a Boone & Crockett buck doesn't necessarily need acres and acres of security cover to save his hide. If he's left undisturbed, the wily whitetail is just as content in a suburban woodlot sandwiched between a housing development and a shopping mall as he is in a sea of trees in an unspoiled wilderness.

The moral of the story: Explore near before venturing far. Put your favorite hunting area under the microscope. Blow up an aerial photo (available from local agricultural extension offices) so that a square mile covers an 8 ½ × 11-inch sheet of paper. You'll be amazed at how many options bucks have right under your nose.

Hunting forested tracts is a little different. Here, going the proverbial extra mile very well may pay off. Few hunters these days are equipped—physically or mentally—to negotiate more than a quarter- to a half-mile jaunt to get to their chosen hunting destination. For many, it's just too much work. Besides, deer populations are thriving at all-time highs in many parts of the nation, so why bother? I'll tell you why: Quality is better than quantity, and I don't mind extra leg-work if it can make a difference.

A case in point is a northern-Minnesota hunt I engineered about five years ago. From a decade of experience hunting a large tax-forfeited parcel, I pretty much knew the exact access routes of local hunters. The area is bounded by a deep river on the north and a lightly traveled road on the south. In between, a series of "ditch bank" trails built by CCC crews back in the 1940s crisscross the rolling stands of aspen, birch and spruce. Invariably, the jump-off point for nine out of 10 hunters would be a fork or dead end along a ditch bank. Smack in the middle of this network of ditch banks is a massive tag alder thicket, and in the middle of the thicket is a five-acre "island" of high ground. This is precisely where I would set up, relying on hunters to push deer into my lap. It worked to a T for 10 years running.

Another favorite hotspot that hosts nary a hunger even during the peak of the season is a relatively small slice of high ground next to a four-lane freeway. I discovered it one day when I noticed a hubcap careening into the ditch in my rearview mirror. A series of calf-sized rubs along the woods line got my attention in a hurry, and after a little snooping around it was obvious that this was a place at least one buck liked to spend a lot of time. Upon further examination, I found out why: A lush alfalfa field kissed the backside. Icing on the cake was the fact that there was no way to get to the field, save a three-mile walk through two different properties. Coincidentally, the landowners were well known for refusing access and hunting privileges. But who cares, if you can hunt a highway right-of-way scot-free?

Getting Close: A Different Ball Game

Now that you know where, you need to know how. It's a different gig when the pressure's on. Prior to pushing the panic button, deer often exhibit inquisitive behavior, especially during the rut; however, whitetails aren't very "curious" once they sense danger. The bottom line is that when they know they're being hunted, their reactions to various stimuli are entirely different than those of unalarmed deer. This point cannot be emphasized enough.

"It's a universal principle of hunting all big game that once an animal is aware of man's presence its disposition changes," said noted trophy bowhunter Myles Keller. "That's why I always go the extra mile to avoid having to hunt educated bucks. I mean, they're a totally different animal from one going through the motions, living out his life in relative bliss.

"For example, bucks on the defensive rarely react to sounds, however enticing, without verifying them with their nose. Rattling, grunting and mock battles need to be re-evaluated, if you think you're dealing with pressured deer. In fact, standard aggressive rutting tactics could even backfire."

Here's a classic example of what Keller's talking about. During a recent Midwest hunt with a reputable outfitter, I discovered that my host was overhunting his ground. In all fairness, it's difficult enough hunting trophy whitetails one on one, let alone hunting these bucks commercially. Add extra hunters to the stew—the outfitter has to host enough clients to cover overhead, including rising lease fees—and it's inevitable that some deer are going to get educated along the way.

Anyway, my first rattling session occurred under idyllic conditions—a crisp, still morning during the pre-rut—with my first responder telling me exactly what I was up against. After five sessions (spaced 15 minutes apart) I picked up a thick-necked nine-pointer in the veiled underbrush below my 25-foot-high treestand. What struck me was his gait: He paused repeatedly, raising his head and licking the air before taking several short, deliberate steps. He repeated this ritual a half-dozen times as he circled into a quartering wind that eventually placed him directly downwind of me. He was barely out of range when he suddenly looked up, apparently hitting my scent stream. About five agonizing minutes later he backed out and vanished, never to be seen again.

Is it impossible to rattle pressured bucks? Not if the timing is right (hormones are raging). But instead of hammering away aggressively whenever boredom settles in, tone it down. Rattle only once or twice to get a buck's attention, then let him find you. If he's able to zero in on your exact location, he's likely to circle downwind and pick you up.

The same goes for grunting and any other calling tactic you've got confidence in. Again, play it conservatively, relying mostly on natural movement rather than trying to pique a buck's interest, which will be in short supply.

Scents remain popular among hunters, and for this reason I rarely rely heavily on them when I'm forced to share my area with other parties. Deer have no trouble associating deer lures—from urines to food scents and masking odors to cover ups—with humans. I learned this decades ago when skunk essence became the rage among zealous bowhunters seeking to masquerade their body odor in hopes of stealing within range of whitetails. Virtually every bowhunter in my neck of the woods experimented with the stuff. At first, it seemed to help disguise our comings and goings. But it didn't take long for us to see fewer and fewer deer.

"I see two problems here," said Mike Weaver, a Virginia bowhunter with 30-something Pope and Young bucks to his credit. "First, hunters back then lacked the means to effectively reduce their body odor; we didn't have odor neutralizers or carbon-lined camo duds. So all we ended up doing was adding one odor to another. Even humans have little difficulty [registering] multiple odors at the same time. Heck, I can easily smell bacon frying and my wife's perfume.

"And second, that many hunters hitting the woods with the same commercial product is doomed to backfire. During that era the concept of cover scents such as fox and coon urine was very popular. Then all of a sudden there was a big move toward skunk essence, which was marketed heavily as a can't-miss hunter's disguise. Now just because I don't use so-called cover scents doesn't mean they can't work. But with so many hunters experimenting with the same strong odor, it was inevitable that deer would learn to associate [skunk essence] with danger."

Today's scent market is different. We've got innocuous odors to complement our arsenal—earth, acorn, pine, cedar, apple, corn, persimmon—as well as the no-scent route of activated charcoal. In addition, today's hunter is better educated. No one really expects to overpower one's body odor with the scent of something else; we know that odor control is an elaborate process, starting with scrupulous personal hygiene, moving on to foreign odor control and ending with intelligent use of deer lures.

Which brings us to the buck-in-the-bottle syndrome. I'll go on record saying that the wise use of deer lures—buck or doe glands/secretions—can be effective—up to a point. That point, from my experiences, is the fine line separating luring a buck from alerting a buck. When in doubt, exercise constraint. For starters, if other hunters in your area use barrels and barrels of doe urine, you might want to reconsider. After all, it takes skill to administer scents without leaving a trace of human odor. Though we preach proper scent use all the time, cutting corners is easy if a guy is running late and it's pitch dark and he's turned around and. . . . You get my drift. Once again, the best-laid scent traps could backfire when the pressure's on.

Escape Routes = Express Lanes

I've known for a long time, at least at the instinctive level, that spooked deer don't bolt haphazardly for parts unknown. Quite the opposite, these deer know exactly where they're going: They're heading for escape routes. No doubt about it, when the pressure's on, deer hightailing for safety stick as much as possible to pre-scribed routes.

Why? Two reasons. First and foremost, these routes are connected to security cover. They're a buck's quickest, surest link to a familiar harbor of refuge. Which leads to reason number two: An uncanny trait of whitetails is their habit of repeat-ing habits. In this case, a buck is much more likely to double back where he came from rather than bound for new ground. It's common sense. His keen senses have already assured him that the area is safe, whereas another place—even if it's a famil-iar part of his home range—hasn't been checked out yet.

The best way to distinguish an established escape route is to intentionally bump a buck to see where he goes. But there's a difference between "bumping" deer and scaring the bejabbers out of them. The most effective method for kicking a buck out of his bed without relocating him altogether is simply standing in one place (not too close, but not so far away that you can't make out his image) directly upwind of his suspected cover. It may take several minutes—or a few more steps closer—to make the buck jittery enough to expose himself, but eventually he will. Compare this with a hunter zigzagging through the woods like a bloodhound. Now that spooks deer!

Veteran game-call manufacturers and popular television and video personal-ities David Hale and Harold Knight are masters at driving deer (another subject for another day). As a result, they've learned a great deal about hunting escape routes.

"Hunters are missing out on this big time," Hale insists. "Nothing always works in the whitetail world, but I guarantee that once you pinpoint a buck's fa-vorite escape routes leading out of a hot food source, you're in for quite a discov-ery. The whole trick is starting with a hot food source, such as tender beans or peas early in the year, a fresh acorn supply later on, or a standing cornfield during the late season."

Naturally, you don't have to drive deer to hunt escape routes. In fact, hunting solo along these notorious "express lanes" can be deadly. You just need to be set up well in advance. Start with a good feel for the lay of the land. Next, look for terrain features that might bottleneck deer movement along the route. Then plug in the direction you expect hunting pressure to come from. Finally, hang a pair of tree-stands at high-percentage spots, one for northerly winds, one for southerly.

Sooner or later it's going to happen. In spite of your best efforts, you're going to have to deal with deer that are on to you. They know their turf is being invaded, and they don't like it one bit. You won't like what they do, either, if you fail to ad-just accordingly. But now at least you know what you're up against. And that's more than half the battle.

The Rut and Pressured Deer: Stay Put

Pressured deer may seem to vanish into thin air. One day you think you're close to scoring; the next day you're fantasizing about next year. In most cases the deer haven't traveled very far but have merely relocated a relatively short distance, most likely within their home territories. So you've got to follow them.

But if the rut's on, you might not have to do all that much improvising. In fact, you may want to stay put, especially if you know the whereabouts of rutting zones that bucks tend to rely on through the years. Why? Because even though resident bucks might have adjusted their travel routes and bedding areas as they sense pressure, bucks from outside the immediate area are likely to replace them.

Interestingly, telemetry studies reveal that estrous does tend to constrict movement to tighter quarters, ostensibly making themselves more easily available to bucks during their fleeting 24- to 48-hour heat cycles. But rutting bucks are another matter. Legend are the stories of "strange" bucks sighted in areas they've never frequented before. Caught out of their home range looking for receptive does, these bucks are as vulnerable as they're going to get.

In other words, the home ranges of does in heat contract, whereas the travel patterns of dominant breeding bucks expand. The net effect of this unique combination favors hunters sticking it out near traditional rutting hotspots. Think about this the next time you're tempted to toss in the towel and launch out for greener pastures.

28   Windy Weather Whitetails

BY THOMAS L. TORGET

Exactly where do you need to set up your treestand to take a buck?
The answer is blowing in the wind.

Not sure wind direction is all that important? Listen to St. Louis
bowhunter Jim Holdenried.

"I was on the Ted Shanks Wildlife Refuge in northern Missouri and my buddies told me there was a Boone and Crockett buck
in there, but I didn't believe 'em," Holdenried said. "I figured they'd seen a good
eight-pointer and badly exaggerated the size of his rack. There was deer sign in the
area, all right, but I honestly wasn't expecting much when I climbed into my stand
that afternoon. After all, this was a public hunting area. Everybody knows you
don't find Boone and Crockett bucks in public hunting areas."

A half-hour later, the monster whitetail stepped out of nowhere and headed
right toward Holdenried's stand. When the 12-pointer paused in a shooting lane
25 yards out, Holdenried drew his bow and released.

As he later lifted the buck's magnificent antlers, Holdenried realized that his
hunting buddies did not need new eyeglasses after all. The buck's rack tallied 173⅜
points, easily qualifying for both the Pope and Young and Boone and Crockett record books.

"I'd scouted the area a couple of days before and picked out a stand site near
a trail that had good sign," he added. "But when I got there to hunt, the wind had
shifted so I had to move my stand 50 yards to stay downwind of the trail. Turns
out, that was the best 50-yard move I ever made. If I'd stayed at my original stand
site, I'd never have seen that buck. The experience really proved to me how important it is to focus on wind direction."

Whitetails pay attention to wind, which is why hunters must do likewise.
Wind helps a buck avoid peril by conveying dangerous scenes and sounds to his
nose and ears. Every deer relies on his nose first and ears second to help him stay
alive. They rarely fail him. Which is why a single sniff of human stink or a subtle
squeak from a treestand will send even a young buck racing for cover. So any
hunter hoping to stage an ambush must choose his venue carefully. Rule One is to
keep your scent downwind of areas where deer travel. Otherwise, the only deer
you'll see will be those running from you.

The Physics of Wind

The atmosphere surrounding the earth is in a state of constant motion. That motion is what we call wind. Put another way, wind is simply air that's moving, either horizontally or vertically. It's produced by differences in atmospheric pressure. Wind currents travel from higher-pressure areas to lower-pressure areas, and when pressure differences are extreme, wind velocities are also extreme. The highest wind speed ever recorded was a blistering 225 miles per hour in New Hampshire in 1934. That's almost enough wind to keep a dedicated whitetail hunter out of his treestand.

Air temperature influences wind direction and speed. As air warms, it becomes lighter and therefore rises. As it cools, it becomes heavier and falls. In hilly terrain, therefore, air currents known as "thermals" drift uphill during the day as temperatures warm. Thermals drift downhill in the evening as temperatures cool.

In summer, land surfaces are warmer than oceans. So land areas become zones of low pressure due to the rising of warm air and the vacuum created beneath that rising air. Cooler air over oceans moves toward low-pressure land areas. In winter, the situation reverses.

Temperature changes throughout the day influence wind. Winds are calmest at night when temperatures are lowest. That's why there's less wind when you reach your stand prior to daybreak than hours later after temperatures have warmed.

Which Way's It Blowing?

Ask hunters in camp about wind direction and most will say something like, "We've got a west wind today." That may be true, but the prevailing direction is only part of the story.

Like a flowing river, wind moving horizontally along the ground travels in a straight path until it encounters an obstacle. Just as river currents swirl and change direction as water passes around and over boulders, wind currents swirl and change direction when they encounter obstacles or changes in terrain. Common examples include hills and valleys, a patch of woods bordering a grain field and a pipeline right-of-way through a forest.

So unless wind is moving across a barren prairie, it's drifting left, right and elsewhere as it flows. And because hunters can't see the wind itself, many pay scant attention to that swirling component. But it is swirling currents that often carry a hunter's scent to nearby deer.

"For years I paid no attention to wind currents and eddies," Holdenried said. "I focused on overall wind direction and ignored the rest. But then I started hunting with people more experienced about the wind than I was. They taught me to recognize that eddies of wind swirl and drift around and that you have to pay attention to them. That's especially important when you consider where to place your stand in hilly terrain. I now know that thermals drift uphill as the morning warms and downhill as the evening cools. So when I place a stand on a hillside for a morning hunt, I'll usually position is on the uphill side of the deer trail."

While bowhunting whitetails in Alberta two seasons ago with Classic Out-fitters operated by Jim Hole, I learned that selecting a stand site at the last-minute can be an effective way to play the wind.

"When temperatures are warm or mild, swirling wind is especially trouble-some," Hole told me. "We face that problem most often in early bow season before the cold weather sets in. We often choose our hunters' evening stand sites later than they're used to doing back home. It's silly to go to a stand four hours before sunset and have the wind right if you know it will shift and be wrong 30 minutes before dark. During warm weather, wind currents can change suddenly as evening ap-proaches. It's frustrating, but that's the way it is. I'd rather have a hunter in the right location for the best 45 minutes of evening hunting than in the wrong location for several hours."

Stand Set-Ups

Playing the wind begins with setting up downwind of where deer are likely to be. Step-one in that process is knowing the prevailing wind patterns in the area you hunt. In much of the whitetail's range, the prevailing wind direction is usually westerly. In south and central Texas where I often hunt, winds generally blow from the south and southeast. As cold fronts arrive, winds shift to the northwest. Over the next several days, winds rotate clockwise until they're once again blowing from the south.

When placing my stands, I incorporate this knowledge into my decision-making. I position some stands knowing that they can be used only for a day or two immediately after passage of a cold front. Others are placed at sites that I can hunt only when winds are in their usual southerly flow.

Sometimes it's wise to place dual stands at a prime hunting site, such as a nar-row woodlot that funnels deer movement between bedding and feeding areas. One stand hung on each side of the trail will allow you to hunt that location when winds blow from at least two directions.

Another way to play the wind is to move your treestands higher. No matter your elevation, gravity will eventually carry your scent to ground level. But if you're sitting 30 feet up rather than 10 feet, your scent will move much farther from your tree before reaching the ground. In the right circumstances of wind speed and stand height, that can mean that a deer passing on your downwind side 20 yards away may not detect your presence.

By placing a stand high enough, there are times when you can use it even though it's upwind of where deer travel. I once hung a stand 25 feet high in an oak that was 10 yards east of a heavily used north-south deer trail. I hunted the stand several times when a brisk east wind blew my scent well past the downwind deer trail. I arrowed three whitetails and was never scented. The key was the stand's ele-vation and my avoidance of it when east winds were light.

Limiting use of individual stand sites is another way to play the wind. That's not likely if you use permanent stands crafted with nails and wood. The time spent erecting a permanent platform leads a hunter to believe he needs to spend time there to justify the effort. So he does, even when the wind direction argues against use of that stand. The inevitable result: what might have been a favorable stand site is ruined. Portable stands are a much better choice because they can be quickly relocated throughout the season, making it tough for whitetails to pattern your movements.

Stay Away When Winds Are Wrong

The willingness to stay away from a "hot" stand site when winds are unfavorable is perhaps the most important tactic for playing the wind. It's not always easy. It's especially tough when you know deer are active in that area and you have only a short time to hunt. But it is always a mistake to be in a location that allows your scent to drift somewhere it should not be.

"I know of a small woodlot in a valley that's a genuine honey hole for good bucks, but I can only hunt there two or three days each season," says Jack Holdenried. "The rest of the time, the wind swirls and drifts around and if I go there the deer will bust me. I've never been able to hunt it two days in a row. One year I was able to get in there just once all season. But every time I'm there, I see several good bucks."

In the course of my hunting in Texas, I've set up several stands in September that I knew I'd not be able to use until late November or December due to prevailing wind direction. But staying away until the wind was right is the reason those stand sites were productive later. In deer hunting, you can never force conditions to be right.

We never actually see wind—only its effects. From a hunter's perspective, one of the key effects is how wind velocity influences deer movement.

Steve Demarais, professor of wildlife biology at Texas Tech University, led a four-year study of the movements of mature whitetail bucks in south Texas a few years ago. The deer were fitted with collars emitting radio signals that allowed researchers to monitor the animals' movements 24 hours a day.

"We found a distinct pattern of how wind speed affects deer movements," says Demarais. "They moved most when winds blew the least. As wind speeds increased, there was a clear reduction in the amount of travel, with deer moving about half as much in a 15-mile-per-hour wind as in a 5-mile-per-hour wind. But when winds exceeded 20 miles per hour, the deer actually moved more, which surprised us. We consistently recorded more deer movement at 25 miles per hour than at 15 miles per hour."

Demarais says that very strong winds confuse deer and make them exceedingly nervous. Whitetails lose the ability to differentiate between safe and dangerous areas. "They get so spooked, they just get up and run," he says. "They might hear a branch break and think a predator or hunter is about to get them so they race away. They're nervous because they feel so vulnerable."

So when winds blow hardest, don't assume the best place for you to be is in camp. If you can tolerate the discomfort that accompanies high-speed gusts, staying in the field can be a great way to play the wind. It happened to me a few seasons back while bowhunting in central Texas. My late-afternoon treestand was swaying badly in the 35-mile-per-hour gusts and there was so much noise that I would not have heard a marching band passing 10 yards to my rear. So I sure didn't hear the six-pointer as he stepped along the trail in front of my stand.

But my eyes could not miss the sight he presented. With ears twisting, eyes wide and head spinning in every direction at once, this buck was experiencing a world-class anxiety attack. He soon twitched his way to within 10 yards of my stand, and at that distance even I can hit the bull's-eye.

Tracking Wind Direction

When winds blow hard, determining direction is easy. But when breezes are light and variable, the task is tougher. A squeeze bottle of unscented spray powder is the best tool I've found for tracking wind. It's especially useful for checking subtle currents of swirling wind, like the ones that float around your treestand at dusk and dawn. Seeing is believing. The first time you use one of these squeeze bottles and observe the degree to which light winds swirl, you'll become a dedicated wind watcher.

Several deer call manufacturers offer bottles of spray powder. Lately I've been using Aerodust Wind Tester by Woods Wise Products (P.O. Box 681552, Franklin, TN 37068; 800-735-8182).

Other useful wind indicators include cigarette lighters, dental floss and small feathers. They reveal overall wind direction, but can't convey swirling currents. I tie a marabou feather to a six-inch strand of thread and tape it to my upper bow limb. It provides a quick and continuous check of wind direction while I'm on stand. A strand of dental floss serves the same purpose.

Rattling in the Wind

Besides having to endure the discomfort of swaying treestands and teeth-chattering wind-chill, high winds create another downside for the hunter: they seriously impede the effectiveness of deer calls, rattling horns and deer scents. Unless a buck is within 30 to 50 yards and on your downwind side, he's unlikely to hear a call blown at normal volume. And blowing it loud is no solution because the higher volume changes the call's meaning. Rattling racket will travel farther than a call, but it still has much less range than when used during periods of calm. The effectiveness of scents is limited because gusty currents dissipate odor within a few yards of where the scent is applied.

So when hunting in high wind, it's usually best to leave calls, rattling horns and scents in camp. Rather than trying to attract a buck to your stand area, concentrate on intercepting one that's on the move in search of quieter, more secure surroundings.

29   Sizzle-Time Whitetails

BY THOMAS L. TORGET

Why wait until it gets cold? Many deer seasons are open early and your hunting options aren't very complicated. In a word—water!

Sometimes I'm convinced that whitetails hide in the treetops with the blue jays—or underground with the ants.

How else can you explain why a grain field that's devoid of deer one moment can look like the site of the annual Deer 'R Us company picnic the next?

But if you really fancy deer crowds, forget that grain field and take a seat near a waterhole on a sweltering early-autumn afternoon. Be careful, though; you could get trampled!

I've hunted deer in forests and woodlots of the West, South, Midwest and Canada. I've done it every month from July through February. I've hunted in temperatures below zero and above 100. Neither extreme was comfortable, but when the mercury sizzled the most, so did the hunting.

Like a lot of the hunters who pursue them, a whitetail buck enjoys a tasty meal, a cool drink and occasional romance. Biologists tell us that bucks go without sex most of the year and can get by with little food for days at a time (no comparisons to his pursuers, please!). But when temperatures and humidity soar, so does a buck's need for liquids. And when it gets really hot and stays that way, a buck's quest for water can be overwhelming.

I've sat in treestands near waterholes in October and had whitetails appear in such numbers that I literally could not keep track of them. And I've sat in water hole ground blinds and watched whitetails parade past near enough to whack 'em upside the head with my bow, were so I inclined. As much as I enjoy rattling, calling and other rut-time tactics, none of them produce whitetails in the concentrations I've seen at a mud hole on a sweltering autumn afternoon.

That's exactly the situation Florida archer Hal Arve encountered a few seasons back when he arrived in Texas for an October bowhunt.

"The weather was scorching hot and it hadn't rained in weeks," he says. "So I figured a waterhole would be the best place to ambush a buck."

Three days into his hunt, Arve was waiting in a treestand near a stock tank when a 10-pointer stepped into range one half hour before dark.

"A smaller buck was already at the water hole when the big one came in, and the two of them knocked heads a bit before the smaller deer ran off," recalls Arve. "Then the 10-pointer took his drink and began moving back toward cover. When he quartered slightly away at 20 yards, I eased back my bow string and released my arrow."

Arve's aim was true and the buck piled up after a short sprint. Its rack tallied 135 points on the Pope and Young Club scoring system, easily qualifying for inclusion in the record book. And before he departed Texas for his Florida home, Arve arrowed a second 10-pointer—also at a waterhole. This one scored 144 P&Y points, giving the happy archer two record-book bucks in a single hunt.

"That experience taught me that staking out a waterhole is the No. 1 way to hunt whitetails in hot weather," declared the 41-year-old insurance salesman. "It all boils down to finding the best waterhole and waiting patiently. Trust me, the deer will come. In fact, when conditions are right, there's a constant stream of wildlife coming in to drink. I saw turkeys, javelina and deer coming and going every time I was on stand. It's a real kick to watch the parade of wildlife."

Waterhole hunting works best when demand is high (hot temperatures) and supplies are low (no rainfall). A deer takes in water from the moisture content of the food he eats, from the early-morning dew on foliage and from the water he drinks from creeks and ponds. When the weather's cool, a whitetail's water needs are modest. When temperatures warm, whitetails drink more often. And when the weather turns choking hot, a buck can get as thirsty as a college football player during August two-a-days.

Continuing hot, dry weather reduces the moisture content of the food whitetails eat, increasing their need to visit waterholes to take on fluids. If the weather remains hot and dry for several months, the lack of moisture reduces the availability of whitetail food, both natural browse and farm crops. Reduced food supplies cause whitetails to travel farther to satisfy daily nutrition requirements. So while drought-like conditions are harmful to a deer herd over the long term, a dry summer and fall can sharply improve near-term hunting prospects because whitetails are traveling farther each day.

Like any other commodity, the water supply/demand balance can be upset when supplies increase abruptly. A single, heavy rainstorm can alter hunting conditions overnight. A buck that had only a few places to drink yesterday now finds water most everywhere. So yesterday's can't-miss waterhole becomes as worthless as a ticket to last week's ball game.

Several seasons ago, I saw how this transformation can occur. After sitting one October evening in a tripod stand 25 yards from the edge of a South Texas stock tank—and watching three dozen whitetails parade past in the hour before dark—I returned to camp just as rain began falling for the first time since early spring. And did it rain! By the time the deluge stopped at dawn, almost six inches had fallen, turning what had been dust-bowl conditions into a veritable swamp. I slogged back to my waterhole for a look. The tripod stand's legs were in three feet of water, while the night before they had been 25 yards from the water's edge!

Needless to say, my waterhole strategy was put on hold for the remainder of that deer season.

Because a waterhole stakeout works best when temperature and humidity are highest, a Dixie deer hunter is more apt to capitalize on this tactic than his Connecticut colleague. And archers use it more often than gun hunters because most state's bow seasons open in September or October, a time when summertime conditions still prevail. But no matter where or how you hunt, a waterhole stake-out can work anywhere whitetails wander. Northern-state hunters will find the tactic most effective during the early days of deer season in years when rainfall is below normal. Southern-state hunters will utilize the tactic more frequently. It all depends on local conditions, and you can't force the issue. But when the weather in the area you hunt is hot and rainfall is below normal, it's foolish not to give this tactic a try whether you're an archer or gun hunter.

There are four keys to staging a successful waterhole ambush: 1) selecting the right waterhole to hunt; 2) placing stands correctly; 3) staying downwind; and 4) timing your shot for success.

From a whitetail's perspective, all waterholes are not created equal. The most attractive ones are those that allow a buck to approach and depart through thick cover so he avoids detection. The thicker the surrounding cover, the better he likes it. A pond that's isolated from protective cover may well be riddled with deer tracks along its shoreline, but almost all those tracks were made at night. Cross it off your list.

Topographic maps and aerial photos are a good place to begin searching for waterholes on the land you'll hunt. Maps may be obtained locally or from the U.S. Geological Survey (Denver Federal Center, P.O. Box 25286, Denver, CO 80225; 303/236-7477). If aerial photos aren't available from a real estate office in your county, you can buy one from the U.S. Department of Agriculture's Aerial Pho-tography Field Office (P.O. Box 30010, Salt Lake City, UT 84130; 801/524-5856).

In addition to studying maps and photos, you'll want to spend a preseason weekend or two investigating your hunting terrain on foot. It's a sure bet you'll discover one or two bathtub-size puddles not shown on your maps or photos. If such a mud hole is near good bedding terrain and is surrounded by thick cover, it may well be your best choice for a whitetail ambush. Don't be turned off by small size. Some of the most active waterholes I've hunted have been as small as a back-yard wading pool.

The more distant a pond is located from other water sources, the greater its importance to area deer. Thus, the greater its appeal to the hunter. If you're lucky enough to hunt land with lots of thick deer cover, abundant food and only one or two water sources, you're as close to deer hunting heaven as you'll ever get.

No matter its size, investigate the shoreline of every waterhole to learn pre-cisely where deer tracks are most plentiful. You'll likely find that one side—and often one corner—has the highest traffic count. That's usually the portion of shoreline that allows deer to approach with the highest level of security. If the shoreline is thickly wooded, deer will usually approach from downwind. If surrounding terrain provides only sparse cover, deer may approach from upwind, relying on their eyesight to detect trouble ahead while their noses cover their backsides.

A pond is usually a better water source to hunt than a creek because a meandering stream gives a whitetail too many options on where to drink. Even a large pond concentrates deer better than a flowing waterway. And concentrating the deer is what makes waterhole hunting work. But a streamside ambush is possible if a hunter scouts carefully and locates the one area where deer traffic is heaviest. Usually this will be a shallow section of the creek where whitetails can cross easily. Concentrated trails and tracks will reveal its location.

When you locate a waterhole that's obviously in active use, it's tempting to place your stand right at its edge. A far better choice is setting up 50–75 yards away downwind of an approach trail. While every whitetail is chronically skittish, a buck headed to water during daylight is paranoia personified. The more sparse the cover along the shoreline, the more nervous he gets as he tiptoes close. By the time he hits the beach, a bullfrog's burp can send him bolting away. Spooky deer make lousy targets, especially for the bowhunter.

While he's never truly "relaxed," that same buck is much less skittish while he's still 50 to 75 yards from the water's edge, particularly if he's moving through thick cover. Which is why a treestand or ground blind placed along an approach route is a far better venue than waiting in ambush right at water's edge.

Another advantage of avoiding the pond itself is that finding a well-concealed stand location is usually easier. Vegetation immediately surrounding most stock tanks and ponds is often a mixture of low brush and medium-high trees—not ideal stand terrain. Setting up half a football field away usually affords the hunter many more options on precise ambush location.

High heat means a steady flow of sticky sweat. That's bad news for the hunter hoping to get close to an animal that carries one of nature's most effective scent-detection systems.

Hot or cold, it's always wise to stay downwind of deer. But when you know you'll be shucking sweat like Michael Jordan in overtime, it's imperative that your stand be downwind of where you expect to see deer. A gallon of cover scent won't help if a buck passes on your downwind side. And his snorting departure will ensure that other thirsty bucks won't be visiting you for happy hour anytime soon.

In early bow season, wind patterns are less changeable than later in the fall. That makes it easier to select which side of game trails to place waterhole stands. Be sure to choose locations that allow you to approach and depart without ever passing upwind of areas where deer might be feeding or bedded.

Shot Timing

Knowing when to pull the trigger is always important, whether you hunt in September or January. But because a thirsty whitetail coming to water has such an elevated sense of caution, selecting the precise moment to shoot can be especially troublesome.

Every deer I've seen at a waterhole seems to regard the whole affair as "nasty work that must be done." There's absolutely no clue that the buck is enjoying himself, as he might while snacking on fresh acorns. Watch his body language and you know he'd rather be somewhere—anywhere—other than here.

It's easy to understand his nervousness. Beginning in his first month of life, a whitetail learns that waterholes are dangerous places where bad things happen. Coyotes and bobcats are frequent visitors and a snootful of their scent doesn't soothe the nerves of an already-skittish buck or doe.

So the deer's objective is to get in, drink and get out as quickly as possible. That means a buck will usually trace his way slowly through adjoining cover until it runs out. He'll pause to visually inspect the shoreline for danger before stepping rapidly to the water's edge. If a final sweep of the area shows no danger, he lowers his head to drink. Depending on conditions, he may drink a half minute or longer before raising his head. Or he may bob up and down, taking quick gulps. When finished, he turns and quickly high-steps his way back to cover.

For the hunter, this approach/departure pattern means that the best time for a shot is usually before the buck steps out of cover and walks to the shoreline. Which is why a hunter on stand 50 or more yards from the water's edge is often in the best position.

If circumstances require that you place your stand near the water's edge, the best time for a shot is often during the deer's last few steps toward the shoreline. You know where he's going and you know you have at least a few moments to take your shot. Once he's finished drinking, he'll depart quickly and may even race away.

Some hunters—particularly archers—prefer to wait until the deer lowers his head to drink. For sure, that's a tempting target. But a buck knows he's most vulnerable at that instant, which is why he'll explode away at the tiniest sound. An archer loosing an arrow at that buck from 20 yards away may see his shaft strike exactly where aimed, but it may miss the deer if it ducked away at the sound of the shot.

Because waterhole hunting is usually an early-season tactic, bucks are often still traveling in groups. That can lead to unique shooting problems. Several times I've had to forego or at least delay an otherwise "perfect" shot at a waterhole whitetail because another deer stood on its far side within inches of the deer I wanted. Because my arrows usually pass completely through a whitetail, I didn't want to gamble that a single shot may fill two deer tags.

While "classic" whitetail hunting conjures up thoughts of snow flurries and long johns, hot-weather hunting has its own rewards. Sizzling heat and stifling humidity may not be comfortable, but they can spell fast action for the whitetail hunter willing to sweat for success.

30   Icebox Whitetails

BY MICHAEL PEARCE

Hunting big bucks in blowing snow and plummeting temperatures requires more than just whitetail knowledge. To be successful now, you need the heart of a hunter.

I must have stared at the sight of deer legs poking from beneath a screen of brush and a set of antlers from above it, for four or five seconds deciding it if was reality or just fantasy. When another set of legs and larger antlers stepped up from behind, I realized it was both.

Like most hunters, I've long been prone to daydreaming on deer stands. Again like most, I've often dreamed the most about what wasn't readily available.

A longtime whitetail fan, I have pursued big-racked bucks countless times on the prairies of my native Kansas, the timbered hills of the Ozarks, in southern swamps and deserts on both sides of the Rio Grande. Through the years and miles, I've never met a whitetail hunt I didn't like. But all along I've longed for one hunt I have never been on.

Call me crazy (my wife does it all the time and she's a clinical psychologist), but I come alive during the dead of winter. Cover the Kansas countryside in white, drop the wind-chills to below zero and you'll get my answering machine if you call. I'll be following pheasants with my golden retriever, chasing cottontails or fishing through the ice. It only seemed natural that I'd want to combine my passions for invigorating weather and whitetail hunting.

After years of waiting, such a hunt began to unfold on, of things, a warm, spring-time day. Close friend and Knight Rifle company representative Toby Bridges called to plan a hunt for the upcoming fall. Bridges laid out an impressive selection, from Wyoming pronghorns to rutting Missouri whitetails. The debate was over when he mentioned an Iowa blackpowder hunt.

"It's a pretty neat situation," said Bridges. "The late muzzleloader season runs from late December well into early January. Though the rut is long over, the deer haven't been pressured and they can be pretty patternable around food sources if we get a little bad weather."

"I know there is no way of knowing, but when do you think my chances are best of hitting some cold, snowy conditions?" I asked.

"There is no way of knowing," Bridges answered, "but being in Kansas you live close enough we can keep our eyes on the extended forecast. If things look like they may get nasty, you can come on up."

We tentatively picked a hunt that would fall between my wife and son's birthdays on the 2nd and 10th, respectively. As luck would have it, a modest cold front was expected on the second day, followed by a regular Arctic blast later in the week. My first stop was at the Knight Rifle factory just outside of Centerville, Iowa. There, I was to meet up with Bridges and the firearm I was to use. Bridges had insisted that I come empty-handed so he could outfit me with one of their new Wolverines.

When I arrived, I found Bridges at the plant's indoor range, working on such a gun.

"I just grabbed this baby off the assembly line less than an hour ago," said Bridges, as he adjusted the settings of the 4 × Burris scope. "Load it up and fire a few shots and let me know what you think."

I eagerly poured 90 grains of Pyrodex Select down the Wolverine's short .50 barrel, seated then loaded a saboted 260-grain bullet and capped the rifle. Unlike any other gun I'd shot, this Wolverine featured a composite stock with a thumb-hole. Like most of the company's line, the gun had a sweet trigger and even sweeter accuracy. The rifle I'd never touched put a three-shot, quarter-sized group about three inches above dead center at 50 yards.

"That'll put you about dead-on at 100 yards," Bridges explained, "We know what the gun can do, now let's go see what we can do."

As we left town, Bridges drove out across the kind of farm country that is the epitome of good, midwestern whitetail habitat. Beautiful hardwoods dotted some hilltops and some surprisingly steep ridges. Down in the river and creek valleys sat some of the world's most productive corn and soybean fields. It was around these fields that our hunt would revolve.

"By now most of the acorns are gone," said Bridges, "a pretty good percentage of the crop fields have been disced. That means all the whitetails in this area, and trust me there are lots, are keying in on a few good fields. The deer are bedding up here in the hills and following these drainages and other travel routes down to the fields."

One look and I knew this set-up blew the old "homebody whitetail" theory right out of the water. You know the one I mean, the ol' "whitetails live and die in the same half-mile." From the looks of things, some of these deer might be traveling a mile or more each way to feed. Though I was new to the area, I already knew that few if any bucks ever saw daylight in the cropfields. Instead, they'd be on the move at dawn and dusk, at the fringes of their bedding areas so not to be caught in the open.

Short on daylight, Bridges and I turned off the highway and followed a farming trail into an area of timber and mixed crop fields where he'd seen lots of good bucks in previous years. Unfortunately, a farmer had tilled the soybean and corn fields, reducing the area's attractiveness to whitetails. Though I saw about everything else native to south-central Iowa that evening, I saw no deer. Bridges, on the other hand, saw some does and a small buck while stillhunting a logging road that bisected the property.

After the hunt, Bridges took me where I'd be staying, and what I found there was almost as exciting as my first deep-winter hunt.

Bridges introduced me to well-known outfitter Steve Shoop, of J & S Trophy Hunts (591 Dale Ave., Hollister, MO 417-336-3690). I'd already heard more than enough about Shoop's impressive stats to know that I was in good hands. One of the finest trophy whitetail bowhunting operations in the nation, last year Shoop's archery hunters harvested over a dozen Pope & Young class whitetails off of his Iowa lease. The quiet, unassuming guide offered opportunities to nearly all who had booked, and an estimate 90 percent of his stands had offered shots at a record-class animal throughout the season.

Every place Bridges and I hunted the following few days was prime trophy whitetail woods, judging from the abundance of huge tracks and old rubs on trees to six inches in diameter. But just because a state produces more trophy-class whitetails than most doesn't mean such deer are easily gotten. Though I had no problem finding does and fawns, my timing was certainly off in terms of bucks.

Time after time, we'd scout out two areas that looked equally productive and, when we met back that night, I'd have seen nothing but does while Bridges had at least passed on a smaller buck. We even tried switching things up, by letting me hunt one of his stands. While stillhunting one morning, bridges glassed a hill-top hayfield where two draws leading to the fertile river bottoms came together.

Through binoculars, he watched three bucks including a dandy, 140-class eight-pointer, cross the tail end of the field as they headed for their bedding grounds. Bridges set up on the field that same evening, and watched as the same bucks, as well as some does, used the same basic path as they headed down for their evening feed.

I was at the field an hour before daylight the next morning, sitting beneath a small hedge tree on a hay bale Bridges brought along to keep me off the cold ground. A steady snow was falling that morning, and by daylight, both the countryside and I were covered in white. Well insulated and realizing the white was the ultimate camouflage, I held still and watched the lower end of the hay field.

Sure enough, an hour after daylight, the same group of does nonchalantly walked the familiar trail back to their bedding grounds. A few seconds later came a small, 1 1/2-year-old, six-point. As only my luck would have it, the better buck was nowhere to be seen. With plenty of days to hunt and the much forecasted Arctic system due in a few days, my confidence and enthusiasm both stayed high.

With cold weather coming, Shoop insisted I hunt one of his honey-holes, where narrow fields of corn snaked their way along the ravines and creek bottoms, some of which purposely hadn't been picked to attract whitetails. The area was also dotted with some off-limit sanctuaries where the whitetails could bed undisturbed. The area had already been productive.

Hunting with a muzzleloader, outdoor writer/biologist Larry Weishuhn saw a variety of bucks, including one super wide-racked behemoth that had been spooked by a pack of dogs chasing coyotes. On video the deer was awesome, and when Weishuhn finally killed it near its bedding area a few days later it was even more impressive. The buck carried a super-impressive 25½ inch inside spread, and unbelievable main beams of over 31 inches each! Though the buck carried six inches of mass, a lack of the number and length kept the main-framed eight-pointer out of Boone & Crockett. The buck did, however, easily make it past Longhunter Society minimum of 135 inches!

That third afternoon of the hunt, the clouds that had blanketed the area broke, giving way to the open skies that would let the cold drop even further. As we set down to a lasagna dinner at Shoop's lodge that night, the temperature was in the teens and dropping in Des Moines, and forecasters were calling for temperatures well below zero all across the state the next morning.

When we woke the next morning, the thermometer outside the lodge read minus 10 degrees and a slight breeze could be felt coming from the north. That morning Shoop blessed me with a ground blind at the back of a lake, where whitetails followed natural funnels and deep trails as they left the corn and headed up into towards one of Shoop's sanctuaries.

"This extreme cold is nothing to play with so I'll drive you in as close as I can," said Bridges, as we climbed into his pickup. "The last thing we want is for you to work up a sweat, get your clothes drenched and then freeze out at the stand." I quietly slipped from Bridges' truck wearing a set of silk and a set of polypropylene long underwear, a layer of wool and other heavy garments. In one hand I carried the Wolverine, and in the other the oversized snow camo I'd slip on once I was at the stand.

I'd no sooner arrived than the top of the sun began to peek over the horizon, coloring the snow-covered valley with pure, early morning light. Well hidden and spacious, the blind was comfortable and big enough that I could sit or stand, with enough cover to wiggle my fingers and toes beneath the snowmobile gloves and packboots to stay warm. As I waited those first few minutes, I studied the landscape to try to pick out the trails and travel routes Shoop had shown on a sketch the night before. I also made some quick distance estimations to be ready if a nice buck came.

Bundled up tighter than a 90-pound bale of straw, I sat up facing where a line of cattails led along where farmground and frozen lake met, waited, wiggled my fingers and toes, and daydreamed. Shadows were still fairly long, when I looked out and saw the legs and little antler described earlier. A quick check through a pair of Zeiss 8 × showed it to be a little 1½-year-old eight-pointer, the kind of buck Shoop insists must be given a chance to grow. But there wasn't time for disappointment. Within seconds. I got a glimpse of another deer trailing behind.

Even with the naked eye, I could see 10-inch tines and a decent main beam over the cattails. The second I realized it was a mature buck, I laid the binoculars aside, and picked up the Wolverine.

The little buck wasted no time walking from the screen of cattails out onto an open area of snow-covered ice and winter wheat. The bigger buck, however, seemed perfectly content to let the inexperienced deer check the open country before he totally revealed himself.

The only possible problem was that the breeze had shifted, and the little buck might catch my scent before the bigger whitetail offered a shot. About the time the little buck put his nose in the air and began to wonder if something was up, the better deer took the few steps I needed.

By then I'd estimated the range at 125 yards and put the scope's crosshairs where I thought the top of the buck's lungs to be. Thanks to the thumbhole stock, both elbows rested firmly on my knees, and not to mention the fact that I was trussed tighter than a Thanksgiving Day turkey, the gun never wobbled when I squeezed the trigger. Even though I couldn't see through the resulting cloud of smoke, I knew the bullet would be on the mark.

Rather than hustling to reload, I laid the gun down to watch the 10-pointer's vain attempt to enter the timber 60 yards away. He collapsed in mid-stride, 10 yards from the woods, in a place where we could drive right to him. Having heard the shot from his nearby stand, Bridges was on the scene in a matter of minutes, wearing smile on a face that featured eyebrows and beard caked in ice from his frozen breath. I remember thinking at the time that I was oblivious to the cold.

No doubt I'll again find myself daydreaming on stands this coming fall. But unlike in the past, I'll be dreaming of something I've already had—ice box bucks.

31 Desperation Deer

BY H. LEA LAWRENCE

When dawn arrives on the very last day of deer season, the time has come to play your best hunch.

I t was T-minus 14 hours and counting, and the tension was already at a fever pitch.

I had wolfed down my breakfast, racing with time as if I somehow could make daylight arrive earlier. Now, as I drove along the country road that led to the place I planned to hunt, my mind was whirling with ideas and strategies. It was the final day of the season, and my score was still a fat goose egg.

My headlights picked up two sets of shining eyes, and seconds later I made out two does standing at the edge of a woods. I slowed in case they bolted in front of the car, but they remained in place as I passed. All things considered, it was a scene I could have done without!

The situation wouldn't have been as severe if several frustrating things hadn't happened earlier in the week. A big buck came in from behind me the first day as I sat in a treestand. It spooked when I attempted to turn around, and all I saw was a white flag and an impressive set of antlers as it departed.

Two days later, a nice six-pointer paraded around within 50 yards of my stand, all the while shielded by two does that remained between us. The deer were in fairly tight cover, and I was never able to get a clear shot. By the time they departed, I was fit to be tied.

The final insult came the next day when I was zeroed in on a buck standing in the open in a harvested soybean field. I was ready to squeeze the trigger when someone on the opposite side of the field took a shot at it. The buck rocketed off and was back in the woods before another shot could be fired. I never saw the other hunter, and it's probably best that I didn't. I wasn't in a very amiable mood!

So I was down to the wire, and desperate is the word that best described my condition. I was determined to make the last day count, but the question was how would I do it?

All kinds of strategies had come to mind, been reviewed and placed on mental file in what I thought to be the order of their importance. There was one thing I wasn't going to do: sit in a stand all day. Instead, if necessary, I planned to use a variety of tactics, hoping one would produce the magic solution I was seeking.

I pulled off the road at my destination, popped the hatchback lid, and started getting my gear together. It was the last day of the season, and the January air was cold enough to make a deep breath painful. There was no wind, and I noticed as I parked that the ground was covered with a thick, furry frost. I was glad not to be looking ahead at a long stay in a treestand.

There was no word from the barred owl that was usually signing off for the night when I arrived at this spot; in fact, there was no sound other than the muffled hum of a jet somewhere high above. I glanced up through the bare trees but couldn't see its running lights in the starry canopy.

I double-checked to be certain the thermos of coffee was in my day pack, zipped it back up, then headed out into the darkness. I figured the first light of dawn would be seeping into the sky within about half an hour.

The leaves crackled under my feet, and as I walked along, the flashlight illuminated the frozen plumes of my breath as it billowed out. The field I planned to look at first was only one-quarter mile distant, and I knew the stroll would warm me up sufficiently for a short period of inactivity. I decided not to linger long at any one spot. If nothing could be seen, or if I felt the potential wasn't good, I'd keep on the move. An arbitrary decision, but one that had to be made.

The plan I preferred was "field-hopping," moving from one soybean field to another. There were several within a mile of where I planned to begin, so I had plenty of territory available. Also, up until the previous afternoon, the weather had been unseasonably warm and deer movement was pretty sluggish. However, a cold front moved in and caused the temperatures to plummet. My guess was that the chilly air would initiate more activity.

I was in southwestern Alabama, hunting in an area the late Ben Rogers Lee introduced me to nearly a decade ago. This was my first trip back in several years, and there was a lot of nostalgia associated with it. The same motel, the same restaurant and many warm memories. I'd set a week aside for this hunt, and making it successful was important in more ways than one. After all, I figured Ben might be up there watching!

As I suspected, I was at the edge of the first field well ahead of first light, so I sat down beside a tree and poured a cup of coffee. The hiatus allowed me the opportunity to run through a final check of my equipment and load the rifle. Long-range shooting over expansive soybean fields requires more sophisticated gear than some other forms of the sport. I felt I had the best: a Remington Model 700 in 7mm Magnum loaded with 160-grain Federal Partition Point ammunition and topped with a Nikon 4-12×scope, along with Bausch & Lomb Elite 10×42 binoculars, an Elite 60mm spotting scope and a Harris bipod. This combination accounted for a couple of nice bucks earlier in the season in my home state of Tennessee. I hoped for a repeat performance today.

By the time I had everything in order, the dim, ghost-like silhouettes of trees draped with Spanish moss began to emerge against the eastern horizon. I brought the binoculars up, but it was impossible to see anything at ground level.

I could hear, though, and somewhere nearby a deer blew. It sent a jolt of adrenaline through my body and put me on full alert. Things take on different dimensions in darkness, and I couldn't determine exactly where the sound had come from. I waited for it to be repeated, but silence prevailed. At the same time, the tension mounted.

In the meantime, an eternity passed as the slowest dawn in history manifested itself. I continued to peer through the binoculars, straining my eyes to make out figures in the field. The letdown came when I was finally able to glass the immediate vicinity. There was nothing to be seen. Either the deer had departed, or it had never come out of the woods.

Full light was required to look over the entire field, because it was several hundred yards long and nearly half as wide. I was sitting at one end where I could see all of it. When all of it could be clearly seen, it was equally as vacant of activity as the portion I viewed earlier.

I decided to give it an hour, but when that much time had passed without incident, I was up and on the move. The next field was on the back side of the strip of woods in which I had been sitting, and I welcomed a leg-stretching and warming walk.

As I walked along, I was again struck by what I consider to be a paradox. It has always seemed strange to be looking at Spanish moss, palmetto fronds and frost at the same time, since the last two are usually associated with semitropical climates. What's more, I've also seen snow and ice storms at this same location, which stretches the imagination even further.

A more positive situation greeted me at the next stop. Before I reached the edge of the woods I could see several deer in the middle of the field a couple hundred yards away. I couldn't tell at a glance if there were both bucks and does present, and I waited until I got settled in to glass them with binoculars.

There were six—four does and two yearlings—and I spent another hour watching them in the hope that a buck might spot or scent the does and come out into the open. A late rut was still on, so that offered a possibility. Another half hour passed without incident, and I decided to move again. The plot I devised included devoting as much as an hour and a half at each of four fields. I'd cover all of them in the morning, then reverse directions and repeat the process in the afternoon. That is, unless I managed to score somewhere along the way.

An old logging road led to the third destination, and fresh track indicated that it had been traveled by several deer quite recently. Most of them were headed in the same direction I was going, which was a bit of encouragement. A pair of fox squirrels playing tag in a gum tree stopped briefly to peer at me before resuming their play. Bushytails are extremely bold during deer season, apparently sensing that they're in no danger. Moments later a hawk came darting through the trees, and when I looked back, the squirrels were out of sight. They paid attention to that kind of hunter!

Falling back on an old superstition, I wished that "third time charms" would apply. In the past, I'd taken a couple of good bucks from the field I was approaching. Now it was time for it to produce once more.

Again, does were the first things I saw. This time there were three, standing in almost the center of the field. From point of vantage I was headed for, they'd be about 25 to 300 yards distant. It was my belief that the chances of seeing a buck were going to be enhanced by having does as magnets.

The place beside an old, gnarled oak I chose as a stand was quite familiar. Ben placed me there on my first hunt at this location, on which I bagged a handsome 8-point buck. For a minute or so I was distracted as my mind was flooded with memories.

The does continued to graze, stopping occasionally to raise their heads and look around. It was like watching cattle, and with nothing else to do, I ate an apple, then drank another cup of coffee. The sky was cloudless, and the winter sun warmed the air enough to make it feel considerably less frigid. Little birds hopped about in the limbs above me, and in the distance I could see a flock of buzzards, slowly swirling high in the air.

For obvious reasons, I had more confidence in this spot than the previous ones, so I took my spotting scope from the day pack and set it up on a tripod. Next, I lowered the bipod arms and extended them for shooting from a seated position. All I needed now was something to shoot at!

As it had done twice before this morning, the passage of time began to wear down my initial enthusiasm. An hour dragged by, then another 15 minutes, and the notion of putting things away and heading for the final field was beginning to take shape in my mind. I was restless, yet something told me to wait out the full period.

Not long afterward, I was thankful for that premonition! At 10:28 a big buck stepped out into the field a full 100 yards beyond where the does were standing. Even at that distance I could see that its rack was impressive, and when I looked at it through the binoculars, I could see a number of high tines. When I eased down and viewed it through the spotting scope, all 10 points were plainly visible.

It was what I wanted, but at close to 350 yards away, it provided a significant challenge. Yet that's where having the "right stuff" counts. I knew the 7 mag was capable of performing well at that range. It was zeroed in at 200 yards, so the business of determining how to adjust for the additional yardage was up to me. I judged that I couldn't go wrong by holding 12 inches high.

The buck wasn't broadside, so once in shooting position, I felt sure that I'd profit by waiting for it to turn. The only problem I could foresee would come if the buck decided to head straight for the does. If that happened, the angle wouldn't change.

I got lucky. Across the field directly opposite the buck, a doe bounced out into the open, followed by her half-grown offspring. At this, the buck turned to face the newcomer. It was all I needed. I took a deep breath, raised the crosshairs to the top of the buck's back and squeezed the trigger.

At the sound of the blast, I could see does and yearlings going everywhere, but the buck dropped straight down like it had been hit from above with a ton of bricks. It may have been dead before it hit the ground.

I couldn't trust that idea, though, and I kept my rifle at ready on the long walk to where it lay. When I reached it and saw where the bullet had struck, I realized I was right. There was a neat hole in the right shoulder.

The buck's rack was wide, with excellent configuration, and as I looked it over, the feeling of elation completely replaced that of desperation present when the hunt began.

There was a bonus, too. The ground was solid, which meant that I could drive down the logging road and right up to the spot. I was whistling as I strolled back to the car.

32   When Deer Disappear

BY JEFF MURRAY

If you're a serious whitetail hunter, you've no doubt encountered that period, each fall, when deer just seem to evaporate. There are reasons why this takes place and ways you can find them.

Every deer hunter worth his salt lick knows that the rut is the best time to hunt bucks. The breeding season increases daytime deer activity, and this dramatically increases the odds for scoring on a decent-racked whitetail. But what if the rut isn't on? What if your schedule doesn't coincide with the fickle estrous cycle of female deer? And what if you have more time to hunt before or after the rut?

Most of us must hunt when time permits. Sooner or later, our days afield are going to coincide with one of the three main periods when bucks seem to vanish. Of course, deer can pull a Houdini act just about any time during the hunting season, but these particular periods really cause hunters fits. I've studied and studied them and, though I can't say I've figured them out, I've learned to adapt. Following are a few strategies that offer some hope for these tough times in the woods.

Hot Weather

The first "reclusive period" generally takes place in early fall, but it can occur at other times as well. Whenever an unseasonably hot spell hits the woods, deer react in ways that befuddle hunters. But the tables can be turned. Hot weather afflicts bucks in the Upper Midwest more than it does their Dixie counterparts. Northern deer, typically the borealis or dakotensis subspecies, are larger-bodied and therefore have a more difficult time regulating body heat when the sun beats down. Moreover, their heavy winter coat is about 75 percent more effective in insulating body heat. No wonder they "cool it" when temperatures rise.

One solution is hunting "mud holes," as Bob Dickson calls them. Dickson, a veteran deer and moose hunter from Manitoba, isn't about to suggest that deer hunters sit over isolated mud puddles like elk hunters have learned to monitor wallows. But Dickson has discovered a tactic that's quite similar. And it works if you plug it into your overall strategy.

"First off, hot spells up north are usually accompanied with calm winds," he begins. "You can't imagine how this can drive deer buggy—horse flies are especially tormenting. Add a buck's thick coat and enlarged neck, and you're talking about one uncomfortable critter. That buck's going to change his ways until the temperature drops."

Dickson claims that buck activity slows to a crawl during these times, with one distinct exception: short feeding forays. A buck still has to eat, Dickson says, but not just any old time.

"Without a doubt, early morning, just before sunrise, is best. That's when it's coolest. If you can pick up on this pattern before the weather breaks, your chances are as good as they're going to get."

Preferred foods can run the gamut—from croplands to clearcuts—so your best bet is scouting with binoculars in open country. This is most efficient because you can cover more ground in less time—and time is limited. If you fail to sight a decent buck, look for large tracks on trails approaching food sources; spoors measuring 4½ inches or better represent a large animal, while rounded tips belong to an older buck.

What if scouting only turns up does? Dickson offers one more tip: "Stick to creekbottoms. That's where you'll find the mud holes. I've watched bucks wallow in them like a pig. The closer it is to thick cover and food, the better."

One time Dickson was checking out last fall's rub line along the edge of a river to see if the buck was still around. He was. All Dickson had was a machete and a compass when he rounded a bend in the terrain and spied a buck lying knee-deep in an oxbow of the creek. It was 90 degrees in the shade that day, but the buck didn't care.

Normally, the best method of hunting creekbottoms is sneaking about like a timber wolf. Binoculars are a must for checking out every fold and shadow before taking the next step. However, during hot, dry spells, sneaking can be next to impossible; curled, dry leaves pop like popcorn underfoot. A trick Dickson uses to get around this is approaching sections of a stream where the rush of rapids dulls the deer's hearing. He's also been known to don a pair of hipboots and slowly wade the middle of the creek.

"You do what you have to do," he says.

The Lull

A second reclusive period occurs just when you expect deer to be gearing up for the rut; they actually wind down a bit. Wise hunters who encounter this snag adjust accordingly.

"What's going on is that other hunters are in the woods now," explains my buddy Noble Carlson, a veteran North Woods deer tracker. "You've got more grouse hunters, now that leaves are down, as well as duck hunters." Squirrel hunters are also active in many areas, and the deer respond in predictable ways.

"Count on more nighttime activity," Noble says. "Once a buck is pushed from his bedding area, even by a passing grouse gunner or a duck hunter from a boat or canoe, it's a different ball game. Nocturnal travel patterns become the rule with few exceptions."

This makes hunting closer to a buck's bedroom necessary if you wish to get a glimpse of him during shooting light. It also means abandoning other traditional areas.

"I rarely hunt field edges in mid- to late-October," adds hunting partner Nick Salzman. "Bucks avoid the fields until the does go into estrus, and that's at least several weeks away. Instead, I hunt the thick stuff."

By "thick stuff," Salzman is talking about areas where the underbrush limits visibility to no more than 20 yards. However, there are thickets, and there are buck thickets. Salzman's all-time favorite is bottomland bisecting a long ridge. "The bucks hit the ridges at night where you see all the rutting sign but no bucks and bed by day in the bottoms," he says. "Most hunters skip these small patches of woods because they think they're too small. But a buck doesn't need much cover to hide out."

Setting up in a small thicket takes some forethought. If you roll up your sleeves and wade in without knowing if the buck's at home, you're taking a big chance. Bump him and kiss the spot goodbye. This is why Salzman lays back from these patches of woods until he's certain the buck's out and on the prowl. Invariably, that means setting up in the dark—either well before dawn, or in the evening well past sunset—to arrange for a later hunt.

Another target with some potential for connecting on a reclusive buck is a "rub belt." For such an area to qualify as a hunting spot during this particularly difficult hunting period, you should find a group of at least a half dozen rubs within about 100 yards. Why? Because you need a spot that's likely to be hit by a buck during midday, not low-light periods. A rub belt is usually the tip-off of a mature buck's preferred 10-acre bedding area.

Now, we're not talking rub lines here. Rub lines more likely mark territory boundaries or travel routes to and from bedding and feeding (or breeding) areas. Also, rub lines are typically found along topographical barriers, such as a river, ridge line or rock outcropping. On the other hand, rub belts are generally associated with ultra-thick bedding cover within the security of a buck's inner sanctum.

Hunters have much to learn about these unique rubs.

"I believe they're made when a buck gets up and stretches from his bed," says biologist Ray Ryan. "The more rubs you find, the better the odds a buck is using the area repeatedly."

Incidentally, September is a good time to locate rubs associated with a buck's sanctuary. Vegetation may be thicker, but at least you can prowl around without fear of spooking the buck; you'll be hunting the area later in the fall. "Telemetry studies show that bucks seem to return to specific areas during their reclusive periods," Ryan adds. "Rubs can give them away, but hunters must exercise extreme caution when poking around a buck's bedroom."

Peak Hunting Pressure

Whitetails that are experienced in dodging bullets and broadheads undergo a radical change when hunting pressure begins to boil over. Once a deer's been shot at with a gun, it's a second season for serious hunters. If you think the October reclusive period is nasty, consider what the cumulative affect of repeated gunfire does. Now, cover alone often isn't enough to tranquilize a reclusive buck. He also seeks distance from two-legged predators to ease the pressure.

A perfect strategy unfolding at this time is going the extra mile—literally. Most hunters stick within one-half mile of the nearest two-track, forming a "human pressure belt" paralleling roads and trails. It's worth getting up a little earlier and walking a little farther to beat the crowds and let them push deer to you.

This ploy works especially well on special management lands—refuges, parks, military parcels—that strictly regulate public access. Hunting-related activities are generally prohibited apart from a few days or weekends in the fall. Some units require hunters to check in and out daily, and most don't allow any preseason scouting. Your game plan is simple. First learn the boundaries, then plug in the main access points. This should tell you where most hunters go and where they don't. With few exceptions, the farthest or most difficult-to-reach region is the best place to set up.

A good example of this is a hunt my barber, Pete Ullrich, took part in several years ago at central Minnesota's Camp Ripley. The army training facility is open for two weekends a year to bowhunters only. Successful applicants of the lottery drawing must check in as they enter a gate in the morning, and everyone must be accounted for in late afternoon when the gate swings shut again. Pete discovered that just about every footpath and artillery lane housed a hunter, so he took a detour. Along the way he learned a valuable lesson.

"I got turned around in a swamp," he admits. "Good thing because I wouldn't have seen so many deer if I'd stuck to the high ground where everybody else was stationed. I stood next to a cedar and let other hunters push deer my way." The tactic works on similar regulated hunts, be they bow, rifle, shotgun slug or muzzleloader.

Of course, sheer distance isn't a panacea. Hunting nearby areas that hunters tend to avoid can be just as rewarding. Over the years I've discovered a half dozen gems that can be counted on season after season.

One is a swath of land bordering a busy freeway. It's a deer magnet when the heat is on simply because parking along the highway is prohibited, forcing hunters to walk a good five miles out of their way. I simply have my wife drop me off on her way to her mother's house. More often than not, when I meet her at our predetermined spot, I've got blood on my hands. I've yet to see another hunter in this patch of woods in 10 years of hunting it.

But my favorite big-buck spot when hunter pressure peaks is an island. Not just any island, though. When I'm really desperate, I head for an island in a swamp. They're obvious on a topo map. The best ones aren't necessarily the farthest back—those near croplands seem to attract more deer.

Find an isolated knoll in the middle of a swamp, and you've got the rainbow with the pot of gold. The swamp serves as an effective barrier, and the high ground meets all of the buck's daily needs, save one: female companionship. This is his Achilles' heel. During the rut, he must venture out to service does, and this is when you can catch him offguard. But you must be as careful when entering a buck's moated castled as you would his daytime bedding lair.

Again, make sure he's off the island before you set up shop. You might be able to hear him sloshing in the mire, but that's a long shot. A trail timing device can make short order out of figuring out his daily routine. One of the sneakiest ways to intercept this buck, once you know the wheres and whens, is with a ground blind; treestands are generally too noisy and time-consuming to erect. A slick alternative is one of the many innovative portable blinds that have hit the marketplace in recent years (see sidebar, "Blind Faith"). They let you set up or take down silently in minutes. And if the wind switches, you can pull up stakes and set up on the downwind side of a trail with little effort.

Whitetails are reclusive enough during optimum hunting conditions. When these tough periods hit, deer can give hunters migraines. Don't give up. These strategies work often enough to make sticking it out to the bitter end a pleasure. It won't be so bitter if you give them a solid effort.

33 Second-Rut Myths That Can Wreck Your Hunt!

BY GREG MILLER

Here's why you should stop dreaming of the rut that may never happen and focus your tactics on deer sign that really pays off!

I first saw the doe when she trotted out of the woods, some 200 yards from my stand site. Unlike the dozen or so whitetails that had preceded her to the snow-covered alfalfa field, this deer showed absolutely no interest in feeding. She was, however, paying a great deal of attention to her back-trail. A minute later I spotted a flicker of movement near the edge of the woods where she had initially appeared. And then I saw the reason for the doe's concern. A big buck was hot on her trail!

The buck galloped out into the field a short ways and stopped. He did a quick visual scan of all the deer in the alfalfa, finally locking in on the object of his trailing efforts. The doe obviously sensed the buck's intentions and started easing toward a distant woods. She never made it. In a series of long, graceful bounds the buck quickly intercepted her. The two deer made a couple laps around the field before running into a small patch of brush 100 yards from my position. I heard several loud grunts and the sounds of underbrush snapping as the chase continued. Then all was quiet. A minute later I actually saw the buck mount and breed the doe. Just before legal shooting time expired both deer walked back out to the alfalfa field and fed side by side.

The above described events took place in my home state of Wisconsin during our late archery season in mid-December. No doubt because of the date, some mid-western deer hunters might naturally assume that the breeding activity I had witnessed was part of the infamous "second rut" that supposedly occurs each season. That's hardly the case, however. Truth is, I hadn't seen any signs of rutting behavior prior to this experience. Nor did I see any additional breeding activity in the days immediately following. But to be honest, I hadn't really expected that I would. As has been the case nearly 100 percent of the time, the secondary breeding activity I saw on that cold December afternoon was a very short-lived, one-day thing.

Experiences and Observations on the "Second Rut"

It's my opinion that no aspect of whitetailed deer behavior has been so mis-understood or as over-hyped in recent years as the so-called "second rut." I'd like to add that this opinion isn't based on speculation or guesswork either. Rather, it's based on hundreds of hours of personal observations of wild whitetails at that time of year when the "second rut" supposedly occurs. Although the bulk of my observations have involved Wisconsin whitetails, I've also had the opportunity to study the "second rut" thing in Iowa, Nebraska, Georgia and Mississippi. My findings from those states run consistent with my Wisconsin data. Simply put, if there truly is such a thing as an obvious and prolonged second whitetail rut, I have yet to see it!

Now this isn't to say that some secondary breeding doesn't occur. It most certainly does. What hunters need to realize, however, is that these flurries of sec-ondary breeding activity are sporadic and totally unpredictable. That's because, in most years, the vast majority of available breeding age does are bred during the ini-tial rut. What's more, there's not much chance that the few remaining unbred does will come into estrous on successive days again a month later. And that's exactly what it would take to induce whitetail bucks into another prolonged rut.

There's a big reason so many hunters believe that a prolonged second rut ex-ists, and it has to do with their beliefs regarding the initial rut. As one such hunter told me recently, "The big bucks in my hunting area can chase, catch and breed only a certain number of does during the first rut. So the way I see it, quite a few does won't get bred the first time around. And all those deer are going to come into estrous again 28 days later, which means there's bound to be a second rut about a month after our first rut."

While this might sound like solid logic, it falls apart upon closer examina-tion. Events I witnessed on a recent Illinois bowhunt will help to partially explain what I mean.

The Role of "Immature" Bucks

The rut was already going full-bore when my two hunting partners and I ar-rived at our Illinois hot-spot. Right from the beginning we all saw some intense big buck/hot doe interaction. And we continued to see this interaction almost on a daily basis. In addition, however, we were also seeing a tremendous amount of immature buck/doe breeding activity. None of us were really surprised at this, however, as it's something we all had seen many times in the past.

Whether you want to believe it or not, the same thing occurs almost every-where whitetails are found. Remember, once a big buck sequesters a hot doe, he can tend only to that one particular doe. Since he's out of the game, so to speak, the buck has absolutely no way to control what goes on in other parts of his range. Obviously, then, he has no way to prevent the immature bucks that live in the area from breeding some of "his" other does. And lest you believe otherwise, mature does will let immature bucks breed them. Once they've been chased to the point where they will finally stand, an estrous doe is going to get bred—regardless what size or age the buck involved might be.

From what I've seen, immature bucks somehow can sense when the dominant bucks in a given area are pre-occupied with hot does. Furthermore, they will immediately seize upon these opportunities to become involved in the breeding process. What I'm getting at here is this: Because of the aggressive nature of 1½- and 2½-year-old whitetail bucks, far more does are bred during the initial rut than most hunters would believe. A couple seasons back I was witness to another affair that perfectly illustrates my point.

Buck Aggression: A Close-up View

It was just shortly after daylight when I heard a deer crashing toward my stand site through the frost covered leaves. Seconds later a doe bounded into sight. The lone deer continued on until she was directly under me, whereupon she stopped running and immediately turned to study her back-trail. A full minute went by, and then I heard a loud crash followed by a deep-pitched grunt. Turning my full attention to the spot where the sounds had come from, I was shocked to see five different bucks come running into view. The biggest of these bucks, a good looking 2½-year-old 9-pointer, was in the lead. Judging from their body and antler sizes, the other four bucks all were 1½-year-old animals.

The doe let the antlered caravan get within 15 yards of her before bolting. The wild chase that ensued lasted a full 30 minutes, during which time the six deer were out of my sight only for very brief moments. In the end, the doe led the bucks back to within 20 yards of my stand site. At that point she finally stood and allowed the 9-pointer to mount her. (It was obvious the 9-pointer was the dominant buck of the bunch, as he did the vast majority of the chasing and, eventually, all the breeding. Had the 9-pointer not been there, however, the most dominant animal of the four 1½-year-old bucks surely would have bred the doe.)

As you might imagine, the six deer made an unbelievable amount of noise during the chase and subsequent breeding ritual. I knew that several mature bucks resided in the area, so I was fully expecting to have a large-racked trophy come charging onto the scene to investigate the source of that noise. The fact that it never happened is proof-positive that the big boys either were already preoccupied with does or temporarily absent from their home range. Whatever the case, the doe still was effectively serviced, albeit by an immature buck. But like I said, such behavior is common, especially in areas with high deer densities.

Opinions of the Experts

Dave Evenson, a wildlife manager for the state of Wisconsin, also is skeptical about the occurrence of a second rut. According to Evenson, "Our facts and figures would indicate that there isn't a whole lot of breeding that occurs in December and January. And contrary to popular belief, there isn't a high incidence of doe fawn breeding that goes on during the month of December either. In fact, the farther north you go, the percentage of doe fawns that get bred decreases dramatically. We've pretty much been able to link this phenomenon to body weight."

Keith McCaffery, another wildlife manager from Wisconsin, agrees with Evenson about the body weight thing. "The findings from a study done in New York some years ago show that doe fawns in northern latitudes need to achieve a minimum body weight of 65 pounds before they can come into estrous the first time," McCaffery told me. "During a normal year very few doe fawns will attain that kind of weight, especially in heavily forested areas. But if they do, then that means the buck fawns also will attain such body weights. And if doe fawns are capable of coming into estrous, buck fawns are fully capable of breeding. If given the opportunity, they most certainly will breed any doe that will stand for them."

I'd be willing to bet that darn few whitetail hunters were aware of that fact!

Evenson and McCaffery both said that the vast majority of Wisconsin's doe herd is bred in November. But they were quick to add that some breeding does occur in December and January. Like me, however, both men are convinced that this secondary breeding activity usually is very sporadic and quite unpredictable.

"Our observations have shown that there normally aren't a lot of does left to breed during the second cycle," McCaffery stated. "I believe this can be at least partially attributed to the fact that immature bucks are doing a fair share of breeding during the initial rut."

Hunting Pressure's Effect on Breeding

Even if a prolonged second rut did occur here in Wisconsin, a couple of factors would keep the bucks from displaying the careless sort of behavior associated with the initial rut. One of these factors has to do with the intense pressure put on our deer herd during the nine-day firearms season in late November. The other factor concerns my home state's seven-day muzzleloader season, which usually runs through the first week in December. From what I've seen you won't likely catch a big buck searching for hot does when thousands of humans are stomping around in the woods. (The same thing applies to several other mid-western states.)

There's another factor that can lead some hunters to believe in the second rut, and it involves a certain aspect of whitetail buck behavior. This behavior sees bucks once again running scrapes and making antler rubs in the weeks after the peak of the initial rut. But rather than being a signal that the bucks are gearing up for a second breeding ritual, these sometimes intense rub and scrape sessions are nothing more than a natural aspect of post-rut behavior. The bucks use rubs and scrapes merely to scent mark certain parts of their home ranges. They do this both to announce their return and to find out if any "new" bucks might have moved into the area during their absence.

Stop Waiting for Something That May Never Happen!

Interestingly, the majority of the rubbing and scraping that bucks do at this time of year will occur along the travel routes they use most often. And just like during the pre-rut period, the travel routines of the bucks will once again be dictated by the location of the most preferred foods. In my opinion, instead of waiting for a second rut that so often never happens, hunters would be far better off exploiting this very predictable aspect of buck behavior. Keep in mind, however, that your best opportunities for some mature buck action will come from stand sites located near bedding areas. Personally, I'll adhere to this kind of approach unless I happen to witness some secondary breeding activity. At which point I'll immediately relocate to stands placed very near to the edges of antlerless deer feeding areas.

Over the years I've taken close to a dozen whitetail bucks during that time when the second rut supposedly occurs. If memory serves me right, only two of those deer were displaying behavior that even remotely resembled rutting animals. The remainder of the bucks I've harvested, on the other hand, were behaving like deer that were locked into very strict post-rut lifestyles. Because of this, I'll continue to plan my late-season whitetail hunting strategies with no thought of the so-called second rut.

Editor's Note: To receive an autographed copy of the author's newest book, *Proven Whitetail Tactics,* send $19.95 plus $3.00 S&H to: Greg Miller, 1828 Duncan Road, Dept. IIP, Bloomer, WI 54724. (WI residents add $1.25) Visa and Mastercard orders, call: (715) 568-3215.

34   Whitetails in the Rain

A little rain never hurt anyone and in the deer woods it can even help you
whether you stand hunt or prefer to have at 'em one-on-one.

The soft, steady drumming sound of rain on a tin roof has to be one of the most hypnotic lullabies in the world. It was certainly working its spell on me. Then I saw something move in the misty grayness outside.

Of all the deer hunting stands, blinds or whatever used over the years, the one in which I now sat while the rain pattered down was both the biggest and most unusual. It was a barn, long abandoned, but still boasting a good roof and sturdy planking on the hayloft floor. An empty bucket made a convenient seat, so there I waited, hoping that the shower would pass and let me get back to my stand beside a distant cornfield. No such luck.

Peering from the loft into the woods, I finally made out the form of a deer. Although it was partially screened by honeysuckle vines and low-growing brush, I could make out antlers large enough to cause me to pay attention. Sitting as I was back in the shadows, the buck failed to notice as I lifted the little Ruger Number One International and used the Bausch and Lomb scope to examine him more carefully. With the 1.5-6 variable cranked up to its highest setting, I could tell that the side nearest me carried four decent tines, so I picked out a handy opening just ahead of the slowly walking animal and waited. He was not a step more than 40 yards from the barn when a 140-grain Nosler Ballistic Tip hit square on the shoulder and dropped him in his tracks. A handsome eight-pointer, the pale antlers almost seemed to glow in contrast to the rain-darkened winter coat.

That rainy day whitetail was the first I had ever taken under such conditions, largely because staying home instead of out in a deluge had always seemed like the sensible thing to do. Like many other hunters, I had assumed that deer preferred not to move around a great deal when the weather was nasty. Hunting from the barn and other sheltered locations has long since changed my mind.

James Dennie, a longtime friend and occasional hunting companion, has no qualms about spending time going afield when things get soggy. He and his brother have erected small, elevated houses near the edges of two clover fields, and regardless of the weather they miss very few mornings or afternoons during Tennessee's rather lengthy muzzleloader and regular firearms hunting seasons.

"Some years you just about have to hunt in the rain or stay at home," he says. "Back in '90–'91 is a good example. The state's harvest figures were lower than had been expected, but that was largely because it seemed to rain almost every weekend, the very time that most hunters have a chance to be in the woods. When wet weather is the norm, it just stands to reason that the deer have to feed in the rain if they are going to eat at all. When hunting in the rain, however, there were very few times when we did not see deer of some description. One fellow who hunts close to us took three bucks in the first three mornings of the season, all while it was raining."

His comments make sense, especially the part about deer having no choice but to be at least moderately active. They have to feed, and unlike the folks who pursue them, they cannot simply opt to stay where it is dry and comfortable. It may diminish the fun quotient, but if you are willing to get wet you have a better chance of scoring than most people realize.

Last season, while the Dennie brothers were warm and dry in their snug "shooting" houses lying in wait for a clover-eater, I was in a less comfortable situation. A hardwood ridge that I had hunted often over the years held two freshly worked scrapes and the ground was littered with acorns. The rut was in full swing, so I hoped that one of the buck's two appetites might bring him by the tree in which I had placed the portable Amacker climbing stand. Naturally, the rain started just about the time I had gotten into position and adjusted the safety belt. Happily, part of my gear that morning was a good rain suit.

Daylight was slow to arrive, made to seem even slower by the inclement weather. No friendly glow lit the east, but finally the gloom lightened enough for me to make out nearby objects. One of the nearby objects turned out to be a small doe who was busy nibbling on some greenbrier vines before starting on an acorn main course. She would occasionally cease feeding to look back into the thicker brush of the hollow. That raised my hopes that the buck might make his appearance soon. Instead, another doe came into the clear followed by a yearling; a button buck. The little fellow was not even legal, let alone the critter that I craved.

The better part of an hour passed during which the steady patter of raindrops continued. Despite the rainsuit, some of the wetness did manage to get through. Admittedly, it was not a comfortable way to spend the morning. The trio of whitetails had fed away up the ridge when another animal came moving my way. This time my luck was better; it was a buck and he was headed straight for the scrape in front of my stand.

The rifle carried on that trip was a Marlin 336 ER in .356 Winchester caliber. Short, accurate and reliable, it delivers flat-nose 200-grain slugs amazingly well and is a quick killer on deer. The buck was angling slightly away when the bullet entered behind the left shoulder, broke the right one. His demise was almost as quick as if he had encountered a stroke of double-forked lightning.

Although a protected "shooting house" is ideal for when it rains, stillhunting is a top-notch tactic. Even the most ham-footed of us can walk quietly when it rains. On one rainy day hunt with my friend, Terry Rohm, I planned to stillhunt slowly to a place that Terry had targetted. Since I would be hunting from the ground, I found a comfortable spot on which to place my Gore-Tex-clad rump and settled in to wait. If nothing came along within an hour of decent light I would get up and still-hunt my way around the ridge and back to the roadside pickup spot where I would meet Terry and the truck.

Our trip had been planned to coincide with Alabama's antlerless hunting season. The normal limit is one buck per day, but during this time we could legally harvest both a buck and a doe each day that we hunted. Reportedly overrun with "slick heads," according to Terry, we were expected to take a doe if the opportunity arose.

Somewhere between 2½-dozen animals of one sort or another, probably deer, passed my hideaway before it grew light enough to make out details. Then a sleek six-pointer made the mistake of stepping into the open. I was carrying the Marlin in .356 Winchester again, and the 1.5-6×B&L scope found the buck nicely. Half of my daily limit lay still on the squishy leaves.

No more than 10 minutes later a pair of does strolled along the same trail, so I bombed the larger of the two and was through for the day except for the chores of field dressing the animals and getting them back to the road. For the latter, I would wait for assistance, hopefully in the form of Terry's ATV. Dragging or hauling deer is much easier on the back that way.

During the time that I was involved with the knife work, I saw seven more deer, at least one of which wore respectable horns. To say I was happy with the "hotspot" that Terry had handed me would have been a major understatement.

As it turned out, there was no mechanical assistance this time, so while my friendly guide growled about the hunter who "shot doe deer the size of polo ponies," he also explained why he had believed that I would find some action there.

"That area below the ridge is low and swampy, real palmetto country. Two small rivers run through it, and when the rains get heavy, especially if they hang around for a few days, that country tends to flood. Most of the time the deer can hole up on grassy hummocks or high spots, but the rising water pushes them out of those places. The ridge where you were sitting is the longest one that pokes into the area and deer moving ahead of the rising water tend to follow it anytime things start getting nasty.

"It also has some good oak timber on it, so the swamp deer are likely to have been feeding up on top at night. Because it is not alien country to them, they aren't really nervous about using it as a travel route."

When asked what drawbacks, beside basic comfort, rainy weather offered Terry responded, "Well, that's one reason I mentioned a travel route the deer had used before. Heavy rain, or even a lot of dripping water off leaves make a noise that can mute danger signals for the deer. I think they are a little more nervous than usual under these conditions simply because their sharp hearing is not as effective.

"On the other hand, I don't think it has much effect on their sense of smell, and of course it has almost none on their eyesight, so you need to be conscious of the breeze and out of sight."

The next afternoon I had a chance to witness the fact that a deer's sniffer indeed works in the rain. Three deer, one wearing a weird three-point rack that was notable only in its ugliness, were feeding in a small clearing where I could watch them through binoculars. There was too much screening cover to allow a shot, plus they were somewhat farther than I was willing to trust a shot with the .356.

I had heard Terry shoot an hour or so previously and when I saw a shape moving in the distance I swung my glasses around to be certain that it was him and not another whitetail. He had indeed connected and was wisely headed back to an abandoned house where he could wait in the dry until reinforcements arrived. There was no way that the deer that I had been watching could have seen or heard him, but there was a light breeze blowing from his direction. Despite the light, steady drizzle, all three heads snapped up as he passed abreast of their position. For a long moment they stood that way, then began moving, not panicked, but alert on their way back into the thicker timber. Unfortunately for them, this also put the ugly-racked one within sight and range of the lever gun. Those antlers now hang over this typewriter as a testament to the need for selective shooting and herd culling.

There is another little trick that works now and then during those rainy deer seasons. One of my old favorite hunting locations is alongside a small hill-country creek, and I have whacked a few in that spot over the years. However, over a period of time it became apparent when the stream was gurgling and making all those watery sounds that follow heavy or prolonged rains. Not being a quick thinker, it took a while before I figured out that the sound of the creek would effectively mask sounds even more completely than rainfall. I stillhunt near creeks and rivers, especially when flooding conditions exist, but you can bet that it will be back away from the edges of running water. This is a self-inflicted handicap that no one needs; getting wet as a muskrat on a hunt is bad enough at its best.

If you decide to try your luck at ambushing a wet-weather whitetail, make sure of your equipment first. A rainsuit is a necessity, of course, but remember that most states require at least some blaze orange. Cover it with a camouflage rain outfit and you are not only illegal but cannot be easily seen by other hunters, one of whom might have an itchy trigger finger.

Also, gloves come in handy because even on days that are not cold, the rain will cause your hands to get both chilly and slick.

Scopes for use under these conditions had better be of good quality, and dependable, quick-release covers are needed to keep water droplets off the lenses. I make it a practice to apply a coat of oil to all metal surfaces prior to heading for the woods. Of course, a thorough drying after the hunt and a wipe-down with a rust preventative will keep the guns looking good and working properly. Just use common sense where your guns are concerned, but beware: Folks will readily question the common sense of anyone willing to sit in the rain no matter what you are doing. That's okay with me, because I know those same folks will be home when it rains. The deer and I will be in the woods.

Part Six
Hunters' Tracks

The Challenges and Rewards
of the Whitetail Hunting Experience

We're going to change the pace a little right here—lighten our grip, so to speak—while we take time to consider some illuminating reflections on some of the things that make whitetail hunting so endlessly fascinating and rewarding.

35 Whitetail Wisdom for the Ages

BY JOHN WOOTTERS

Author of the wonderful book, HUNTING TROPHY DEER, respected whitetail authority John Wootters shares some poignant observations on what makes a great deer hunter. This article originally appeared in the November 2000 SPORTS AFIELD.

The topics listed here aren't your common, entry-level stuff like "white-tails like 'edges,'" but they're hardly secret to an expert hunter. Still, now and then I'm startled to meet hunters who misunderstand or ignore these truths. I learned them the hard way during 60 seasons of chasing bucks across three nations and eighteen American states, and they apply anywhere in the North American whitetail range.

The First—and Best—Deer Hunting "Secret"

The first and most important "secret" should be the most obvious: The activity most essential to deer-hunting success takes place between a hunter's ears—not in his boots.

Hunting, especially for mature bucks, is far more mental than physical. Most of us can't run a deer down, but we may be able to think our way to getting the drop on him. With a thorough knowledge of local whitetail habits, state of the rut, terrain, weather, deer responses to hunting pressure, moon phases, and the status of seasonal food and water resources, a hunter can churn out good predictions—sometimes spookily accurate ones—about when, where, and how to hunt. Without that knowledge, he's back where we all started—stumbling around in the woods, hoping to run into a buck by accident . . . and accident is an unreliable partner in an enterprise as subtle and complex as a deer hunt.

Passing Up the Spikes

It sounds too simple, but the greatest secret to shooting a big buck is not filling your tags with little bucks.

If you dump the first thing with antlers that trots by each season, you'll probably grow a long gray beard waiting for your wallhanger. Old (read "trophy") bucks are scarce everywhere, and live according to very different rhythms from those of young bucks and does—which is why it's easy to be out in the garage skinning a forkie when the mossyhorn ambles by your vacant stand. Learning to pass up immature bucks is the most basic step toward taking that career deer of your dreams.

The All-Important Rut

Our deadliest weapon is an understanding of the process hunters call "the rut" in all its phases and manifestations.

This is the critical component of buck-hunting knowledge, especially when the target is a mature buck. For half a century I've watched our body of knowledge about the rut grow and change. What "expert" deer hunters taught me about the rut when I was a boy was a pretty primitive and in some ways skewed version of whitetail reproductive rituals. It may be that 50 years from now hunters will find themselves looking back on the state of today's knowledge with amused condescension, but we can only go with the best information available.

It's out there somewhere in the veritable avalanche of whitetail how-to being published these days. The problem comes in sorting out the real McCoy from the, er, Meadow McMuffins. Beware of false prophets. I regularly read discussions of the rut that include statements I believe to be the exact opposite of the facts. Accept nothing blindly (not even what you find here); compare authors' statements with your own observations. You'll soon identify those writers whose reports agree best with what you see happening in the woods and whose theories, explanations, and advice offer helpful insights for your own hunting. Ignore those who only boil the pot—merely filling white space month after month, or rehashing their own or others' material. Beware pundits who reveal a very narrow regional focus, especially if that focus is not on your region.

Keep in mind that the timing of the rut varies as much as a month or more with latitude and other factors. In my home state of Texas it's usually almost over by opening day (first week in November) in north, central, and northeast Texas but still at least a month away from ending in the famed Brush Country of South Texas.

Know-How, Not Gear, Takes Bucks

Equipment does not kill bucks; hunter know-how does. This means that the most powerful and accurate long-range rifle wearing a space-age scope is useless in the hands of a hunter who does not know how to find a buck. Likewise, rangefinders, grunt calls, decoys, the slickest new tree stands, the current "irresistible" scent, the hottest camo pattern, the latest canyon-crawling ATV . . . none of these—nor any other technological wonder—will, by itself, get you a buck. They're useful aids for a skilled hunter, who knows them to be simply refinements and not basic hunting techniques. Even the best of them are not substitutes for knowledge and personal hunting skills.

I hate to say it, but you can't purchase skill; you can only buy the means to apply your own skills more effectively.

Weather or Not

Weather, though certainly significant, is probably much less so than we've believed. Like all wildlife, deer are tough animals, able to live and function in an often-harsh environment from which they have no escape. Certain activities must go forward, regardless of weather. They have to eat and find water. Their biological programming insists that they participate in the rut, not just when the weather's nice but whenever the rest of the local herd does.

You may, therefore, find a whitetail on the move even when you think it's too hot or too cold or too windy for deer. A plummeting barometer just before a cold front comes close to stalling herd activity, and days on end of steady rain will sure slow them down. Bitter weather can keep deer in their beds all day, but only when the cold is truly abnormal for the region. But most of the weather "rules" of deer hunting are violated pretty regularly by the deer themselves.

Just one example: I've often found lots of bucks out and about during a windy, dry norther when orthodox wisdom says the strong gusty wind should suppress movement. In each case, the rut was peaking and it was cold—but not unseasonably so. In other words, the bucks' drive to leave no doe unbred just overwhelmed their traditional dislike of howling winds. This reminds us that no single weather parameter perfectly predicts deer activity; we have to consider all factors together to make an educated guess.

Prevailing weather conditions, therefore, may alter your hunting location or method but should not keep you in camp except perhaps in extreme circumstances. I've killed several of my finest whitetail bucks on days when, due to the weather, I almost didn't go hunting at all!

Moon-Struck Deer

Moon phase, on the other hand, may affect deer movement even more than we thought. The trouble is, we do not understand exactly *how* the moon exerts its influence. There are plenty of personal opinions and theories around (often conflicting and a few preposterous) . . . but not much hard evidence.

I believe I do possess hard evidence, in the form of a database of correlated moon and deer-movement observations comprising more than 13,000 individual deer sightings collected over 21 seasons. It's much too complicated a subject to examine here in detail, but based on the information in my database I strongly urge you to pay attention to the moon phase. Plan your most important hunts during dark-of-the-moon periods if possible, and never miss a chance to hunt on a morning following a moon-dark night. If you have no choice but to hunt on a full moon, be sure to remain on stand and alert at least through the midday hours.

Is Your Gun Ready?

The critical knowledge most often disregarded by hunters is that the gun was personally, recently sighted-in with the identical ammunition to be used in hunting.

Guns—even today's super-rifles in plastic stocks—do change their zeroes unexpectedly and for mysterious reasons. Occasionally these changes can be quite large—even large enough to miss a deer altogether at 50 yards. Although it's admittedly better to miss cleanly than to wound, neither should occur. If it does happen, I guarantee it will always be on a deer that's terribly important: your only chance at a buck all season, or maybe the biggest buck you ever saw. The only assurance that it won't happen to you comes from sighting-in your rifle carefully, yourself . . . and then checking the zero at least once a week throughout the season! I do this without fail, even with rifles that haven't changed zero since I've owned them.

Seeing Deer

As illogical as it may seem to beginners, the hardest thing in deer hunting may be simply to see a deer that's there to be seen. Mature whitetail bucks are seldom caught standing in the open in broad daylight, so don't expect to see them there. Instead, learn to look into and through bushes, instead of at them. Try to pick bits and pieces of a deer out of the brush and to assemble them mentally into a buck. It's a knack that takes a little practice and a lot of patience, probing back into the screen of undergrowth with eyes and/or binoculars, looking not for a deer but for some suspicious abstraction: a shape, color, line, shadow, reflection, or mass that doesn't quite fit into the scene. The clue may be nothing more than six inches of antler beam, the angle of a hock, or the bright blackness of an eye. Suddenly, as if by magic, the whole animal takes shape.

Remember: Every hunting guide has horror stories about clients who could never be made to see a wallhanger buck standing motionless for a long time, in more or less plain sight and easy range.

What Deer See

Never forget how easy it is to underestimate a whitetail buck. I've read "expert" opinions, for example, to the effect that a deer's powers of vision are inferior to those of a human. To put it delicately: horse hockey! Most mammals, including man, tend to overlook motionless objects that blend with their surroundings. That's what makes camouflage work. But a white cane is the last thing a whitetail deer needs; his eye can be riveted by the flutter of a bird's wing in a bush at 100 yards, and he may be able to detect the contraction or expansion of the pupils of your eyes at 20! Likewise, the keenness of his other senses, his sheer nerve, and his gift for choosing the correct hunter-evasion tactic for every situation are often underrated by the unwary hunter.

There's no point in handing a buck an even greater advantage than he already has, is there?

Confidence

On the other hand, the consequences of overestimating the powers of the beast are equally discouraging.

We can, after all, defeat ourselves before we ever set foot in the woods, psyching ourselves out with awe of the almost magical elusiveness of an old white-tail buck. He's a real load, all right, but neither his intelligence nor his wariness is supernatural. His brain is good, but not as good as the human brain. He may be able to out-smell, out-hear, and out-sneak us, but we still retain one immense advantage over any wild animal: the power of human imagination.

An old warhorse of a whitetail buck can show you some astonishing tricks and he'll demand the very best you have, but he is not invincible. He may seem so, but he can be had—by a good hunter who goes to the woods armed . . . with knowledge.

36   The Rack

BY JAY CASSELL

Former Senior Editor of SPORTS AFIELD and now Senior Editor at The Lyons Press, Jay Cassell has written about topics as diverse as caribou hunting in Alaska and mayfly identification on Eastern trout streams. In this story from Sports Afield, December 1992, he writes about his 6-year-old son's initiation to hunting.

I found his antler, Dad," the throaty voice of my 6-year-old son, James, crackled over the telephone. "I saw it in the woods when Mom was driving me home from school, right near where we went hunting! Are you coming home tonight?"

When I told him that my flight wouldn't get in until 11:00, and that I wouldn't be home until midnight, there was a disappointed silence over the phone. Then, "Well, okay, but don't look at it until morning, so I can show you. Promise?"

I promised. We had a deal. I told him I'd see him soon, then asked to talk with his mother.

"Love you, Dad."

"Love you too, James."

Unbelievable. My son had found the shed antler of the buck I had hunted, unsuccessfully, all season. The big 10-pointer I had seen the day before deer season, the one with the wide spread and thick beams. He had seen me that day, having winded me as I pussyfooted through some thickets for a closer look. I think he somehow knew that he was safe, that he was far enough away from me.

I had scouted the 140-acre farm and adjoining woods near my home in suburban New York, the farm that I had gotten permission to hunt after five years of asking. "You can hunt this year," Dan the caretaker had said to me during the summer, when I asked my annual question. "I kicked those other guys off the property. They were in here with ATVs and Jeeps, bringing two and three friends every day they hunted, without even asking. Lot of nerve, I thought. Got sick of 'em, so I kicked 'em off. Now I'll let you hunt, and your buddy John, three other guys, and that's all. I want some local people on here that I know and trust."

When Dan had told me that, I couldn't believe it. But there it was, so I took advantage of it. Starting in September, I began to scout the farm. I had seen bucks on the property in previous years while driving by, but now I got a firsthand look. There was sign virtually everywhere: rubs, scrapes, droppings in the hillside hayfields, in the mixed hardwoods, in the thick hemlock stands towering over the rest of the woods. I found what were obviously rubs left by a big deer. In a copse of hemlocks near the edge of the property, bordering an Audubon nature preserve, were scrapes and, nearby, about five or six beech saplings absolutely ripped apart by antlers.

With James's help, I set up my tree stand overlooking a heavily used trail that seemed to be a perfect escape route out of the hemlocks. James and I also found an old permanent tree stand, which he and I repaired with a few 2×4s and nails. This would officially be "his" tree stand—or tree house, as he called it.

Opening day couldn't come fast enough. James and I talked about it constantly. Even though he's only 6, and can't really hunt yet, he couldn't wait for deer season. He knows what deer tracks and droppings look like; can tell how scrapes and rubs are made; can even identify where deer have passed in the leaf-covered forest floor. My plan was to hunt the first few days of the season by myself while James was in school, and then take him on a weekend. If luck was with me, maybe I'd take the big buck and could then concentrate on filing my doe tag with my son's help.

Opening day came and went, with no trophy 10-pointer in sight, or any other bucks, for that matter. A lot of other days came and went too, most of them cold, windy and rainy. Three weeks into the two-month-long season, on a balmy Sunday in the 50s, James and I packed our camo backpacks with candy bars and juice boxes, binoculars and grunt calls, and at 2:00 P.M. off we went, on our first day of hunting together. When we reached the spot where I always park my car, on a hillside field, I dabbed some camo paint onto James's face, which he thought was cool. Then we started hiking up the field and into the woods, toward the hemlocks.

We saw one white tail disappear over a knob as we hiked into James's stand. I didn't really care, though. This was the first time I was taking my son hunting! It would be the first of many, I hoped. I wouldn't force it on him, just introduce him to the sport, and keep my fingers crossed.

At James's stand, we sat down and had a couple of candy bars. "Can I blow on the deer call now, Dad?" I said yes, and he proceeded to honk away on the thing like a trumpet player.

"Do it quietly," I advised. "And remember, always whisper, don't talk loudly. And don't move around so much!"

What with James honking on the call and fidgeting—checking out my bow, looking around, pointing to the hawk soaring overhead, crumpling up his candy bar wrapper and stuffing it into his pocket—I was sure no self-respecting deer would come within a mile of us. None did, not to my son's stand, or to mine, or to the rocks where we later sat, overlooking a trail and those ripped-up beech saplings, until darkness finally settled over the woods. But that was okay.

Hiking out of the woods, we met my friend John coming from his tree stand.

"I saw that 10-pointer today," he began, giving James a poke in the ribs with his finger.

"Where?"

"Up near those hemlocks, the same area you and I have been hunting. We were probably 100 yards away from each other."

"Well, what happened?" Part of me was saying, *Great, he got the buck!* The other part of me was saying, *Pleeeease tell me you didn't shoot him.* John looked at me sheepishly.

"I was watching that trail, and I saw a doe headed my way, right where I always put my climbing tree stand. Then, right behind her, I saw a buck—you know that 6-pointer we've seen over by the lake? Well, I started to draw back on him—he was only 30 yards away—but then I saw some movement to my left. It was HIM! Cutting through the hemlocks. That 6-pointer and doe got out of there fast, and the 10-pointer got to within 10 yards of my stand, stopped broadside to me, and then looked up straight at me!"

"Did you shoot? Did you shoot?"

"I couldn't. I was shaking too much. I mean, I could even hear the arrow rattling against the rest. Eventually, he just took off down the trail. Man, he was something. Must weigh 200 pounds!"

Later, driving the short ride home, James said, "Hey, Dad, how come John didn't shoot that deer?"

"Shooting a deer is a lot harder than many people think. Even if everything else is right, sometimes you can get so nervous that you just can't shoot, no matter how much you want to. John's time will come, though. He works at it."

★   ★   ★

I didn't see the buck until two days after Christmas. Hunting by myself, I left my normal tree stand and circled around to the backside of the hemlocks. At 4:00 P.M., I was wedged between some boulders that overlook a well-used trail. It was 20°F, getting dark, and I was cold and shivering uncontrollably. But I kept hearing a rustling behind me. *Another squirrel.* But it wasn't. Suddenly, 60 yards through the trees, I could see a big deer headed my way. It was moving with a purpose. It stopped at what appeared to be a scrape, and I could see a huge symmetrical rack dip down as the buck stuck his nose to the ground. Then he stood up, urinated into the scrape, turned, and headed back into the hemlocks. If he had kept coming down the trail, I would have had a clean 15-yard shot. It wasn't meant to be.

That was my season. I didn't see that 10-pointer again, and I missed my only shot of the year, a 35-yarder at a forkhorn that sailed high. Such is deer hunting.

★   ★   ★

So now I was returning home from my trip. I walked in the door at midnight, quickly read through some mail on the counter, soon slipped into bed. My wife rolled over and whispered, "Don't forget to wake up James before you go to work. He really wants to show you that rack."

The alarm went off at 6:30, and I got up to take a shower.

"Psst, Dad, is that you?" came a sleepy voice from my son's room.

"Yes, buddy, how are you?"

"Wait here, Dad!"

Before I could say another word, he jumped out of bed, put on his oversized bear-paw slippers, and went padding down the stairs to the basement. When he returned, he had the biggest grin on his face that I've ever seen.

"Look, Dad!"

And there it was, half of the 10-pointer's rack. A long, thick main beam, four long, heavy points, the back one eight inches. Amazing. And that buck will be there next year.

"Dad, can I put it on my wall?"

"Of course."

"And can we go look for the other half of his antlers tomorrow, because tomorrow's Saturday, and I don't have school, and you once told me that their antlers usually fall off pretty close together. Please?"

"Sure, James. If you're good in school today."

The deal was made. We never found the other half of the shed, though. It snowed, and we couldn't really look. Mice probably ate the other half.

But you know what? I think maybe my future hunting companion was born this past season.

Part Seven
Gearing Up

Tools of the Experts

This old chestnut is really true: By itself, the newest and most expensive gear in the world won't make you a consistently successful whitetail hunter. On the other hand, the stuff you're using for hunting—what the legendary Nash Buckingham always called "the ropes and tools"—can help you a great deal when you know how to use it properly. The gun or bow you shoot; the boots and clothes that keep you warm and dry and quiet; the treestand you sit on—these are critical elements in any hunt.

Entire books are written on this vast subject, and it is not our intention to try to match them here. Instead, whitetail authority, photographer, and hunter Charles Alsheimer covers some basics (and beyond!) on what to look for before you buy.

37   Gearing Up

BY CHARLES ALSHEIMER

From an equipment standpoint I'm a firm believer in the idea that form follows function. This is not to say that I don't have nice equipment, because I do. When I returned from Vietnam in 1970 one of the first things I purchased was a beautiful Weatherby Mark V rifle. Though it looked great in the gun cabinet, it was less than functional in the field because of its high gloss finish. To remedy this I had the metal surfaces matte-blued and the stock refinished in an oil finish. This toned down the glare, making the rifle far more practical in hunting situations. Over the years I've worked hard at trying to make all of my hunting gear more practical for the field. It hasn't always been easy to do this, but in most cases I've succeeded.

Guns

Though I own a beautiful Winchester Model 94 in 30-30 caliber, I long ago stopped deer hunting with calibers such as the 30-30 and the .35 Remington. I fully realize that both are legendary deer calibers. However, in my opinion these and calibers like them are marginal deer rounds when compared with calibers such as the .270, .280, .308, and .30-06. To adequately and consistently kill a whitetail, it's generally felt that a bullet should have at least 1,200 foot pounds of energy at impact to get the job done. Calibers such as the .30-30 are marginal in this regard. So with this in mind, bullet weight and velocity are important factors to consider.

I've been in a lot of deer camps over the years and the most popular whitetail calibers have been the .270, .280, 7mm Remington Mag., .308, and .30-06. These are the choices of serious whitetail hunters. When loaded with the proper bullets, they are lethal from 30 to 300 yards and beyond, and more than enough for even the biggest whitetails roaming the continent. Though I've seen a fair number of 300 magnums sitting in camp gun racks, they are simply too much gun for a white-tailed buck and the hunter pulling the trigger. The problem with using magnums for whitetail hunting is that excessive muzzle blast and recoil overwhelms the average deer hunter and causes poor shot placement due to flinching.

I've rifle hunted whitetails with everything from a .243 to belted magnums, but my favorite calibers are the .270 and .30-06. I guess this is partly because I was a big Jack O'Connor fan growing up. It's also due to the job I've seen each do on trophy class bucks. I use rifles suited for the terrain I'm hunting. If I'm hunting dense forests such as New York's Adirondack Mountains, I use a modified Remington 7600 slide action .30-06. The rifle was reworked by Harold Torre of The Whitetail Gun Shop in Essex Junction, Vermont (802-878-7133). These folks specialize in reducing the weight of slide action Remington rifles by remilling the barrels and removing wood from the buttstock. My scoped 7600 handles like a dream and weighs less than seven pounds loaded. It's just the ticket for big woods whitetail hunting. Several of my other whitetail rifles have been worked on by Tom Fargnoli of Naples, New York (716-374-2814), who specializes in building custom deer and elk rifles.

When I hunt in country that offers shots out to 300 yards and beyond, I use either a .257 Weatherby Magnum or a .270, both of which are equipped with synthetic stocks. Though it isn't the nicest looking gun I have, the .270 Model 700 Remington bolt action is my pride and joy. It fits me perfectly and the 130 Nosler Ballistic Tip bullets (pushed by 55 grains of IMR 4350 powder) I hand load are extremely accurate and lethal on whitetails. In spite of the recent advancements in factory ammunition, I hand load for all my rifles, including the .30-30. I push the .257 Weatherby's 100 grain bullets with 64 grains of IMR 4350 powder. With a muzzle velocity of over 3,500 feet per second, this load is excellent for open country whitetail hunting. The load I use in the two .30-06s I own is 165 grain bullets pushed by 57 grains of IMR 4350. This load exceeds 2,800 feet per second and is an excellent whitetail load out to 300 yards. After years of use I feel the 165 grain bullet is the best all around .30-06 load and an excellent choice when bigger animals such as bear and moose can also be hunted.

I'm not a long distance shooter, and would not think of shooting at a buck over 300 yards away, unless conditions were perfect. Deer hunting is not woodchuck hunting and prone shooting is seldom possible in the deer woods. For this reason I sight in my rifles to hit an inch-and-one-half to two inches high at 100 yards (it depends on caliber), which makes them dead on at about 200 yards. By sighting in for 200 yards my loads are dead on at 50 yards, an inch high at 175 yards, and approximately six inches low at 300 yards. I sight in for 200 instead of 300 yards because I've hunted whitetails across North America and the average distance of all my rifle kills has been 115 yards. Frankly I've never attempted a shot further than 225 yards as I feel it's too risky under normal hunting conditions.

Fortunately it hasn't happened to me, but I've witnessed some real horror stories with damaged rifles on deer hunts. On more than one occasion I've seen a hunter's rifle stock break or scopes malfunction. For this reason I always carry two rifles when hunting away from home. Murphy with his infamous Murphy's Law seems to always be in the camp I'm in. It never fails. So, I prepare for the worst and hope for the best.

I cut my whitetail teeth hunting with shotguns and rifled slugs. While growing up on the farm I loved to hunt woodchucks with my .222 and .243. Then, when deer season rolled around I'd get depressed because I had to switch to a slug gun. In my formative years I viewed this as a real downer because few shotguns were accurate shooting Foster style slugs. But, no more.

In the last five years slug gun technology has taken a quantum leap. Manufacturers, realizing there are more slug gun hunters than rifle hunters (because of game laws), have rushed to provide more accurate slugs and guns. I currently use a Remington 11/87 deer gun, equipped with a Hastings rifled slug barrel and a 227 power Leupold shotgun scope. This particular gun has no problem grouping three slugs into a two-and-one-half inch hole at seventy yards, which is the distance I zero in my slug guns for. I also occasionally use a Mossburg Model 835 that, like the Remington, groups most sabot slugs very well. Also the 11/87 shoots Winchester's Foster style slugs nearly as well as sabots, which is an added bonus because Foster style slugs are less expensive than sabots. So, with this kind of accuracy I no longer feel handicapped when New York's gun season arrives.

Because shotgun hunting involves foul weather and close quarter encounters with whitetails, my 11/87 is equipped with a synthetic stock and matte finish. The Mossburg 12 gauge has a Realtree finish on a synthetic stock.

In order to make my deer rifles more functional during inclement weather, I do a few extra things. Even though most synthetic stock manufacturers say their stocks don't need extra work, I've had all of my synthetic stocked rifles' actions bedded and the barrels floated by a gunsmith. This improves accuracy immensely. In addition I have all my rifles' triggers adjusted to a three pound trigger pull. This has given me more confidence and made me a much more accurate shooter. And lastly, rifle hunting for whitetails often means cold weather snow hunting (especially in Canada). Because of this more than one hunter has lost a chance at a trophy of a lifetime when a firing pin froze up. For this reason I have all my rifles' triggers and bolts degreased so they will not freeze up in cold weather.

The most important rifle in my arsenal is a .22 Ruger Model 77/22 equipped with a Leupold .22 four power scope. This gun's importance might seem odd but it's the gun I stay sharp with. As deer season approaches I take a few minutes each day (rain or shine) to shoot twenty rounds off hand at a flipper target from a distance of 25 yards. The target has three different size metal circles and when I can consistently hit the three-quarter-inch circle my confidence soars. This gun, with its three pound trigger pull and big game style scope, allows me to fine tune my shooting skills so I'm the best shot I can be by the time the season rolls around. Getting in my daily rounds with the .22 is just as important as daily archery practice prior to bow season.

Archery

Though I grew up with rifles and very much enjoy shooting them, my first love is archery hunting. Simply put, the challenge of hunting whitetails at close quarters with a bow and arrow is what whitetail hunting is all about. To get a white-tailed buck within twenty yards is no easy task and requires that the hunter and equipment be one. Because I strive to become better each season, my choice of archery tackle has changed over the years.

My first bow was a simple forty-five-pound fiberglass recurve. After one fall with it I moved to a Bear recurve and found that could shoot considerably better.

However, it wasn't until I started using a compound that my proficiency increased to where I was consistently killing deer with arrows.

From the standpoint of what is available on the market, my preferences in archery tackle could be construed as pretty basic. Though I occasionally shoot with a release, I do all of my serious deer hunting with fingers (tab or glove). I currently shoot a top-of-the-line Golden Eagle sixty-pound compound equipped with two sight pins. One is set for ten yards and the other for twenty yards. I prefer a wheel compound to a cam because a wheel bow is quieter and easier for me to shoot.

I do not shoot with an overdraw. Currently I'm shooting 31 inch 2216 aluminum arrows topped with 125 grain Satellite Titan heads. This four blade broadhead not only has a large cutting surface but also flies the same as 125 grain target points.

In spite of all the hype and advertising, most bows are pretty much the same when it comes to quality. However, the sound they make when shot is not always the same. A key in successful whitetail hunting is how quiet a bow is when the moment of truth arrives. Whenever I get my hands on a hunting bow I go over it to see where the noises are. After pulling it back a few times and then shooting it, I'm able to determine if there are any noises in the bow's eccentrics. Often, when pulled to full draw, a wheel will squeak. To eliminate the sound I apply unscented Pledge or vegetable oil to the wheel axle or string channel. Some people suggest using a light lubricant such as WD-40. However, I shy away from any petroleum-based lubricant because of its odor.

After silencing the bow's eccentrics I go to work on the arrow rest. Having a silent arrow rest is critical when it comes time to draw on a buck. I cut a piece of rawhide and glue it below and above the arrow rest so that if the arrow falls off the rest it does not hit any metal surface. When it comes to the actual arrow rest there are a number of ways to go. Though metal spring rests are popular with 3-D shooters, I stay away from any metal rest as nothing is louder than the sound of metal to metal coming together. I keep things simple and use a rest compatible with aluminum and carbon arrows. In other words the rest must be dead silent when I pull the arrow back.

Once the arrow rest is taken care of, it's important to make sure the cable guard slide performs in both wet and dry conditions. Most bow manufacturers skimp when it comes to cable guard slides, so it's important to find one that is quiet in all weather conditions. There are several aftermarket slides available and I've had great success using a Townsend speed slide on my bows. If you want to go with the slide that came on your bow, it can be made to slide quietly by spraying silicone on the cable guard to eliminate friction. Also, if you get in a pinch, wipe facial oil off your nose with your fingers and rub this oil on the cable guard. It works quite well.

If precautions are not taken, a lot of noise can be created when an arrow is released from a bow. Due to the shape of cams, the string almost always slaps when an arrow is released, thereby making more noise than wheels. For this reason wheel bows are quieter, which is one of the reasons I shoot a wheel bow. I use two rubber cat whisker silencers to quiet the string. Avoid using fabric puff silencers because they take on moisture when it rains and the added weight slows arrow flight up to five feet per second. Should noise in the bow persist, I opt for a bow stabilizer.

The last step in a bow's noise creation comes when the arrow clears the bow. When this happens vibration is at its peak. To eliminate as much noise as possible, I tighten most screws on the bow and quiver with Loc-Tite to make sure they stay tight no matter how much I shoot. I also make sure the arrows in my quiver are aligned in such a way that the feathers or vanes are not touching. If they do touch, they will rub together during the release, causing unwanted noise.

Though I hunt with arrows fletched with both vanes and feathers, I prefer feathers. To waterpoof feathers and make them perform better, spray them with unscented hair spray. This keeps them from picking up moisture and adding weight to the arrow.

Stands

When I first began deer hunting nearly all of my stand hunting was from permanent wood stands that I built. As I became a better hunter, I realized that permanent stands limited the way I could hunt whitetails, especially mature bucks. For added mobility I purchased my first portable stand (a Baker climber) in the early 1980s. I immediately fell in love with the concept of using a portable stand to put me where the action was hot.

Though I own and occasionally use climbing stands, I shy away from them because they're noisy. A mature buck is cagey and the least little foreign noise will send him into orbit, so I'm noise conscious when I hunt. For this reason I rely on lock-on style stands for the bulk of my hunting. Also, lock-on stands are strong. Though lock-ons have been my stand of choice for the past ten years, I'm starting to use more ladder type stands. Why? Because I'm getting older and safety is an increasing consideration.

When I first began using portable stands, weight was a big factor in considering which stand to use. No more! Today most manufacturers use lightweight aluminum that is strong. The light weight of aluminum stands also allows them to be hung easily. For this reason I choose aluminum over steel stands.

A key feature I look for in a portable stand is platform size. In a cold climate, where I'm typically standing for long periods of time, I insist on a stand with a large platform. Cold temperatures require that you stand a lot in order to stay warm. I do toe raises and all kinds of minimal-movement exercises to keep warm in a stand. The reality of it all is that after three hours in sub-freezing temperatures, one's body starts to do unusual things. Reaction time and eye focus begins to slow. Hand flexibility diminishes. In all, the prospect of losing one's balance is very real. Therefore, it is important to have as big a platform as possible. I look for a platform with at least 576 square inches (24 × 24 inches) of surface area.

In addition to platform size, make sure the stand's seat can be folded up when you stand up, otherwise the seat will continually cut into the back of your legs. Also, I like a seat that is higher than the normal 17-inch seat height. By having a seat at least 20 inches high, you'll be in better position when a buck shows up. And lastly I continually look for a better safety belt. As a result I seem to be using a different one each year to ensure my safety when hunting above the ground.

Clothing

Down through the years I've hunted in about every kind of clothing imaginable, from blue jeans to cotton work coveralls to wool. During the last few years I've discovered that none of my early hunting garments can stack up to what's available today. Probably the greatest advances in hunting (aside from the compound bow) have been in the area of clothing. When I began deer hunting in the sixties, wool was the ticket. But wool became heavy when wet, and trying to dry it was often impossible in a hunting camp. Today synthetics abound and the hunter has an array of clothing options to choose from.

The key to handling deer season's endurance test is dressing right for the occasion. I have several different patterns of camouflage I like to wear during bow season. None of it is waterproof. In order to stay dry and warm, I purchase it large enough to wear over waterproof and warm clothing.

It may seem simplistic but layering is the key to beating inclement weather conditions. The secret to layering your clothing is to trap air between the layers of garments, thereby insulating your body. To keep from perspiring I never head for a stand with all my clothing on my back. Rather, I have a fleece backpack that contains the bulk of the clothing I intend to wear. If I'm bowhunting from a stand, I stop and put on the required clothing when I'm a couple hundred yards from the stand.

Temperature, moisture, and the length of time I intend to sit dictate what I will wear. On cool damp days I wear polypropylene underwear that wicks the moisture away from my body. Polypropylene is an amazing fabric that enables a person to stay dry and warm longer. Generally it comes in three weights: light, medium, and heavyweight. To eliminate bulk I recommend the medium weight polypropylene for general hunting purposes.

Beating the rain often requires good rain gear. As mentioned previously, wool picks up weight in rain. Down clothing is warm and lightweight but worthless once it gets wet. In attempts to come up with a lighter garment many hunters have turned to Gore-Tex to stay dry. The beauty of Gore-Tex is that it is able to breathe so that moisture doesn't build up in the undergarments. When first introduced Gore-Tex was noisy. Now many manufacturers have taken the noise out of Gore-Tex hunting gear by covering it with fleece or wool, allowing the hunter to be quiet in the woods.

During bow season when the temperatures range from 32 to 60 degrees, I layer my clothing to allow for a four-hour sit. If it's in the thirties I'll wear polypropylene underwear and fleece garments under my camouflage. I also recommend a nylon or polypropylene inner sock and a wool outer sock. The inner sock wicks perspiration away from the foot to the outer sock, allowing one's feet to stay warm and dry.

Well over 50 percent of heat loss is through your head. Therefore, I go to great pains to make sure my head is well-covered and warm. My favorite hat for hunting in the rain and snow is a watch cap made of polypropylene and Gore-Tex. It not only keeps my head warm but also dry. They come in various camo patterns and are marketed by the larger catalog outfitters.

Nothing forces a hunter out of the woods faster than cold feet, so keeping the toes warm is a must. During bow season I often wear knee-high rubber boots to hide human odor . . . a carryover from my trapping days. The boots are big enough to slip over my lightweight hunting boots. The socks, hunting boots, and rubber boots work as an excellent layering system and are more than enough to keep my feet warm.

If I'm hunting in extreme cold, I layer my clothing to the hilt. Here's an example of how I dress when hunting in Canada, where the temperatures are often around zero. First I put on lightweight polypropylene underwear. Over this I put on a heavyweight layer of polypropylene underwear. Next I put on a heavy wool shirt (Maine Guide Shirt, sold by L.L. Bean) and a pair of sweatpants. Over this I wear a "dry plus Thinsulate" Cabela's Super Slam camouflage fleece suit. In my pack I carry a fleece warm-up jacket should I need extra warmth. On my feet I wear polypropylene socks next to my skin and a pair of heavy thermal or wool socks over them. My boots are L.L. Bean cold weather packs with wool liners. I also make sure that I have extra dry liners so I can put a dry set in the boots each day. Though I carry disposable air-activated hand and body warmers, I use them only on rare occasions.

From an equipment standpoint I rely heavily on three other things. First, when gun hunting from stands in cold weather I use a sleeping bag. Actually it's a bag I've modified for deer hunting and is just the ticket for staying warm in temperatures below 35 degrees. I've been using this technique for a few years and in the last two years have killed seven whitetails while sitting in the cozy confines of the bag.

Over the last few years I've refined the way I use a bag to make it more efficient and less awkward. It's critical that a sleeping bag be quiet when used for hunting. As a result an inexpensive cotton bag is the best. Because most cotton-lined bags have a nylon outer shell, I advise hunters to turn the bag inside out so the cotton inner liner is on the outside. Doing this keeps things quiet, should the bag rub on the stand platform or the edge of the stand.

If you want to modify the bag you can do a couple of things to make the concept even better. I've purchased fleece material and had an upholsterer sew the fleece on the nylon side of the bag. Doing this makes the bag super quiet on both sides so that I can keep the cotton side inside the bag where it belongs. Also I have two two-inch elastic bands sewn on the open end of the bag so they can go over my shoulders (like suspenders) after I get into the bag. This keeps the bag from falling down.

Lastly I have a sixteen-inch slit sewn into the non-zippered side of the bag. The slit allows me to get my arm out of the bag quickly when something shows up. The other side of the bag has the zipper so a slit isn't needed. By sliding into the bag (with all my clothes and boots on) and pulling it up to my shoulders, I'm able to stay warm as toast in temperatures near zero. It is the ultimate in layering.

Based on experience there are two cautionary notes that need to be stressed when using a sleeping bag. First, if you are hunting from a tree stand, a good safety belt must be used. When you are in a sleeping bag, mobility is limited and it is easy to lose your balance if you aren't careful. Secondly, because of the bag's bulkiness, this technique is not well suited to bowhunting unless the bag comes no higher than your waist. To keep the bag from taking on a mildew smell, I open it up and hang it to dry each night. Once you try a bag you'll undoubtedly ask the same question I did: "Why didn't I do this before?"

Because of the amount of equipment I carry (camera, small tripod, drag rope, etc.) I use a small specialized day pack. The pack I use is called a BackSeat and is tailor-made for my needs. Not only is it compact but it also has a collapsible seat that doubles as a packframe.

One of the last things I want to mention is the cover-up scent I use. In order to consistently kill whitetails you have to beat their noses. Let's face it, in spite of all the best laid plans wind currents often change, so controlling body odors, keeping clothing clean, and using a good cover-up is essential. Though there are many good ones on the market, I've been using Essence of Fall since it came out and am amazed by how well it works. I spray it on all my gear to kill human odor and it works great on the sleeping bag, keeping it free from mildew odor. It's a part of all my hunts.

Because a person exhales over 250 liters of breath into the air each hour I go out of my way to cover up mouth odor. There are two ways a hunter can keep a whitetail from detecting breath odors. One way is to chew a chlorophyll gum, like Golden Eagle Archery's Breath Away gum. The other way is to carry an apple in your pocket and periodically break a chunk of it off and suck on it while on stand. Apples are known as "nature's toothbrush" and take away bad breath.

Part Eight
Shots at Whitetails

How to Meet Whitetail Hunting's
Most Unforgiving Moment!

You blew it! You missed! You can't believe it, but he's gone. You'll see that white flag waving back at you in your nightmares for months to come. One shot in two years' hunting, and now he's gone!

How much does it hurt? Trust me: You don't want to know.

Even though missing a shot eventually happens to everybody, you'll feel better about it knowing you had studied up on the subject and that you were well-armed and ready.

You won't feel much better, but even a little bit will help!

38 Let's Talk Sense About Deer Rifles!

BY JON SUNDRA

Debates over which rifles and cartridges are best for whitetail hunting will never be completely settled. Jon Sundra's opinions, however, will go a long way toward helping you make up your own mind.

Picture in your mind's eye a gun rack containing the following: a Marlin 336 lever action .30-30, a Remington Model Seven in .260 Rem., a Browning BAR in .30-06, a Remington 7600 slide action in .308 Win., a Winchester Model 70 Classic Laredo in 7mm STW and a Ruger No. 1 in .300 Wea. Magnum. A pretty eclectic mix of rifle types and calibers to be sure, yet all would qualify as terrific "deer rifles" under certain circumstances. And under certain other circumstances, any one of 'em could make a miserable deer rifle. Like the man says, "It all depends."

Maybe I shouldn't be pointing this out, but of all the various topics there are to write about, my colleagues and I get the most mileage by presuming to prescribe the "right" guns and calibers for a given hunting situation. Most of us, however—and I do it as often as anyone—fail to mention that the terrain doesn't always have to dictate hunting method, rifle and caliber choice. The facts are that the man behind the gun has a great deal to say about hunting tactics and the kind of shooting that's likely to be required. With that in mind, let's now take a closer look at those guns in our rack and see under what deer-hunting scenarios each would excel . . . and suck.

First available in commercially loaded form in 1948, the .300 would be followed by the .375 and .340, all three based on full-length H&H cases blown out to minimum body taper with shortened necks and venturified shoulders.

The first conventional-shouldered equivalent would not appear until 1976 when Remington unveiled its 8mm Re. Mag. This same case would eventually serve as the hull for the .416 Rem. Mag. and the 7mm STW. All three are of true magnum length and differ only in the neck and shoulder dimensions that change as a result of the case being necked up or down. Other than that, we're talking an identical case that will hold approximately 92.0 grs. of water when measured to the base of the neck.

What we have, then, are four distinct families of belted magnums based on the Holland & Holland case of 1912: There's the Remington 6.5/.350 family at

63 grs.; the Winchester short-magnum family at about 82 grs.; the original .300/375 H&H at 87 grs.; and the .300 Wea./8mm Rem. at 92 grs.

There's always one bastard in the bunch to foul up what would otherwise be the orderly categorization, just described, and in this instance it's the .300 Win. Mag. Though based upon the H&H case like all the others, the .300 Win. is based on a hull that measures some .120 longer than the nominal 2.5″length of a .264 or 7mm Rem. As such, its body, hence powder capacity, is commensurately greater, but it is still commercially loaded to an overall length that is the same as the others and will therefore cycle through standard-length actions.

Again for the sake of historical accuracy, I should also mention that there are three other commercial cartridges that belong to this long list of H&H progeny— cartridges that achieved a modest degree of success before the Winchester short magnums appeared. I'm talking about the .308 and .358 Norma Magnums, and the 7 × 61 Sharpe & Hart, all of which were loaded by Norma of Sweden.

That about brings us up to date. As for the future of the belted case, it looks pretty grim. I don't believe we'll ever see the introduction of another commercial cartridge based on the H&H case; it has had its time in the sun. Today's thinking is that the belt is an inferior method of headspacing compared to the head-to-shoulder system used for non-belted cases. From the handloading standpoint it is useless; indeed, knowledgeable handloaders adjust their sizing dies so that cases will headspace on the shoulder as determined by the individual chamber. Also, the belt easily takes on burrs which can cause sticky chambering; there's no such problems with rimless cases.

Today's new crop of commercial magnum cartridges reflect the foregoing facts. Whether based on the .404 Jeffery, .416 Rigby, or unique head sizes like the Lazzeroni family of cartridges, all share the common characteristic of no belt. And I don't look for that to change. This new crop of super-performance cartridges, however, is a story in itself that we'll have to save for another time.

For the first half of this century, the Marlin 336, along with its spiritual twin, the Winchester Model 94, personified the term "deer rifle." As for the .30-30 cartridge, well, it's become so synonymous with the lever action rifle that we almost assume the two must go together by law. Today this 104-year-old cartridge is no longer "fashionable," but it, along with other lever action calibers like the .32 Spl., .38-55 and .35 Rem., are as good at harvesting deer as they ever were. Nothing's changed really, other than the mind set of typical hunters living in those regions where these guns once reigned supreme. Where once sportsmen used to think only in terms of local deer hunting, today they think on a broader scale. Few hunters today buy a rifle with the idea that deer is the only big game they're ever going to hunt. "One of these years I'd like to go out west on an antelope (or mule deer or elk) hunt. If it happens, I'll need more gun than a lever action .30-30."

Such was the reasoning behind so many eastern whitetail hunters opting for bolt action .270's, .30-06's, even 7mm and .300 magnums. It wasn't that they felt they needed such guns for regional deer hunting, but when you can get so much more power and reach for virtually the same investment, plus having a rifle they know will serve them well for just about any hunting they're likely to do in their lifetime, why not?

The fact remains, however, that so long as one doesn't expect too much of the traditional lever action rifle, it will get the job done as well as always. By "asking too much" I mean purposely putting yourself in a situation where the shooting can be longer than, say, 125 yards. If truth be told, probably 90 percent of all whitetail deer taken east of the Mississippi are shot under that range. Think about that for a moment.

Experiences and Observations

On any number of occasions I've hunted whitetail in places like Pennsylvania, New York, Michigan, South Carolina, Maine, Quebec and New Brunswick where the brush and timber were so thick that 75 yards would have been considered a long shot. And let's face it: Come opening morning and the hunting pressure's on, that's where the deer are—the big bucks anyway. It's here that the shooting is close, fast and offhand . . . and usually at a running animal. Under those circumstances, an iron-sighted lever action .30-30 is probably as effective a deer harvester as any other rifle type and caliber . . . and better than most.

Which brings to mind a story. Back when I was a lot younger I thought I knew a thing or two about guns, and wasn't hesitant about proving it at the slightest provocation. Anyway, as a guest in a Pennsylvania deer camp one season I was introduced to an old gent everyone called "Pop." Now Pop owned one of the raunchiest-looking guns I've ever seen outside of Africa. It was a Marlin lever action in .35 Rem. wearing an aperture sight. The only bluing visible was a thin strip on the underside of the barrel between it and the tubular magazine. A patina of powdered rust accented the otherwise dull gray of bare metal with splotches of brown. The stock looked like it had been used as a spool for barbed wire, and exposed wood screw heads indicated that it had cracked in the wrist.

Thank goodness it wasn't I who chided the old guy about his sorry-looking rifle, but it wasn't because I didn't want to. Another kid in camp, even younger and dumber than I, beat me to it. I think he was a relative and therefore felt he could get away with it.

"See this here box of ammo," Pop asked, shoving it in the kid's face and shaking it for emphasis. "It's got five rounds left in it. With the 15 that ain't here, I got me 11 bucks in as many years. The other four were fired at paper to check my sights."

I often think about that incident whenever I find myself disparaging "old-fashioned" guns and cartridges. Can you imagine telling Pop his deer rifle wasn't "modern" enough or was lacking in performance?

At the opposite end of the spectrum from Pop's traditional lever action we find the "beanfield rifle." Representing this newest genre among rifle types in our gun rack is the Winchester Model 70 Classic Laredo in 7mm STW. With a big 4-14× or 6-18× variable aboard, this gun would look awfully silly in a whitetail stand where you couldn't see beyond 50 yards in any direction. But take that same rifle and put it in a treestand at the edge of a bean field that stretches for 500 yards, or on a power line right-of-way, or on one Arizona mountain where you're glassing for Coues deer on another, and suddenly our 11-1/2 lb., 46″Laredo becomes the best of all possible choices.

What under most other deer-hunting scenarios would be considered an excessively long, heavy rifle, and a needlessly powerful cartridge and scope is precisely what you need if you want to maximize your chances of hitting that 10″vital zone under field conditions from 400 yards or more. Rarely does one have a rifle rest that is as steady as a concrete bench and sandbags, so the added weight and the accuracy edge a heavy gun provides simply adds a few more chips to your stack when the time comes to take the shot.

Let's now turn our attention to the Browning BAR in .30-06. Actually, the BAR represents a category of rifles into which we can include another resident of our gun rack, the Remington 7600 slide action. These guns and the relatively few others we can put in the same category—the Remington 7400 semi-auto, the Browning BLR and BPR, the Savage 99—may be first seem a lot different from one another, but they share a common distinction: They are not the kind of guns gun cranks buy. They are, however, the kind of rifles deer hunters buy. By that I mean simply this: If my primary goal was to put venison in the freezer rather than a braggin' buck on the wall, something from the aforementioned category would probably be my choice.

Any time a snap shot at running game is likely—such as in still-hunting (stalking), or as part of an organized drive—all you have to do before pulling the trigger is to determine that it's a legal deer you've got in your sights. Once that's confirmed, any of these guns will get off a quick follow-up shot . . . and a third and fourth if needed, as fast as you're capable of aiming 'em.

Trophy Hunting and Other Options

If, on the other hand, one is strictly a trophy hunter, firepower is of little concern, because evaluating the quality of the head comes first. In fact, most trophy hunters are incapable of making a swift decision about a shot. They're more concerned about using up their tag on an animal they didn't want to shoot than they are pulling the trigger at all. It often happens that while evaluating a head and listening to the guide's opinion as to your chances of finding a better one in the time you have remaining, that you blow the only chance you have. But then that's trophy hunting, and that's why today's typical trophy hunter is rarely seen shooting anything but a bolt gun or a single shot.

It's unfortunate that we gun cranks look down our noses at lever guns, slide actions and semi-autos. Hell, I often find myself referring to other guns as "contraptions." After all, other than their ability to spit lead faster, there is little about these guns to tweak our aesthetic sensibilities. Let's face it, you don't dote over a pump, lever or semi-auto; you don't customize 'em in any way—re-stock 'em, rechamber 'em, rebarrel 'em or fit 'em with after-market accessories. (There are no after-market accessories for such guns!) Nor do we spend hundreds of hours at the range and loading bench searching for the component recipe that will produce one-hole groups. And there's nothing elegant or refined about such rifles—no pedigrees born of competition or a legacy of custom gun-making traditions.

The fact of the matter is that these are the pickup trucks of the rifle world. Yet for all the things they are not, when it comes to putting a deer down for the count anywhere from the muzzle out to 250 or more yards under any conceivable field conditions, these "contraptions" get the job done as well as any other rifle type, and better in situations where a running shot is needed. And let's face it: Doesn't that take in about 95 percent of all deer taken in North America each year, east and west?

The Single-Shot Option

On the other side of the firepower spectrum we find our Ruger No. 1. Here's a gun type not generally thought of as a "deer rifle," but again, if it does the job, who's to say it isn't? So long as you dismiss entirely any thoughts of running shots, I can't think of a single deer-hunting situation where a single-shot like any of the several permutations of Ruger No. 1, Browning Model 1885 or Dakota Model 10 couldn't do a great job. Not only are these guns handier by virtue of their being about 4″shorter on average than a bolt rifle sporting the same length barrel, they can be just as accurate. They are also chambered for today's most potent, long-range calibers such as the .25-06; the .270, 7mm and .300 Weatherby Magnums; the 7mm Rem. and .300 Win. Magnums and the 7mm and .300 Dakotas. In fact, a single-shot can be just as good a beanfield rifle as . . . well, a beanfield rifle.

And it's not like you're absolutely limited to one shot. With a little practice and a spare round handy—like under an elastic band on your offhand wrist—you can get an aimed second shot off in less than five seconds. I wouldn't say that's putting oneself at any great disadvantage, would you? There's also the added satisfaction—a certain panache, if you will, to hunting and taking a trophy with a one-shooter. It's a way of telling the world that putting meat on the table is not your top priority.

Grabbing our Remington Model Seven now, if there's one rifle type in our gun rack that has supplanted the classic lever gun as being the quintessential 21st century deer rifle, this is it. Of course all the other gun makers offer their equivalent versions of the Model Seven, i.e., slender barreled carbines based on short actions and trimmed-down stocks of wood or fiberglass. But it was Remington that truly defined the genre by taking it a step further than everyone else. Instead of simply using the short version of their standard bolt action like everyone else, they built this carbine around the even shorter, lighter receiver of the XP-100 pistol, then designed a new and lighter trigger guard/floorplate unit to boot. The result is the lightest, shortest barreled action of any major manufacturer.

Like I said though, everyone offers a similar model(s)—Winchester, Browning, Savage, and Ruger, all characterized by short, slender barrels of 20″or less and weighing between 5-3/4 and 6-3/4 lbs. All are chambered exclusively for the various .308 Win. family of cartridges—the .243 Win., .260 Rem., 7mm-08 Rem.

and .358 Win., as well as the .308 itself. In more open terrain and where one chooses to set up a stand that can require long-range shooting, the .243, .260 and 7mm-08 are the better choices. For the heavier cover one finds in still-hunting and for organized drives where shots are apt to be close and at running game, the .308 and .358 would be better suited. In any case, these carbines are lighter than any traditional lever gun and far more capable ballistically.

When you consider all the attributes of the bolt action carbine and the fact that it can easily handle all but the most specialized requirements, it's easy to see why so many eastern deer-only hunters are turning to these light, handy guns.

Bolt Action Sporter

Now we come to the one gun type that isn't represented in our rack, yet is the most common of all: the bolt action sporter. Here we're talking a gun with a 22″or 24″barrel of medium contour in standard chamberings, and 24″or 26″in magnum chamberings. Depending on barrel length, contour and type of stock, these guns will average between 7¼ to 7¾ lbs. sans scope and mounts. As for calibers, virtually any chambering can be had, though for deer hunting a .300 magnum would be a sensible limit even for long-range western hunting.

Fitted with what has almost become the mandatory variable scope, the bolt action sporter in chamberings like the .270 Win., .280 Rem., 7mm Rem. Mag. or .300 Win. Mag. have long since become the standard for western mule deer hunting, yet they're not that out of place in whitetail turf, either, or for that matter, hunting any other critter North America has to offer.

Despite the fact that hunting rifles are becoming more and more specialized, it's hard to say no to the kind of versatility the plain ol' workhorse sporter provides. It may not do anything perfectly, but it does so many things so well that you and I will never see the day when its status as the most popular rifle is threatened. And that goes for deer hunting as well as anything else.

39 Shotgun Slug Savvy

BY WAYNE VAN ZWOLL

Understanding how slugs perform is the key to choosing the right one for your hunt.

It was 1963, and coming up on deer season. In southern Michigan, deer hunters couldn't use rifles (and still can't). Shotguns were safer where farms were small and cattle grazed between the woodlots. The most coveted guns among farm boys back then were Ithaca's Model 37 Deerslayer pump and Browning's Auto 5 Buck Special. Both came with short, cylinder-bore barrels and iron sights. They were costly, so most youngsters carried the same cheap shotguns they used on pheasants. You had to take a fine bead with a bird barrel, otherwise the slug would hit high at 50 to 75 yards—where a lot of the deer were shot.

Some remarkable shooting was done with the worn pumps and autoloaders pulled from mud-room racks in Michigan's rural hinterlands come deer season. One farmer I know killed a buck at 147 paces offhand with his 16-gauge Remington 11-48.

In this enlightened time, we might not feel justified launching shotgun slugs at deer that far away. But there's no question that the lumbering Foster slug in a 12- or 16-bore repeater could reap venison. Developed in the early 1930s by Winchester ballistician Karl Foster, the slug that bears his name consists of soft lead and features side ribs that mash down easily as the slug passes through the barrel's choke constriction. The heavy nose and hollow base allow it to fly accurately for short distances, and the hollow base permits the slug to expand upon firing to fill the bore.

Back then, the only other slug available to hunters was the Brenneke. It was developed in Europe in the late 19th century, but it didn't arrive on our shores until after World War II. It has ribs like the Foster, but the wad is screwed onto it and there's no hollow base.

Ironically, most deer-load development in my growing-up years was aimed at increasing the effectiveness of buckshot. It wasn't until the 1980s, with the advent of rifled shotgun barrels and specialized scopes, that slugs began to attract more attention. While Foster slugs still account for 60 percent of all slugs sold, the real news in slug technology today is the sabot (pronounced *saybo*). A projectile within a projectile, sabot slugs are smaller than the bore; they're housed in bore-diameter capsules that fall away upon leaving the muzzle.

The advantage to the sabot is that the slug itself can be just about any shape, and it can be made lighter because it is the housing that fills up the bore. Less weight means faster, flatter flight. Now, you may not care about long shooting. Maybe you want all the weight you can get for close shots in thickets. Sabots that weigh as much as Foster slugs are the answer. They penetrate better because they're skinnier and have a higher sectional density.

The sabot's main advantage, though, is that plastic capsule. You can fire it in rifled barrels that spin it for better accuracy. You can't shoot a hard lead or jacketed slug in thin-walled rifled shotgun barrels at high speed because the friction could cause too much pressure. Soft lead would strip. With sabots, there's no mark on slug or bullet.

Some sabot slugs are actually bullets. Nosler's pistol bullet for the .454 Casull goes into Winchester's newest shotgun sabot loads, and it has proved to be a real winner.

The shift to sabot ammunition began when California-based Ballistics Research Institute (BRI) developed an hourglass-shaped slug in a two-piece plastic sleeve split along its length. Originally designed for police use, by the mid-1980s it had been packaged for deer hunters. I remember shooting prototype rounds through a Benelli autoloader with a rifled barrel, and coming up with a one-hole group at 50 yards. I was impressed, and so were folks at Winchester, which later bought BRI. Federal followed with its own hourglass slug.

What kept the sabot from burying the Foster slug? Well, the Foster shot as accurately or even more accurately in smoothbore barrels. It flattened readily in deer, opening a bigger wound channel than the slender sabot slugs. Not every shotgun could be fitted with a rifled barrel. And a lot of casual hunters chose not to spend the money for a new tube. Besides, sabot slug ammo costs considerably more than shells loaded with Foster slugs.

In 1993, a small New Jersey firm developed the Lightfield Hybrid sabot, an almost-bore-diameter slug in a thin-walled, two-piece capsule. Designed by Tony Kinchen, the Lightfield expanded readily and proved deadly on deer-size game. Like the Brenneke Magnum, this slug had an attached wad. Meanwhile, another New Jersey shop, Gun Servicing, continued its experiments with .45-caliber pistol bullets (300-grain Hornadys) in a 12-gauge sabot cup.

That same year, Remington introduced the first commercially successful bullet-shaped slug: the 50-caliber Copper Solid. It had a notched, hollow nose to initiate expansion, but the light body of a whitetail deer wasn't enough to cause upset. So Remington revamped the slug by using softer metal.

By then Barnes had unveiled its Expander MZ bullet, developed for muzzleloaders but soon added to the slug market. Federal adopted this 50-bore solid copper hollowpoint for its Premium slug ammunition in 1997. That was the year Hornady shouldered its way into the slug market with a sabot design. Hornady's new 300-grain .486 H2K Heavy Mag appeared just last year.

The turn of the millennium brought a new Brenneke sabot slug into the PMC lineup. This Nevada firm loads the 1-ounce slug to 1,600 fps. Winchester earned the spotlight about the same time, with a 385-grain Partition Gold hollowpoint bullet pushed from a 12-bore shotgun at 1,900 fps. The Nosler bullet delivers more than 1½ tons of energy at the muzzle, and at 200 yards it still has 1,500 ft.-lbs. more than a .243 Win., 6.5×55 or a .300 Savage.

Of course, ballistic performance depends not only on slug design but also on its weight and the load in the shell. When I was young, only 12- and 16-gauge shotshells were thought suitable for deer. The 20 (then only a 2¾-inch shell) drove a slug as fast as a 12 (to 1,600 fps), but a lower ballistic coefficient resulted in quicker deceleration with an attendant loss in energy.

At 100 yards, where a 1-ounce 12-gauge Foster slug still carried 1,255 ft.-lbs. of energy, the 20-bore slug managed only 835. The 12 at 100 yards hit like a .30-30 bullet at 125 yards, while the 20-gauge at 100 yards mustered only the snap of a .30-30 at 250. However, some of today's 20-bore slug loads do a fair bit better.

Chart Lessons

The accompanying chart shows some useful information. First, the most sophisticated sabot slugs do not deliver the meanest punch up close. A 1¼-ounce Foster slug from a 3-inch 12-bore shell generates 1½ tons of smash at the muzzle—40 percent more than the 3-inch Barnes sabot load. Second, there isn't a lot of difference in muzzle velocity across gauges and slug weights. With a few exceptions, slugs leave the gate at 1,400 to 1,680 fps, most between 1,450 and 1,600. Differences in slug weight among gauges translate to energy differences downrange.

Notice too that for all its machismo at the muzzle, the Foster slug gets tired in a hurry. In fact, that powerful 1¼-ounce magnum 12-bore load can't match the Barnes sabot for energy at 100 yards. Over the length of a football field it loses 470 fps to the Barnes' 255, giving up all of its 850 ft.-lbs. of initial advantage. The Hydra-Shok (hourglass) sabot slugs can't maintain speed like the Barnes, but they don't decelerate as fast as Foster slugs either.

It's worth noting that the plain 2¾-inch 20-gauge Foster load outperforms the newer Hydra-Shok sabot in the 3-inch 20-gauge hull, even at 100 yards. Why would anyone pick the sabot? Better accuracy from a rifled barrel, perhaps.

Among slug types, the trajectory of the Barnes bullet is the flattest. Zeroed at 100 yards, it flies roughly two inches high at 50 and three inches low at 125. Hydra-Shok slugs are half an inch higher at mid-range and strike almost an inch lower at 125 steps.

Foster slugs don't warrant a 100-yard zero because they would climb too high between 50 and 70 yards; better to zero closer when shooting Foster slugs. A 50-yard zero will keep you within two vertical inches of your aim out to 75 yards. At 100 yards those slugs will land about five inches low. If the gun shoots Fosters accurately, it makes more sense to zero a little farther out—say 70 yards. That way you'll be able to hold center on a deer's ribs to 100 yards and be sure of a solid hit. Beyond that, shot placement becomes a problem.

Killing Power

How much energy is needed for a quick kill? Not as much as you might think. Slugs kill by destroying vital tissue. The more you destroy, the quicker the deer will expire. The main thing is to put that slug where it will do the most damage to the vitals. Dumping a ton of energy in the wrong place can leave you with only a blood trail. A 20-gauge slug sending 700 ft.-lbs. through a deer's lungs will quickly turn out the lights.

Some hunters assume big, heavy slugs will hit like a cement truck, throwing a deer to the ground. That can happen when you shatter bone structure that supports the deer, or destroy its spine. In my experience, a lightweight, high-speed expanding bullet from a .243 gives more dramatic results than a 12-gauge slug. One deer I shot through both lungs with a 16-gauge Foster slug showed almost no reaction. It ran off as if unhurt. I followed and found it dead within 60 yards.

Other hunters have told me they've seen deer drop as if flung down by the impact of a big slug. Soft slugs that flatten and stay inside the animal can give quicker results. Because whitetailed deer do not require a deep-penetrating slug, I prefer sabots that expand readily. Foster slugs don't have to expand to plow a big channel; they're still a great choice for close shooting.

Foster slug accuracy from smoothbore barrels can vary a great deal. The notion that open chokes yield better accuracy than tight chokes makes sense, but individual guns don't always follow this rule. I cut the full choke off my Remington 870 16 gauge years ago and mounted a scope. My expectations for rifle-like groups were unfulfilled. At 80 yards the gun would keep Foster slugs inside a six-inch circle—but it had shot almost that well with the choked barrel.

Rifled barrels and sabot ammunition deliver better—and more uniform—results. Most barrels are rifled one twist in 24 inches to 1:34. Fixed-barrel bolt-action shotguns can be expected to outshoot pumps and autoloaders with lightweight, interchangeable barrels. However, I prefer pumps and autoloaders to the bolt-action shotguns, which seem a bit unwieldy. It matters not to me whether a shotgun punches three-minute groups or makes all the slugs jump through one hole because I'm not going to use a shotgun at long range. While bullets from sabot loads can be deadly at 200 yards and even a bit farther, slugs are at their best in the thickets, where ranges are measured in feet, not furlongs.

A lot has been said about shotgun slugs driving undeflected through thickets that would turn a Panzer. My tests with 12-gauge Foster slugs showed deflection to be less than that of rifle bullets commonly used for deer. But thick screens of brush still turned the slugs. Holes in the targets showed that some also flattened and otherwise deformed. Tipping was evident, too. So while big, heavy projectiles are less susceptible to deflection than small, lightweight bullets, you can't shoot confidently through dense brush or tree limbs. If the slug deflects, a crippling hit may result.

Slugs have certainly come a long way since I was a young hunter. With today's variety of accurate guns and efficient loads, no shotgun-toting deer hunter should feel like he's handicapped.

40 Drop Them in
Their Tracks!

BY RICHARD P. SMITH

By aiming for the **"magic spot,"** *you can put deer down where they're standing.*

On some cold, crisp fall mornings, the origin of sounds that come to the ears of waiting whitetail hunters can be deceiving. One such morning I was posted along the edge of a thick patch of evergreens bordering a stand of hardwoods when I heard heavy footsteps in the leaves. I thought they were being made by another hunter, so I looked to the hardwoods, expecting to catch a glimpse of orange.

I saw nothing, but the footsteps continued.

Once I turned my head, it sounded like the noise was coming from the opposite direction, among the evergreens. I swiveled my head back toward the spruces, and my eyes immediately focused on movement. A buck with a decent rack was approaching.

Through the scope on my .30-06, I watched the deer angling from right to left no more than 25 yards away. I was concerned that the buck would detect me at any moment, so I decided to take the first good shot I had.

I typically try to shoot deer behind the shoulder, taking out their lungs, but I couldn't be that choosy this time. I put the crosshairs on a small opening the buck was about to enter, and when they fell on the buck's left shoulder blade I pulled the trigger.

To my surprise, the buck dropped instantly. At the time I thought I had made a lucky shot. It wasn't until years later that I learned that any whitetail can be dropped in its tracks with a hit high on the shoulder, provided you're using an adequate caliber-bullet combination.

I dropped that eight-pointer with a 150-grain pointed softpoint Remington bullet. I've had good results with that bullet out of my .30-06, which is all I shoot.

For many years when I saw a deer I wanted, I normally took the first killing shot I was offered, as I did on that eight-point. You learn to do that when hunting in the woods because shot opportunities can be few and far between. A buck that is in front of you one minute acting carefree can be gone the next, heading for another county without a clue about what spooked him. Hunters who wait for a perfect shot may have to wait a long time.

I experienced enough "lucky shots" on whitetails through the years that a pattern started to develop. For example, one year I was scrape-hunting on the afternoon of November 21 when a big buck chased a doe into view. The doe went through an opening in the brush, and I had my scope covering that spot when the buck followed her. A bullet to his left shoulder ended his life faster than it takes to tell about it.

It was fellow Michigan deer hunter Jack Eddy, of Owosso, who helped me recognize the value of always trying for hits like I made on those bucks to drop them in their tracks. I had accumulated enough similar experiences before talking to Eddy to reinforce what he told me. His advice made sense and was based on a lifetime of successful whitetail hunts.

"If you shot your deer in the right place by accident, remember how you did it and do it from now on," Eddy wrote me a letter. "If it was by choice, welcome to the club! You will never have to follow up on any whitetails you shoot in the 'magic spot!'

"My last 57 bucks have all been shot in this spot, and all of them dropped where they stood, except three that were running. Those three all pulled their legs up under them and somersaulted along the ground for some distance, but never moved again.

"The magic spot, as I call it, is located about four inches below the top of the back on whitetails and directly above the center of the shoulder, horizontally. That's where the top of the lungs are. The backbone also dips down in this area before joining the neck. It's the center of the nervous system. When you hit any deer there, everything stops.

"The shot was introduced to me by Conservation Officer Clarence Roberts, of Grayling, in 1950. I have used the shot since that time and have never had a deer get out of sight before collapsing. Most went down in their tracks."

When you think about it, it's not surprising that whitetails seldom go anywhere when hit in the magic spot. A hit in this location will potentially break one or both shoulders and the spine in addition to taking out the lungs. A broadside shot offers the best opportunity to maximize damage from a hit in this location, but Eddy said that angling shots can be just as effective.

On deer that are either angling toward you or away, try to visualize the magic spot on the opposite shoulder and aim for that. Most hunters try to angle their shots through the center of the chest cavity on deer that are facing at an angle. Eddy's recommendation is to aim for the upper chest rather than the center.

Some hunters don't like shoulder shots on broadside animals because they claim such hits ruin a lot of meat. However, this doesn't happen when connecting on the magic spot, according to Eddy. A properly placed bullet connects on the upper portion of the shoulder blade. The bone is thinnest there, and that's also where there's the least amount of meat. Eddy said that there is only about a half-inch of meat on the upper shoulder.

And there's plenty of margin for error if a hunter's aim is a little off. A hit on the high side will break the back. If a bullet strikes up to a few inches to the left, right or low, it will still enter the chest cavity, causing a fatal wound.

Always be ready for a follow-up shot on big game that drops instantly on the chance that they are only stunned or simply have a broken back. Shots that graze the spine can drop deer just as quickly, but they will soon recover from the shock and leave when they regain their feet. Your job is to not let that happen. An insurance shot is highly recommended, especially if the animal shows any signs of life. I've heard plenty of sad tales about whitetails that were only stunned that lay motionless for minutes before they recovered and caught the unlucky hunters by surprise.

Never let your guard down on a deer that drops like a ton of bricks until you are absolutely positive it is dead! If it doesn't move, check for breathing or eye movement. The eyes on animals that are dead are wide open and glassy.

The objective of all deer hunters should be to make clean kills that are instantly fatal, and the shot discussed here is one of the best ways to do that. There are other considerations that can be important when it comes to putting animals down in their tracks, too. In crowded deer woods, for example, dropping a whitetail where it's standing can reduce the chances of the animal being claimed by another hunter if it runs off. When hunting near private property you don't have access to, it can be important to drop game quickly so it doesn't cross property lines.

Any time a whitetail you've shot runs out of your sight, recovery can become difficult due to any number of variables. It could fall off a cliff or die in a river or lake. Failing light may delay recovery long enough for a bear, wolves or coyotes to claim your prize or heavy rain to wash away the blood trail.

When bucks aren't dropped in their tracks, they can break—or even lose—their racks trying to escape. That happened to me on one of my biggest whitetails. It was an 11-pointer that ended up with an official score of 148-6/8. He would have netted at least 150 if he hadn't broken one of his tines after I shot him.

The buck was broadside, moving from right to left at a fast walk when I saw him. I picked him up in my scope as quickly as possible and put the crosshairs behind his shoulder for the shot. The buck took off in high gear when my bullet connected, and seconds later I heard the unmistakable sound of his antlers slamming into trees as he started losing control.

Not all rifles and loads are recommended for use on the magic spot, especially on broadside shots. Most rifles that are at least .30 caliber shooting softpoint bullets that weigh at least 150 grains will do the job. One exception that Eddy mentioned is the .30-30 with 150-grain bullets. He added, however, that 170-grain bullets from a .30-30 will have the desired effect.

Some popular big-game calibers besides the .30-06 and .30-30 that are recommended include the .308, the 7mm Magnum, the .300 magnums and the .338. Eddy has had excellent results with 150-grain bullets out of his scoped .270, and the .280 should work just as well. Eddy uses his .270 when hunting from a stand and used to carry an iron-sighted .35-caliber pump rifle with 200-grain Remington bullets when stillhunting.

Shotgun slugs that are at least 20 gauge also have the desired effect. Eddy has successfully used a 12-gauge with Brenneke slugs. Heavy bullets out of .50- or .54-caliber muzzleloaders being pushed by 100 to 110 grains of powder should also get the job done.

Although the 150-grain bullets I've used in my .30-06 have worked perfectly on deer, some hunters may prefer heavier bullets like 180s. They are more likely to produce better penetration after breaking through the heavy shoulder blade.

Light, fast bullets in calibers smaller than .270 are simply not meant to bust through heavy bone, and that's why they shouldn't be used on the magic spot for broadside deer. On deer that are angling, however, when a bullet doesn't have to bust through the shoulder blade before entering the chest cavity, smaller-caliber rifles like the .243, 6mm and .25-06 can be used. They will also work on whitetails or muleys facing directly at you. When offered this type of shot, Eddy recommends aiming two inches below the white throat patch—a spot that's on a line with the top of the chest cavity.

After talking to Eddy about dropping deer in their tracks, I've concentrated on aiming for the magic spot. I've shot three more deer there, each of which dropped in its tracks. This method can work for you, too.

Editor's Note: When hunters don't connect on the magic spot and big game runs out of sight, Richard P. Smith has plenty of advice on following up in his book Tracking Wounded Deer. Copies are available for $19.50 from Smith Publications, 814 Clark St., Marquette, MI 49855.

41   How to Get Your Scope on Target!

BY WAYNE VAN ZWOLL

*Step-by-step, we'll walk you through everything you need
to get your scope on your rifle—and on target!*

There's more to attaching a scope to a rifle than many shooters think," he told me, as if missing a buck had something to do with the sight. "Lots of scopes are put on wrong. Lots are put on right but paid no mind after the ring screws are snug." He gave the screwdriver a twist. "These weren't. 'Course"—and he caught my eye—"that doesn't mean the scope was off." I must have turned red, for he added kindly, "Probably was, though."

The old gunsmith told me to remember that scopes help you most when you set them up properly.

I have remembered!

The first step is finding the right mount. Manufacturers make it easy, with bases to match most rifles. You needn't drill and tap as was the case when rifles were made for shooting with iron sights only. But you're still smart to consider enlarging the standard 6–48 holes to 8–40, and reaming base holes to match. Reasons: First, 8–40 screws are much stouter, a consideration if you're scoping a hard-kicking rifle. Secondly, factory holes aren't always properly aligned or drilled the proper distance from their mates. An oversize drill can fix misalignments so the base fits perfectly and the screws tighten squarely. This isn't a job for a hand-drill. Pick a gunshop that's black with big, greasy machinery that might have been used to manufacture 1917 Enfields—a shop manned by a dour, equally greasy machinist who looks old enough to have designed the Enfield. If he growls at you, so much the better.

Steel bases are better than aluminum because steel is less easily deformed than aluminum. But if you tighten a properly-radiused aluminum base (like the Weaver) securely it will anchor your rings. I like Dave Talley's scope mounts, but there's nothing wrong with standard Redfield-style dovetail bases now manufactured also by Leupold and Burris. Conetrol makes the sleekest mount-ring combo in the business, one that's particularly appealing on slender, lightweight rifles. Weatherby offers the mount designed and sold for years by Maynard Beuhler. Various European mounts have been pointed out as engineering marvels. But it seems to me that simpler is better. I want few parts firmly mated. Never needing both iron sights and a scope on the same rifle, I avoid quick-detachable mounts. Scope failures once made an iron-sight option necessary; scope failures are now extremely rare.

To my mind, there's no difference of any importance between one-piece and two-piece bases. Just make sure they're very snug to the receiver before installing rings.

Rings should be the lowest that will allow your scope's objective bell to clear the barrel and the ocular bell to clear the bolt handle. Low-mounted scopes keep a rifle's center of gravity low between your hands and put the target in front of your eye when your cheek is tight to the stock. Tucked to the rifle, they're less susceptible to banging on rocks and trees, and they slide in and out of scabbards more easily than high-mounted scopes. Some shooters argue that higher scopes give you quick finger access to the ejection port (a point made also by people who favor two-piece bases). My question: What are you doing jamming your fingers in the ejection port?

Ring Spacing

Ring spacing is important. You want the rings to give the scope as much support as possible. You don't want them crowding turrets or bells or forcing you to move the scope to or from your eye to accommodate them. Sometimes extension rings or bases are necessary, more often these days with short-coupled variable scopes. I steer away from them, mostly for cosmetic reasons. They're no less solid than ordinary rings.

Rings must be perfectly aligned to clamp the scope most securely and without damaging the tube. To "turn in" a dovetail ring, clamp it on a 1-inch dowel and use the dowel as a lever. Scope tubes weren't made for that job. If the scope won't snuggle into the bottom halves of split rings when you gently lay it in place, the rings aren't aligned. If they resist alignment, check the bases. It may be time to chuck up an 8–40 drill bit.

While split ring halves shouldn't have to be matched to fit perfectly, I still do it. No fit is as close as that of pieces rejoined. Make sure those rings are secured to the base. I recall a scope working loose on a .416 Rigby at the bench and finally jetting off the QD bases upon recoil. It ricocheted off my skull to land some yards away.

Eye Relief Adjustments

A scope is best positioned so you have to slide your head forward to get the correct eye relief. Thrusting your head toward the scope is a normal movement when you take quick aim, concentrating on a target. If you must move your head back and forth to find the place that gives you a full field of view, you've lost valuable time. With the scope well forward you also reduce the chance of a cut brow when you're shooting prone or uphill.

Tip: Position the ocular lens even with the rear guard screw, then inch the scope back if you must to find the proper spot. Snug the scope into the rings when you think you're satisfied, then mount the rifle quickly several times. Next, don a sweatshirt, then a jacket and try it again. If you have a variable scope, change magnification during these trials. Eye relief can change with power. I want a variable placed so that at 4× its full field hits me as naturally as if I were looking over iron sights. If you commonly shoot at higher powers, check eye relief at those settings.

Before you establish the scope's final position, wipe the tube with a silicon rag to remove grit and lint. Some shooters clean scopes with solvent and dry rags to nab all traces of lubricant. I've never had a problem with rings losing their grip, though the inertia of heavy variables under heavy recoil can break the bond, enabling the scope to slide. A dry scope with a trace of silicon to keep ring surfaces from rusting makes sense to me.

Reticle Positioning

Now you're ready to position the reticle. Give yourself time to do this, as a hurry-up job will surely result in a tilted reticle. Rotate the scope as you think it should be, then clamp one ring just tightly enough to hold it in place. Shut your eyes and shoulder the rifle. When you look through the scope, the crosswires should be horizontal and vertical. If they aren't, loosen the screws and turn the tube. Repeat. When you can't think of how to make that reticle any more square with the world, set the rifle aside for a few minutes, then go through the closed-eyes routine once more. You may find that you canted the rifle earlier. You've no doubt looked through scopes that were.

Rings should be tightened like the lug nuts on an automobile wheel: each a little at a time until all screws are as tight as you can get them without stripping threads or tearing heads. The new Torx screws allow you to apply much more pressure than on slotted or Allen heads.

Securing the scope to rifle is only the mechanical part of setting up the scope. Now you must work with optics. The first step is to bring the reticle into focus. Many hunters—probably most hunters—neglect this. They adjust bicycle seats, computer screens and toasters but ignore the ocular adjustment on their rifle scopes. Result: they can't aim well. It's as important to bring the reticle into sharp focus as it is to peg your stirrups at the correct length before you ride horseback into the mountains.

To do this, loosen the lock ring, just forward of the ocular (rear) bell of your scope. Some scopes have ocular adjustments like those on binoculars—you rotate a ring in the ocular housing until the reticle becomes crisp. Regardless of the design, start by turning the lens out (rearward) to a point at which the reticle looks very fuzzy when you point the rifle skyward. It's essential that you train the rifle on empty space so your eye doesn't try to focus on an object. Now lower the rifle and turn the housing in (a full turn if your scope has the traditional lock ring, but only a fraction if it adjusts like a binocular with double helical threads that quickly move the lens in and out). Repeat the pointing exercise. If the reticle is not sharp (it shouldn't be if you've turned the housing out far enough to begin with), repeat again. Do this until the reticle appears sharp against the sky. Your first impressions count. If you stare at the reticle for more than a second or two your eye will try to bring it into focus. As with eliminating tilt in a reticle, it's smart once you've focused the scope to leave it for a while, then check it again before you tighten the lock ring.

No, this operation does not bring your target into focus. Most scopes are designed so that for normal vision a target will appear in focus over a wide range of distances, as it might to the unaided eye. Very close targets may seem blurry. You'll have to live with that or aim only at targets far away. Some scopes have parallax adjustment—a focus option of sorts. You'll see it most commonly as a sleeve with yardage markings on the objective (front bell). A few makers now put parallax adjustment on the left side of the turret, in what looks like a second windage knob. It's easier to reach there, though engineers tell me the mechanics are more involved.

Understanding Parallax Correction

The purpose of parallax correction is to eliminate aiming error caused by misalignment of your eye behind the scope. If your eye is perfectly centered in the scope's axis you'll have no such error at any range. But when cheek and comb don't place your eye dead center, even if you're still getting a full field of view, the reticle may not show where the bullet goes. You can see how this works by purposefully moving your head up and down and side to side as you look through the scope with the rifle steady over sandbags. The crosswire will seem to shift slightly unless your target is at the parallax-corrected distance. Most hunting scopes without adjustments are set parallax-free at 150 yards. The best way to eliminate parallax error is to ensure a perfect stock fit to your face so your eye always lines up effortlessly with the scope axis.

Using the Reticle to Estimate Range

Knowing your scope's reticle subtension will help you estimate range. Many catalogs list the space in inches that a reticle or part of it subtends (covers) at 100 yards. European companies specify reticle subtensions, like windage and elevation adjustment values, in metric terms. If you know that half the slender wire of a "plex" reticle—the distance from the bottom post to the intersection—subtends 16 inches at 100 yards and you're hunting whitetail deer with an average chest depth of 16 inches, you can quickly gauge yardage just by looking through the scope. You know that if a deer's torso just fits between the horizontal wire and the tip of the post, that deer is about 100 yards away. An elk just squeezing between top and bottom posts would also be about 100 yards distant because a mature bull measures roughly 30 inches from back to brisket, with the hair. A deer that fills the post-to-post gap is only 50 yards away.

You can do the same with a dot, or with a post whose tip extends above the horizontal wire. Range-finder reticles, such as those sold by Redfield and Shep-

herd, employ stadia wires or circles to help you "bracket" animals and thus determine range. Mil dot reticles for tactical use offer a more sophisticated ranging
method, but it's predicated on the same principle.

A mil dot reticle comprises a crosswire with a series of tiny dots strategically
placed along both axes. The spaces or interstices between dots each subtend one
milliradian, millradian or mil. That's 1/6400 of a degree in angular measurement.
The span is 3.6 inches at a hundred yards or 3 feet at 1000. So at 1000 yards two
mil dots subtend about 6 feet.

To use this reticle as a rangefinder, you divide the target's height in mils by
the number of interstices, subtending the target to get range in hundreds of yards.
A man or a moose (20 mils by linear measure) that appears in the scope to be four
dots high is thus 500 yards away. Actually, the official method is to divide target size
in yards by the number of mils subtended and multiply by 1000. That's a lot for me
to remember. Naturally, scope reticles with mil dots are calibrated for one magnification.

This one-magnification rule, incidentally, applies also to variable hunting
scopes with non-magnifying reticles, such as American hunters prefer. If you boost
power from 4× to 8×, the size of the target image doubles, but reticle sizes does
not change—meaning reticle subtensions are now half what they were before. European scopes with reticles in the front focal plane make range-finding easy because the size of the reticle in relationship to the size of the target stays constant no
matter the power. The disadvantage of this option is that at the high magnification
you'd want for small, distant targets, the reticle is much bigger than is desirable. At
low power, where you'd peg the scope for quick shooting in timber or to boost
exit pupil in poor light, the reticle shrinks and can be hard to find right away.

You may discover that at a certain magnification your plex reticle will allow
you some tricks that can extend point-blank range. For example, one of my low-
powered scopes has a plex reticle with a vertical post-to-post gap of about 32
inches at 200 yards. An elk filling this gap is thus 200 yards away and dead when I
shoot because my rifle is zeroed at 200, at the intersection of the crosswire halfway
between top and bottom post. At 300 yards I know the elk will appear about ⅔ as
big. I can figure out holdover if I want—or I can again rest the top of the bottom
post against the bull's brisket. The horizontal wire than cuts across the elk about ⅓
of the way up the ribs. At 300 yards the bullet drops about 7 inches, or ¼ of the
depth of the chest. So I hit only slightly below where I did at 200 yards, given the
post tip as my aiming device. Another fatal shot. No range estimation necessary.

At 400 yards a bull elk will just fit between the horizontal wire and the top
of that bottom post. Again, I could estimate the 20 inches my bullet will drop, but
I can also keep the tip of the post against the brisket, just as I did at 200 and 300
yards. The intersection is now on the bull's back, where it would be if I were to
purposefully hold high. The bullet drops into the lungs.

This technique also works at 100 yards, incidentally. It breaks down beyond
400 yards where trajectory becomes very steep. But shooting beyond 400 steps
rarely makes sense anyway, because even if the hold is perfect, slight errors in shot
execution magnified by that distance can easily move your bullet out of the vitals.

Wind also becomes as problem. If you're sure of wind conditions all the way to the target, plus your bullet's rate of deflection under those conditions, and have a mil dot reticle and lots of time and a very steady position, you can snake a bullet to the bull's eye through wind beyond 400 yards. Usually, however, wind causes misses and crippling at such long range.

Zeroing In

The last thing to do in setting up a scope is zeroing. I save money by bore-sighting first. You can do this with a collimator—an optical device with a bore-diameter spud you stick in the barrel. Using your scope adjustments to center the reticle on the optical center of the grid in the collimator's screen, you get a rough zero. I do the same thing with bolt and dropping-block rifles by securing the rifle on a bench and looking through the bore out the window to the top of an orchard windmill a mile away on a hill. With the rifle motionless and the windmill's tip centered in the bore, I adjust the scope's reticle onto my "target." That's all. Now the scope's optical axis is in line with the bore.

At the range, I place the rifle on sandbags, either using an adjustable rest under the front bag or building a stack of bags so that with the rifle at rest the crosswire quarters my 100-yard target. Having bore-sighted, I'm confident those first shots will be on the paper at 100 yards, so that's where I start. I position the front bag where my hand would be under the barrel, and the rear bag just ahead of the toe of the stock. The barrel never rests on the sandbag (it will bounce hard off the surface), nor does the bag go where the swivel or swivel stud will tear into it on recoil. I hold the stock's grip firmly with my right hand, using my left to squeeze the rear bag to make slight adjustments in my sight picture.

I fire one shot, then adjust the scope and repeat, my goal being to land a bullet 2 inches above point of aim. After I'm there I complete a three-shot group. Next I go to a clean paper at 200 yards. At this range I want the bullets hitting center. I shoot three-shot groups, letting the barrel cool between groups, adjusting until one cluster shows up in the middle.

With most big-game and varmint rounds, I then shoot at 300 yards to confirm a 6- to 8-inch drop, depending on the load. If I had access to a 400-yard range I'd shoot at that distance, too. It is not good enough to shoot only at 100 yards (or as some shooters do, at 25!), then look at a chart in an ammunition catalog and assume you know where your bullets will strike at long range. For one thing, small deviations at short range become significant far from the muzzle. For another, the height of your scope mount affects the relationship of bullet trajectory and sight-line downrange.

Not long ago a fellow came to hunt with me with a rifle he said was zeroed for 200 yards. He missed an outstanding elk. Later at the range I benched the rifle and found it zeroed at 325. He had popped a few rounds through paper at 100 yards and figured that since most landed about 3 inches high they'd hit center at 200. That's what everyone had told him. But the scope's big objective bell had forced the use of high rings. The flat trajectory of a hot .300 Weatherby load, combined with the sharp pitch of a high sight-line, pushed his zero far from the muzzle.

Testfiring Your Scope

When you've set up a scope the way you want it, you're smart to give it a test. You've had a go from the bench. Now step to the side and fire two three-shot groups each from sitting, kneeling and offhand at 200 yards. Sitting and kneeling, you'll want to use a sling—one with a shooting loop so you can snug the rifle hard against your shoulder and take some weight off that forward hand. Sling tension will steady the rifle, reducing wobble. But it will also pull the forend away from the barrel and tug against the upward thrust of recoil. That means bullets may strike lower than they did when you shot from the bench. If the forward swivel is mounted on the barrel, the effect can be great indeed.

Some years ago I zeroed a Ruger Number One in .300 Winchester Magnum. At the zero range of 200 yards I was astonished to find its point of impact drop 9 inches when I shot from the sit with a tight sling! I managed to cut that disparity in half by relieving forend pressure up front and cushioning the pull of the forend screw in the rear. Most rifles don't show such a dramatic difference, but almost every rifle I've shot with a tight sling prints lower as a result. It's important to know that, because you won't have a bench in the field. Maybe you'll want to adjust your zero to compensate.

One last tip: When checking zero, reserve one target for "cold, clean-barrel" shots. Shoot only the first bullet per session into this target, duplicating the first shot you'll fire at game. After five sessions at the range, with cleaning in between, compare that five-shot group with the others you've compiled. It should be a relatively tight cluster and, more importantly, in the same place as warm-barrel groups relative to your point of aim. If first shots from that clean, oiled bore go "wild," you may want to consider hunting with a dry or even a dirty bore.

There's nothing complicated about setting up a scope. But neglect it, or neglect practice from field positions, and you'll be hunting with a sight that is much less helpful than it could be.

42　The Stillhunter's
Ultimate Rifles

BY STAN WARREN

When your deer hunting means walking, not sitting in a stand, your rifle had better be easy to carry and potent enough to get the job done. Here are one expert's top picks.

It was back in the days of Jack O'Connor, whose passionate writings about the .270 Winchester had novice whitetail hunters like me salivating for one. Unfortunately I could not afford anything of that order, but I did scratch up the wherewithal for The Great One's second favorite: a 7mm Mauser. The fact that mine had been produced for some Banana Republic army and still wore its ungainly, full-length barrel and military woodwork did not bother me at all. So I thought.

Bear in mind that at this time it was about as easy to get a shot at a whitetail buck around home as it is to find a diamond in a gravel driveway. I had almost frozen my backside off every morning for a week, perched in my treestand consisting of a shipping pallet nailed to a white oak limb. Back in those days, either mornings were considerably shorter or youth combined with anticipation helped time pass. Finally the incredible happened: A buck walked out not over 40 yards away.

Since he was directly to my right, it was quite the chore to turn quietly while fighting to control a heart that was hitting runaway speed, not to mention the mental demon shouting, "Hurry, hurry! He's gonna run!" Then the unthinkable happened: I found that the rifle was simply too long to be brought to bear. The limbs that had provided great cover would not let me move the doggone thing the necessary few inches required. My first almost-buck wandered away unaware that he had nearly lost his life.

A hacksaw and some crude down-home gun whacking (I almost said gunsmithing) made the old '93 Mauser more portable, new sights made it as accurate as it would ever be and removal of considerable wood, along with all but 20 inches of barrel, reduced the weight considerably. I later sold the thing for $50, a little better than twice what I had paid for it. Prior to its departure it had accounted for about a half-dozen whitetails.

Move the calendar forward a couple of decades. Improved financial conditions had allowed me to acquire a rifle that handled a potent and racy-looking belted magnum cartridge. Certainly it would be enough and more for the mule deer I would pursue on the horseback affair. I was mentally rehearsing my acceptance speech, to be made after acquiring my one-shot trophy, when the guide ahead of me ducked to pass under a limb. I also ducked, but failed to allow for the 24-inch barrel sticking above my shoulder. Tail over teacup, I made an interesting if not graceful dismount. The Long Barrel Demon strikes again.

Before both gunmakers and lovers of long-barreled rifles descend upon me, skinning knives drawn and with evil intent, let me add that I still own and use the big boomers. Hardware with lengthy tubes goes along for most everything from elk to prairie dogs; they just don't go to the whitetail woods.

Although a few acquaintances think anything lighter than a .300 Magnum is inadequate for a 150-pound whitetail, most folks realize that anything from a 6mm through the lighter .30 calibers will get the job done if the hunter does his part. Goodness knows enough deer of both sexes have gone to their rewards due to cartridges as small as the .223 and .22-250, which are legal in some states these days. If I shy away from the .243 and 6mm, it is simply because by preference I am a woods walker rather than a stand sitter. Many times the only shot possible in the timber is of the angling variety, which may call for driving a bullet from the hindquarter area into the business district, where things like the heart and lungs can be found.

This establishes the guidelines for power. Portability has already been mentioned, and practicality includes several factors, of which price is one. We may all dream of expensive shooting irons, even custom jobs, but the truth is, the vast majority of deer hunters select rifles off the retail rack. Let's take a gander at what's generally available.

The Ultra-practical Lever Action

It is impossible to discuss easy-to-carry deer rifles without mentioning the venerable Winchester Model 94. Its reputation was made primarily using the .30-30 round, which, although adequate for whitetails and even larger game, certainly is not an earth-shaking cartridge. But it is well suited for a light rifle that can be carried a lot and pointed quickly regardless of the cover. With a 20-inch barrel on a standard model, the whole affair is just over a yard long and weighs about 6¼ pounds out of the box.. The Timber Carbine version is exactly a yardstick long and pulls the scale an even shorter distance. Chambered in the .444 Marlin, this is no pussycat. It is not a grizzly bear round when used with commercially available ammunition, but a whitetail within 150 yards or so is in serious trouble.

What can be said for the Winchester can also be said for the Marlin lever rifles. I have used a Model 336 ER in .356 Winchester since the round was introduced and dearly love the thing. Far more potent than the popular .30-30, the cartridge was sadly dropped from the line a few years back. That does not mean Marlin cannot provide some extra oomph for those who want it. Versions in .444 Marlin and .45-70 are available, and handloads in the latter make it suitable for use on any deer (including moose and elk) if the hunter sticks to shots of less than 200 yards. I have carried a Marlin in .45-70 a couple of times when chasing wounded elk in black timber and on one occasion took a bolting bull completely off his feet with a through-the-shoulders shot at about 40 yards. He was defunct before his chin hit the snow.

The problem with both the .444 and .45-70, for some people at least, is either real or perceived recoil. This puts them on the very edge of our practicality scale and probably explains why far more conventional lever rifles are sold in .30-30 and even .35 Remington.

Browning's BLR in the short-action design fits our working scale too, for those who prefer its styling and detachable clip magazine. Deer hunters can opt for either the .243, 7mm-08 or .308 Although it does not quite fit here, this rifle in its long-action arsenal is chambered for some heavy hitters.

Before leaving the subject of lever rifles I must touch quickly on a personal favorite. In the days before slings became virtually standard equipment and hunters wanted their firearm in their hands rather than hanging on their back, an odds-on favorite was the Savage Model 99. I snatched a circa-1930 version off the used rifle rack at Cabela's out in Nebraska and have since come to truly appreciate both the rifle's design and the .300 Savage chambering.

Its first trial in the woods came on a misty, drizzling day on the family farm. Where deer had been scarce not too many years back, they are now plentiful, and I intended to pot a doe for the freezer. A gnarly racked seven-pointer changed my mind. I was standing beside a twisted and ancient white oak, watching and waiting, when he came down the ridge about 100 yards away. At half that distance he was coming uphill and pretty much directly at me. Perhaps he sensed something was wrong. He stopped, his head came up, and a 150-grain Federal bullet caught him on the point of the chest. The "obsolete" cartridge had destroyed the heart/lung area and was recovered against the spine in front of the hams.

Finding a Savage 99 in its original version, with the wonderful rotary magazine for the .250 or .300 Savage, or a later one with the detachable clip and .243 or .308 chambering, will probably call for scrutinizing of used-gun racks. The company apparently dropped it in favor of more profitable bolt-action rifles since it does not appear in recently published gun roundups. What a shame. Even when carried suitcase style, the 99 is a real speedster to use and delivers some punch.

Before moving on the bolt guns, there is one more special rifle that bears mention. Against all odds and probably against conventional wisdom, I rate the Ruger Number One International as the finest rifle for the "walking around" hunter. The stubby Farquharson-type falling-block action and 20-inch barrel make this little full-stocked gem just 36½ inches overall. If it were any faster to handle I would probably have beaten myself to death with it by now. Instead it seems to fly to the shoulder and the six-MOA dot reticle installed in the 1.5 × 6 Bausch & Lomb scope by the T.K. Lee Company of Birmingham, Alabama, practically finds the target by itself. If you have ever swung a good ruffed grouse gun, you will get the idea.

This particular deer stopper actually rests only a few feet from where I peck at this keyboard, and a handful of cartridges for it, carrying 140-grain Nosler Ballistic Tips, are not far above on a shelf. I occasionally get a whack at a marauding coyote from the office window, and thus far precious few have escaped once spotted. Both the International and Light Sporter models of the Number One come in .243, .270 and .30-06 for those who want something lighter or heavier than the 7257. To each his own.

Easy-to-Tote Bolt-Action Rifles

Dog paddling into safer water I can now address the bolt actions, which are by far the favorite of most big game hunters everywhere. Generally accurate, reliable, strong and capable of multiple shots when needed, bolt guns are certainly the practical choice. The fact that they come in a wide variety of workable calibers is certainly an asset, ensuring that even the lightest ones can handle a lengthy shot if one comes along.

Picking a favorite here is like having multiple daughters in a beauty contest. There are no easy answers, even if we limit our choices to those that cost less than $1,000, weigh in at seven pounds or less and are 42 inches or shorter overall. Most major gunmakers have something to fit the criteria for the stalker or stillhunter.

Perhaps it is just as well to start with the Winchester Model 70 Classic Featherweight. A trade I now regret involved one of these (again in 7 × 57, which is no longer available), and this graceful design is based on the much loved pre-'64-type action. How is the accuracy with the whippy-thin 22-inch barrels? A buddy has one in .22-250, and prairie dogs, along with other varmints, better allow a 300-yard cushion between them and the muzzle.

Whitetail hunters can opt for the .243, .308, 7mm-08, .270 or .30-06, but there are two additional chamberings that have real merit. If I were using one strictly to stalk deer, East or West, there would be a strong temptation to select the 6.5 × 55 Swedish Mauser. Its pedigree may not read very loudly—a 120-grain bullet at just under 2,900 fps and a 140-grain bullet at around 2,650—if numbers are your thing. It should be pointed out, however, that this little rig has taken uncounted numbers of big game animals in Europe, including bear, boar and stags. Minimal recoil makes it delightful in a featherweight rifle, and with premium-grade bullets like the Nosler Partition and Speer Grand Slam, it "kills bigger than it is," even according to avowed big-bore fanciers like Elmer Keith and Colonel Charles Askins. These guys knew a thing or two about guns, I might add.

In the highly portable Winchester one can also request the wonderfully versatile .280 Remington. You want versatility, maybe a rifle that will whomp whitetails at ranges from a few feet to 300 yards and beyond, then take on elk, sheep or anything short of dangerous game? Consider the words of long-time Outdoor Life shooting editor Jim Carmichael, who said, "I have taken so much game with this one (a particular 160-grain load) that I sometimes wonder why I carry anything else."

Speaking of my fellow Tennesseean and gun-related guru, Jim was also the major force behind the introduction of the .260 Remington. This relatively new offering is available in the Savage 16FSS Weather Warrior and Remington's Model

Seven and Model 700 Mountain Rifle. More about these guns and their various attributes in a moment; for now the cartridge gets some attention.

The .260 is nothing more exotic than a .308 Winchester case necked down to hold .26-caliber bullets. Users can expect an increase of 50 fps or so over the velocities delivered by the 6.5 × 55, partly due to higher allowable maximum pressures developed by the ammunition. After all, there are no surplus military rifles around chambered for the .260 that are apt to come apart at the seams if treated too roughly. They can also, for now at least, expect better over-the-counter availability of ammunition. What one round will do, the other will do equally well. Neither will stomp you even when used in a featherweight rifle, and both will send any whitetail now walking the earth to visit his ancestors with surprising rapidity.

The Savage bolt action just mentioned is proof positive that this company has shed the "cheap but serviceable" rap it carried for a while. The retail price may be a dab less than the competition still, although that does not detract from the usefulness of the M16FSS. Even with a man-sized synthetic stock and 22-inch barrel, it still spans less than 41 inches and tips the scale at around six pounds. I once had a Savage varmint rifle, and it felt as if the action weighed that much. If the only one you can find is shiny stainless, buy a camo paint set and make things better. You'll have enough money left after the purchase to do so. Other chamberings here are .243, 7mm-08 and .308.

Enter the Remingtons, the Model 700 Mountain Rifle and the Model Seven. I have been lucky enough to play with both of these since their introductions, and for portability the latter is hard to top in a bolt action that fits into our price guidelines. With the 18-inch barrel, the overall rig is a mere 37¾ inches, while a 20-inch tube edges out to 39¼ inches overall. Weight runs around 6¼ pounds, depending on the density of the hardwood stock. Synthetic models are a bit lighter. Certainly the .308 Winchester, .243, 7mm-08 and .260 chamberings are suitable for use on deer.

The Model Seven's price is similar to the Mountain Rifle, but for my money the Model Seven finishes second in this race unless you are outfitting a youngster or other small hunter. The Mountain Rifle has a 22-inch barrel, which puts it in the 41-inch overall-length class—not a bit of a drawback because of some design characteristics that make this rifle well suited for the stillhunter. Weight is less than seven pounds prior to the addition of a scope, and I have found that the low-pitched pistol grip holds and handles well and points as fast as any commercially produced rifle around. Maybe the stock was designed around someone of my approximate size and bulk. Whatever the reason, the Mountain Rifle points as quickly as any deer gun on my rack, with the possible exception of the Ruger International versions.

The 22-inch barrel also means better velocities out of the .25-06, .260, .270, .280, 7mm-08 and .30-06 chamberings. Recent tests using factory .260 ammo in both of these rifles showed that the Model Seven gave up as much as 150 fps, according to my Pro-Chrono sitting 10 feet in front of both muzzles. If restricted to whitetail deer at moderate ranges, this is not much of a deal. Should the hunter occasionally walk into sizable openings that might have a buck at the far end, the more potent choices have a decided edge. I might also be swayed by a lot of testing on the range, where the Mountain Rifle, in whatever caliber used, delivered outstanding accuracy despite what the company calls its "lean-contoured" barrel.

There are also a pair of bolt guns from Ruger that make the walkabout hunting list, and both sport that company's top tang safety for added speed in getting into shooting position. First is the M-77RL in the Mark II Series. At six pounds and just over 40 inches with its 20-inch barrel, it comes in three of the most popular whitetail calibers, plus it is also available to handle one of the best balanced, least-used cartridges around: the .257 Roberts. With +P ammunition or good handloads (I had mine altered to .257 Ackley Improved), it is no trick to toss 120-grain bullets at well over 2,700, while 100-grain pills can be boosted to over 3,100. The only problem with this personal choice is ammunition availability. Run out of cartridges in rural America and you could have a problem. This is just what happened to me in the hinterlands of Nebraska when an airline lost part of my luggage. I had to borrow a rifle to go hunting.

Finally it is time to detail a rifle (bolt action, of course) whose weight, length, balance and features, such as caliber versatility, make it an odds-on choice for stalking or stillhunting. Certainly it will handle work from a stand when required and even take on game larger than whitetails. Why not the Ruger M-77 RSI MKII, or just the M77 International as it is better known? Rounds like the .30-06, .270, .308 and .243 suffer little enough when run through an 18-inch barrel and can be found just about anywhere ammunition is sold.

The rifle, with its Mannlicher-style stock, carries and handles like proverbial lightning, and the safety is under your thumb all the time when you're carrying the shooting iron at port or high-port position. Mine weighs right on seven pounds with a 1.5 × 6 B&L scope. I can even carry it on a sling while riding a tall horse, should the need arise. If you can think of anything that fits the bill better, please let me know: I can always use another rifle, given the proper excuse.

43   The Spiteful Crack of the
.250–3000!

BY JIM BASHLINE

Pennsylvanian Jim Bashline passed away shortly after he wrote this article in 1995. He was one of the finest writers, editors, and human beings I've ever known.

It was mid-afternoon when the tourist hunter drove into the parking lot of the Old Hickory Tavern on November 31, 1941. His dark blue Packard was encased with frozen slush containing fragments of coal cinders, which was what the Pennsylvania Highway Department used to dump on icy roads before calcium chloride and limestone chips became standard treatment. There were lots of cinders then; soft coal was the number one fuel for home and industry. The Marylander had driven to Coudersport, Pennsylvania, to be part of the area's most important economic annual event—the opening day of deer season.

The hotels, boarding houses, and tourist cabins (motels hadn't been invented yet) would be full by nightfall. The Old Hickory's eight double rooms and bunkhouse annex had been booked a year in advance, and this Baltimore dude had reserved the best room in the house for himself and his buddy.

"Hey, kid," he said in my direction as he exited the Packard. "Are you next in line for bellboy?"

I was. The town kids who were too young to have a hunting license served as baggage carriers for the out-of-state "sports." As a gunstruck, ten-year-old, this was my second year on the job. We got the chance to carry their duffle and, oh the thrill, their gun cases and maybe hang around long enough to actually see the artillery. Good tips too. Some of these guys actually popped for a half dollar, which was serious money to an Appalachian urchin. The Great Depression of the '30s was barely over in north central Pennsylvania.

The dudes always had nicer guns than most of the local talent. From the looks of the unsoiled, leather-trimmed canvas case the Maryland hunter handed me I assumed that something wonderful was inside. After I made five trips up the narrow stairway to his room with his and his pal's gear, he fished three quarters out of a vest pocket and pressed them into my hand. It was the biggest tip I had ever received.

"What kinda rifle you got, mister?" I asked.

Maybe my recollections are a bit fuzzy, but it seemed like adults were kinder to kids in those days. At least this guy was.

"Well, I've got a brand new Savage 99 with a telescope on it. Do you wanna see it? I guess so."

With great care and obvious pride, he unbuckled the case and withdrew a shiny, lever action rifle with an equally shiny scope perched on its receiver. He opened the action, closed it and thrust it at me. "Here take a look through the telescope."

I aimed the rifle through the window glass and killed a ten-point buck on the other side of the street. Heart shot. Lowering the rifle, I squinted at the numbers stamped on the barrel. Oh, double thrill. It was a .250-3000 Savage. I knew all about them. I had memorized every word about every rifle and caliber mentioned in Stoeger's Shooters Bible. Among my family members and my father's friends plenty of .30-30s, .32 Specials, Krags and Springfields had been seen and touched. But a 99 Savage chambered for the mythical .250-3000—with a telescope yet— was heady stuff at age 10. Wishing him good luck at hunting (required protocol, since you might get to carry his gear again when he was ready to depart), I went back outside to hustle some more business. As I turned to leave, he handed me a cartridge. "For your collection," he winked.

Yeah, people were nicer to kids then.

The Memories Begin!

I thought about that rifle a lot during the next couple days as I wrestled with the fifth grade conundrum of decimal points. While I understood what the digits stood for in .250 and that "3000' meant feet-per-second, how to apply that information to practical arithmetic eluded me. My gift cartridge was studied with more care. I thought it was the deadliest looking package in the world and that I must have a rifle to fire it one day.

Another thing I didn't know much about in 1941, was that the wonderful .250 Savage was already on the way out as being the darling of the high velocity crowd. It wasn't even "modern," with its official birth year being 1915. The sizzling .220 Swift and Winchester's flagship .270 had already taken over first and second places in the velocity race. No matter, the first round in my cartridge collection set the stage for a long term romance.

The well-trodden path of exactly who created the .250 Savage cartridge has been travelled so often that we're now convinced no one knows for sure. Charles Newton probably sparked the idea when he necked a .30-40 Krag case down to .25 caliber. Harvey Donaldson, father of many wildcat cases, was involved too when he began to tinker with a cut-off "ought-six" case. John Pierce, a Savage engineer blended the thinking and lo, the .250-3000—or .250 Savage—was made whole.

It has seemed curious to me that the .250 Savage hit the hunting scene before the .300 Savage did. While no one can doubt the .300's effectiveness on deer and slightly larger game, it didn't create the stir or inspire the rifle/shooter love affairs that the .250 was responsible for. It wasn't just the advertised 3000 feet-per-second speed of that little 87-grain bullet that did it. It was the impressive manner the cartridge killed stuff with either the 87- or 100-grain bullets if their jackets weren't too thin. When the .250 went "bang," creatures of deer-size or so dropped quickly, if not sooner.

This is not hyperbolic cow flop. The .250 Savage is a more efficient deer-class round than the .243, .244 or a pile of other cartridges that are close to the hearts of American venison seekers. Why is this so? Only the hunting gods know for sure. A platoon of other smart alecs know this is true and while all of them have theories about it, they eventually admit the mystery.

In his excellent book, "Shots at Whitetails," Larry Koller heaped praise on the .250. He killed many deer with his Savage rifle and with one exception, they all dropped "as though struck by lightning." Legendary Alaskan guide Hosea Sarber killed every big game animal the north country offers with his .250, including several huge bears, and didn't get chewed up either. In his informative and entertaining book, "Popular Sporting Rifle Cartridges," Clay Harvey writes, "I can think of nothing better for use on game up to 250 pounds. Nothing."

The Legend Grows

Two departed gun writers of biblical status, Jack O'Connor and Townsend Whelen, went into spasms of delight over the accuracy of the .250. Long before bench rest shooters got into carrying one-hole groups in their wallets, these two gurus told the world about the minute-of-angle targets their .250 rifles could produce. As if those endorsements weren't enough, Don Robbins, half of the rifle building team of Taylor and Robbins, held the 200-yard bench rest record for more than 20 years: ten shots into .760 of an inch with a .250. There aren't many rifles around today or any other day that can do that.

A balanced combination of bullet, case capacity and design was, most likely, among the happiest of accidents in the weird world of rifles. Later whiz-bang rounds were the result of long hours spent by smart folks over drafting tables and sophisticated instruments that did much of their thinking.

The .250 just kind of happened. The sad thing about this is that it happened well before advertising hype reached the "thin air" region it now occupies. If the hoopla that announced the arrival of later cartridges had been laid on, the .250 might still be riding high today. As it is, the job of keeping it alive falls to the balding and greying ones who insist on carrying a rifle that punches our shoulders gently and places animals dead on the ground before the echo of the shot subsides. Forget lengthy loading experiments. Pour 32 or 33 grains of 4895 into the case, seat a good 100-grain bullet on top and go hunting. If you don't handload, the factory ammo will group almost as well and kills deer just as fast.

In addition to doing its job with distinction, the hardware chambered for the .250 is an additional reason for song and verse. In its pure and original form, no lever action rifle can top the sex appeal of the old 99 in its many configurations. Carbines, long barrels, lightweights, Monte Carlo equipped, you name it, Savage made it at one time or another. Even the re-introduced straight-grip 99F which appeared briefly during the early '70s, with .250 stamped on the barrel, is an exquisite hunting piece. Winchester chambered its pre-64 icon, the Model 70, for it, and for a time Savage built .250s on their unusual Model 40 and 45 frames.

The caliber also enjoyed a spurt of popularity with custom makers and several European firms. Later, Ruger offered its Model 77 in three styles for the .250, with the full stocked, RSI carbine in .250 being as cute as a cub bear. A wonderfully accurate .250 is the Remington 700 Classic, made for one year only (1986, I think). It's fair to say that a short ton, at least, of excellent quality .250s have been cranked out by some of the world's best rifle builders. All past tense rambling of course, but it may be too soon for the "fat lady to sing" about the passing of the .250.

The mystique of sectional density aside, .25 caliber bullets in a number of cartridges do exceptionally well on game and paper. The ancient .25-35 is extremely accurate when matched with a good barrel. While the .257 Roberts has never been the performer the .250 is on targets, it's a wonderful hunting round. The .25-06 is a sort of grown-up .250 that has few equals beyond 250 yards. The same can be said for the .257 Weatherby. I suppose it's obvious that I'm fond of all .25 calibers. Correctly used, one or the other of them would suit me fine for 90 percent of all big game creatures. But it's still the .250-3000 Savage that brings on the warm fuzziness of happy nostalgia.

The deer hunters who had rooms at the Old Hickory for the 1941 season did well. By Wednesday evening, ten tagged bucks were hanging on the meat pole that was erected for "show and tell." Yeah, no one protested seeing dead deer hanging in full view of passersby in those days. I made a daily check of the meat pole after school and read the information on the tags. None yet bore a Maryland address.

The dude with the new .250 scored on Thursday of the opening week. I was there at four in the afternoon when that 1939 Packard pulled up with a decent 8-pointer draped between a chrome-plated headlight and the fender-mounted horns. I "supervised" as the hunter and his pal added the deer to the display. The one hole in the hide told the story. Lung shot. "Took out both lungs, just like that." He snapped his fingers for emphasis. "Never saw a deer drop so quickly and you know what else?"

"What?"

"The bullet didn't come out. This is all I found when I dressed him."

The dude reached into his black and red Woolrich coat and came up with five fragments of lead and jacket metal. He dropped them into my hand.

"Add these to your collection, kid. And get a two fifty-three thousand some day. It makes a spiteful crack. I did OK for a 'flatlander,' right?"

Flatlander was what we termed nonresident hunters back then (and still do). Yes, he had done well, and I got another 75 cents for helping him load up the next morning before school. Flatlanders weren't so bad after all. This one would be in his 80s by now. He'd have been at prime military age at that time. Like everyone else he had no idea of what was going to happen on the coming Sunday morning, December 7. I hope he's still around to read this and remember.

I still have those shards of the "dude's" .250 bullet stored in an aspirin tin. In a variety of small containers, I've also saved fragments from other .250 bullets that have killed deer for me. Most of them look just like his did—shrapnel from miniature bombs that came apart as they usually do when fired from rifles chambered for this 78-year-old cartridge.

The .250 really does have a "spiteful crack" and carries more than a little magic with it as well.

44   Outer-Limit Whitetails!

BY BOB McNALLY

Big bucks are cagey, but a long shot with a dead-on rifle can quickly cut your odds!

Even in the first light of dawn Stacer Helton of Sandersville, Georgia, knew it was a helluva buck. The deer was a long way off, in an open pasture chasing does, but its rack was impressive. He was in central Alberta, the rut was rocking, and plenty of buster Canadian bucks were on the move. Stacer had seen several good deer and passed on a number of them. But the heavy whitetail he watched through binoculars looked like the kind of buck he had traveled across the continent to collect.

The buck sported a tall rack, and had plenty of antler mass, but there wasn't a great deal of spread to it. Yet Stacer knew the body size of the buck was enormous, so rack perception was likely altered. He set down his binoculars and picked up his long-trusted rifle, a customized Remington in 7mm STW caliber. It was a long shot, but he had planned for that. There was no wind, and he had a solid ground-blind rest, with a rifle he knew well.

He figured the distance at 250 yards, so he settled the crosshairs of the 3×9 Zeiss scope high in the kill zone of the large buck, and touched the trigger.

The rifle roared, and as it recoiled Stacer bolted another round in the chamber, and in a fluid, lickety-split motion was back on target. The deer was down for good, however, taken with the first shot behind the shoulder. It had only moved a few steps from where it had stood—a measured 350 yards from Stacer! The 140-grain Ballistic Tip bullet had done devastating damage to the 300-pound buck, passing completely through the animal, without the deer ever knowing Stacer was anywhere near.

The 5×5 buck sported split-brown tines and gross scored an impressive 172%.

Just two days later in nearby Saskatchewan, Stacer took an even bigger 180⅛ gross (171⅛ net) Boone and Crockett buck with the same rifle and round at 145 yards, anchoring the 280-pound deer on the spot. Back home in Georgia, just before the state season ended in January, Stacer shot yet another dandy 200-pound buck scoring 140 points using his 7mm STW. The 8-point buck was taken stem-to-stern, at 175 yards, because it was the only long-range shot the deer offered. That buck also was pole-axed by a 140-grain Nosler Ballistic Tip bullet—from a gun Stacer has learned to rely on for long-range whitetail hunting.

Stacer's Magnificent 7

"I've tried them all for whitetails, and I don't think there's a better deer caliber available for my long-range buck hunting than the 7mm STW," says Stacer, who runs Skinner's Guide Service for deer and turkeys in Sandersville. "It's incredible for long-range shooting, which I'm convinced is the best way to collect an older, heavy-rack buck in today's hard-hunted woods. I handload 140-grain Ballistic Tip bullets, which have a muzzle velocity of 3560 feet per second out of my customized 7mm STW. It is unbelievably accurate. I have it sighted to hit 2 inches high at 100 yards, and at 400 yards I just settle the crosshairs along the back line above the kill zone. This rifle takes all the guess work out of judging distance for me."

Ballistically, the 7mm STW is awesome, according to Stacer. he's taken dozens of deer with the rifle, and incredibly has never lost one. Often the animal's entire chest area has contusions from damage inflicted by the 140-grain Ballistic Tip as it passes through. Frequently the bullet does not exit a deer, thus expending all its energy inside the animal, to make for a quick, clean, humane kill—even at ranges well beyond 200 yards.

Such long-range power on whitetails is available from many different, and long-proven calibers, such as the 30.06, .300 Winchester Magnum, 7mm Remington Magnum, .270, .280, 284 Winchester, .308, 25.06 and even the newer .260 and 7mm-08 Remington. All can do an admirable job on deer at 200 to 300 yards, provided the right man is on the trigger. Additionally, most long-range riflemen insist on highly-accurate guns, mostly bolt-actions, or special single-shot tack-drivers.

Most hunters are proud of such firearms, and delighted in the fact they easily can shoot 1-inch groups at 100 yards, or 3-inch groups at 200 yards. So why do so many whitetail hunters set ambushes for deer that produce 50 to 70 yard shots? It's just as easy to drop a buck at 100 or 150 yards with a quality scoped rifle, than at half those ranges. And be assured you'll see more deer, and particularly more mature bucks, if ranges are increased.

Breaking Down Big-Buck Defenses!

Hunting deer at longer range is such a ridiculously simple tactic for taking older, bigger bucks, it's amazing more riflemen don't consciously do it. Human scent is less of a factor when hunters select stand sites well away from areas they expect to find bucks. Locate a scrape line, for example, and if possible, hang a treestand far up a ridge, or on a facing ridge, so as not to disturb the hot whitetail spot you've discovered. Walking to and from a stand too close to a deer hot spot can spook game, and no hunter can be completely scent free on stand. So the farther you are from whitetails, the more likely you'll see them.

"I use a .270 Weatherby Magnum and 140-grain bullets for my whitetail hunting," says Don Moultrie, well-traveled hunter and owner of Moultrie Game Feeders in Alabama. "This is the same rifle I use for elk, bears, everything. The caliber is fantastic, devastating on deer well out to 300 yards. Those are long shots to some people, but good bucks often only offer fleeting glimpses to hunters at even those ranges. Your best chance at a good buck is from long range, and you've got to have a rifle up to that task.

"At 200 yards a hunter can get away with a lot more mistakes with older whitetails than he can inside 100 yards. A lot of sportsmen have no idea just how smart a three-, four-, or five-year-old buck is. The slightest scent of man, the slightest movement, alerts him. The farther a gunner is from the place he's hunting, the less likely a buck is to detect him.

"If you're hunting a rub line that's 50 yards away, it's even money that a buck coming to that area will wind you or cross the tracks you made going to your stand. Likewise, a rutting buck coming to a scrape usually comes in downwind. But he's alert, and often circles the area, so a close hunter normally will be detected, and the shooter won't even know a buck has come and gone. That's why I take a stand 150 to 200 yards away from the place I think I can see good deer. And once I find such a place, I stay away from it, and make sure other people stay out, too.

"An old buck has a sixth sense about him for survival, and your best chance of killing that deer is if he has no inkling you're anywhere within his world. If a big buck is disturbed he'll move out of an area, or become completely nocturnal. He'll move around only at night or in places where he isn't exposed, and then he's almost impossible to kill."

To prevent this, hunt from long range, insists Dan.

A top-quality pair of binoculars may be the most valuable aid in long-range whitetail hunting. Lightweight portables are nice, but full-size models with excellent light-gathering optics make more sense. You'll pay a high price for good binoculars, probably as much as your rifle. But that classy gun does you no good until binoculars locate a target.

Quality Optics Stressed!

It makes more sense to put an expensive scope on an inexpensive rifle, than to do it the other way around. The point here is even the best caliber bullet shot from a great rifle can't perform like it should if the scope used is of poor quality. Buy the best optics you can afford, from companies like Zeiss, Nikon, Swarovski, Steiner, Leupold, BSA, Burris, Simmons and Redfield. A good rule of thumb is to spend at least as much on the scope as on the rifle itself. Crystal-clear, shock-resistant, fog proof scopes are vital to accurate bullet placement in whitetails at long range.

Large-diameter scopes that gather a lot of light are in vogue today, with many hunters wanting 50mm models with 3-to-9 variable magnification. Don't overlook the style crosshairs the scope has. I like the duplex type, which has heavy crosshairs, leading to finer ones near the center. But there are many styles, like the target dot and the post, and one of those may look best to your shooting eye.

Tripods

Another accessory some experienced long-range shooters employ is a collapsible bipod that attaches to a rifle forend sling-swivel post. A bipod offers a benchlike, steady gun rest for a shooter when none other may be available. Good ones made by companies such as Harris are light, easy to use, quick to handle and won't change the zero of an accurate, long-range rifle. They also are height adjustable, which is advantageous when shooting over high prairie grass or brush. Some bipods are designed to stay mounted on a gun while hunting, others are made to quickly attack to the forend sling-swivel post (while detaching the sling) once game has been seen.

Wayne Nelson, with Cabela's Outfitters in Sidney, Nebraska, uses a bipod religiously in hunting open-country deer in his native state. Long shots of 200 to 300 yards are common. In the grasslands of that plains region much of the time hunters stalk into the wind, so no stands or trees are available for a solid rifle rest. Nelson has taken a number of dandy Nebraska deer thanks to long-range rifle accuracy resulting from bipod use.

Wayne uses a bipod that attaches to his rifle for prone shooting, but there are "taller" models designed for shooters kneeling, sitting or standing. These have longer legs than ones made for prone shooting. Another version bipod by "Stony Point" has telescoping legs and does not attach to the gun forend sling-swivel post. It's simply carried by a hunter in a pack or pocket, then readied for use as a rest when a shot is made. Weight of the rifle on a bipod "yoke" steadies it for accurate shooting. Stony Point also make an aluminum monopod (one leg) that telescopes up to five feet.

One of the best portable rifle rests on the market for long-range whitetail shooters hunting from tree stands is the "API Shootin' Rest." It's unusual looking, but once tried, it's loved forever by hunters wanting accurate bullet placement at far distances. The all-plastic rest has a large half-circle base that fits snugly over a sitting hunter's upper thigh. A single plastic, telescopic post is adjustable to different heights, and a padded, smaller, plastic half-circle at the top of the unit cradles a rifle forend. The unit pivots easily with a gun, and offers a rock-solid rest, especially useful to hunters in fixed-position treestands that have no railing to rest a firearm. It also can be used on the ground, in monopod fashion.

Long-range hunting for whitetails naturally demands additional responsibility for sportsmen. Marginal shots at deer at ranges beyond practiced limits are inexcusable. To wound and lose a deer is among the most heart-wrenching experiences outdoors. Sportsmen who purposefully shoot from 200+ yards must be equipped to do so, and plenty of practice at the range is mandated. That said, increasing the distance between you and your buck hot spot should also increase the odds of paying a hefty taxidermy bill at the end of the deer season.

45 Running Deer: Straight Talk on Critical Shooting Decisions

BY RICHARD P. SMITH

The arguments are heard in every deer-hunting camp: Should you take a shot at a running deer.
If so, how? Some sensible and illuminating answers are right here.

Just when I thought the Pennsylvania deer drive was going to end without any whitetails coming my way, one of the drivers hollered, "Deer coming off the hill! Deer coming into the hollow!"

I was near the bottom of the hollow, posted next to a tree to help break my outline. Immediately after hearing the warning, I saw a number of deer running off the hill on the opposite side of the hollow, coming my way. No antlers were visible on the heads of the two whitetails that were in the lead as they temporarily went out of sight in the bottom of the hollow, but a small set of antlers were obvious on the first deer to reappear, charging uphill toward me at close range.

The buck's eyes widened as it spotted me. I knew there was no way it was going to stop. If I didn't take a running shot, I wasn't going to get a shot at all.

I quickly found the fast-moving target in my scope, swinging through the animal from the rump forward. As soon as the crosshairs were on its shoulder, I pulled the trigger. Although the whitetail was covering ground, its speed was nothing compared to the velocity of the 150-grain bullet from my .30-06.

The deer dropped immediately, adding another buck to the list of those that I've taken on the run over the years. Many of them were taken on drives like that one, but others have been shot as they fled from other hunters who weren't part of an organized drive. Still more were dropped with a second shot after the first round fired at a stationary target missed, usually due to a deflection, and they tried to escape.

Ethical Shooting

Shooting at moving deer isn't something I take lightly, nor should anyone else. I prefer to shoot at deer that aren't moving, but that's not always possible in the real world, especially when participating in drives or afield in areas where there's heavy hunting pressure. I only shoot at running deer I'm confident I can kill. Questionable shots are avoided.

Hunters who are uncomfortable shooting at running whitetails or lack confidence in their ability to connect on moving targets, obviously should not do so. If you are interested in learning how to do it, to boost your confidence level for those times when the only buck you might see is hoofing it for parts unknown, read on. There's a secret to hitting moving whitetails in woods that George, a hunting partner of mine, began discovering after a frustrating season years ago. The technique is different than the approach I used to take that little buck on a Pennsylvania drive.

George's lesson on how to hit moving whitetails started out by finding out how not to do it on the second day of firearms season in Michigan. We were positioned several hundred yards apart on the ground, watching an evergreen thicket bordering a stand of hardwood trees that whitetails frequently traveled through. George was on the top of a ridge and I was at the bottom where the pines filtered into a lowland swamp.

I heard my partner shoot about 10:30 a.m. After waiting a while to make sure no deer came my way, I went to George's blind to check on his success. He told me that a forkhorn and a doe had come by at a steady walk or trot. He followed the buck in his rifle sights until he felt they were lined up properly and fired. However, his bullet hit a tree he hadn't seen instead of the deer. We chalked the miss up to bad luck and continued hunting.

When George's "back luck" repeated itself on the fourth and fifth days of the season, we began to realize he might be doing something wrong. The situations were similar in each case. A buck came walking or trotting past George and he swung with the animal, firing when he felt he was on target. His bullets found trees he didn't realize were in the line of fire every time, instead of the bucks he was shooting at.

The buck George missed on day number four was the same one that got by him the second day, but the third opportunity was at a trophy buck with a large rack that may have had as many as 12 points. Understandably, George was disappointed about not connecting on the big buck, although he felt bad about the earlier misses, too. It was apparent that my partner was doing something wrong to miss every time. After I thought about it a while, I figured out what it was.

Over the years, I had taken a number of whitetails that were either walking or running, including a yearling buck the previous season. I was posted in a cedar swamp when the buck appeared in front of me, moving from left to right at a brisk walk. The variable power scope on my rifle was on the lowest setting (3X), which is important to be able to pick up moving whitetails quickly. When I found the buck in the scope, I swung the crosshairs ahead of him to an opening in the trees that he would soon enter and held them there.

When the buck walked into the opening and my sights, I squeezed the trigger. He dropped dead on the spot. I touched off the shot when the crosshairs were on the forward edge of his shoulder. That deer was 40 to 50 yards away when I folded him.

To Swing or Not to Swing?

The difference between my approach and George's is that I selected an opening ahead of the buck and held my sights there rather than swinging with the animal as he did. While following the bucks with his sights, he was concentrating on aiming and not obstacles that might be in the way. Even if there were no trees in the way at the moment George decided to shoot, the split second delay before the bullet was actually on its way, and his follow through, resulted in the bullet actually hitting forward of where he thought it would. There happened to be a tree between the bullet and deer in each case.

By aiming through an opening and letting the deer do the moving rather than the rifle, the hunter knows no obstacles will be in the way when he or she shoots, thereby increasing the chances of connecting. The technique is simple, but it can be difficult for some hunters used to swinging a shotgun on running rabbits or flying game birds to adopt. Many deer hunters who also hunt birds and small game with scatterguns do what comes naturally when faced with a shot at a moving deer, and that's swinging the rifle or shotgun with the game. Precise aiming isn't necessary when using shotshells because there are enough pellets that even if some hit trees or brush, there's a good chance others will score hits on the intended target.

It doesn't work that way with bullets or slugs. A single branch or bush, as well as trees, may deflect the single projectile off target or stop it altogether. When moving deer are in the open like the young buck mentioned at the beginning, swinging with them isn't as much of a problem as it is when they are in cover. In fact, swinging through them like I did in that case, is a perfect way to score, as long as hunters don't swing too far ahead of them.

I well remember the first trophy deer I ever shot at. I missed him because I led him too much. I was walking up a steep slope at the time when I jumped two deer on the edge of some timber. I got a glimpse of them as they disappeared from sight, then looked around and spotted the body of a third animal barely 50 yards away. The entire body looked so large I thought it had to be an elk, but if it was a deer I wanted to make sure it had antlers before shooting.

I took a step or two in an effort to get a look at the animal's head and it took off bounding, going uphill and across the slope in front of me, still about 50 yards away. It was obvious then that I had passed up an easy shot at a trophy buck and now had to take a running shot or nothing. I found the buck in my scope right away and swung out in front of him with plenty of daylight between the intersection of my crosshairs and his chest before firing. I shot in front of him and he was gone before I could rack in a second round.

If I had tightened my finger on the trigger when the sight was on his shoulder, he would have been mine. That 150-grain, .30-06 bullet was traveling around 2,900 feet per second when it left the muzzle. That's fast. Fast enough to require little lead at 50 yards or less.

Under those circumstances, lead is measured in inches. This means the sights should be on a deer's body when shooting, not in front of it. Even at 100 yards, not as much lead is required with centerfire rifles as most hunters realize. At the 100-yard velocity of 2,600 feet per second, it only takes a bullet from my rifle .11 of a second to cover 300 feet. The slower 150-grain, .30–30 bullet reaches the 100-yard mark in .15 of a second at around 2,000 feet per second.

If a deer hunter shoots when his or her sights are on the forward edge of a walking buck's shoulder that's broadside at 100 yards, that should put the bullet in the chest cavity. A running buck would require a little more lead so there's daylight between the sights and the deer's chest when firing. The lead I used on that huge buck I missed was probably good for a 150-yard shot.

Shotgun slugs are slower than centerfire rifle bullets, so hunters will have to take that into account when shooting at moving deer. However, Remington's 12 gauge rifled slugs still cover 100 yards in approximately .25 of a second. Consequently, I would shoot when my sights were on the chest of a walking whitetail that's broadside at 50 yards and about six inches in front of the chest on a running animal at the same distance. Double the lead for 100-yard shots.

On deer that are angling away, allow for a lead that will put a bullet or slug either through or behind the ribs where it will angle forward into the chest cavity. When bucks are bounding, try to time your shot to coincide with when they touch down and present a level profile.

George and I did a lot of talking about shooting at moving whitetails among ourselves and with other hunters after the season. George missed those three chances at bucks, and he realized how to better handle the situation the next time it arose. He's used the knowledge to tag a number of bucks since then, one of which was an eight-pointer. The rack buck appeared with no warning 20 yards behind George.

He was afraid the buck would see him and spook if he raised his rifle, so he let the whitetail walk by, then got up as slowly as possible and turned around. The buck heard George make his move, snorted and broke into a run. An open lane was in the buck's path, so George swung his rifle to it and waited for the antlered deer to reach it.

Just as he was about to squeeze the trigger the buck stopped on the edge of the lane. George quickly adjusted the crosshairs to the buck's exposed shoulder and filled another tag. Although the buck was not moving at the time he shot it in this case, his success was assured by using the proper technique for shooting at running deer.

If George had swung his rifle with the buck, anticipating on sending a bullet its way when it entered the lane, there's a good chance he would have shot as the buck stopped and his follow through would have put the bullet in front of the whitetail, resulting in a miss. And if the cover where the buck stopped had been too thick to get a bullet through, he would have been ready for a shot at the moving deer as it crossed the lane by holding on the opening.

Another time I had a chance at a running buck myself that could have made the difference between filling my gun tag or ending the season with a story about one that got away. I heard the buck bounding my way from behind. The whitetail was clearing a windblown tree as I turned around and immediately saw a small rack on its head.

The buck was coming almost directly at me when I covered an opening with my scope between trees he was about to enter. When the center of his chest was in the crosshairs at a distance of 18 yards, I hit the trigger. The five-pointer faltered, but stayed on his feet and passed by me seven steps away before stumbling and going down. When I dressed the buck, I discovered there was little left of its heart due to damage from my bullet.

Deer hunters who use scopes on their rifles or shotguns aren't at any more of a disadvantage than those with iron or peep sights when it comes to hitting moving deer. In fact, I think it's easier to score on moving whitetails with a scope than iron sights. The key is to use the lowest magnification possible so the field of view is the largest available. I haven't had any problem with 3 × magnification, even at close range, although 1½ or 2½ × glass is better.

Hunters who have a hard time finding deer in a scope should practice looking at an object then throwing up their rifle and aiming at it as quickly as possible. This exercise will help find a buck in your scope in the critical time sometimes available when hunting. Photographing running whitetails with a telephoto lens is the same as shooting at them with a telescopic sight, so keep that in mind for practice, too.

There are a few ways to get actual practice on moving targets with a rifle or shotgun. Some sportsmen's clubs have deer silhouette targets mounted on tracks or pulleys, giving their members a perfect opportunity to bone up on shots at moving deer. Old tires can be used for similar practice sessions by putting cardboard centers in them and having partners roll them down inclines. However, this should only be done in areas where safety requirements are met, meaning protection for people pushing tires and a suitable backstop for bullets.

The next time you get a shot at a whitetail on the move through wooded terrain, remember there's a good way to increase your chances of connecting. Simply try to pick an opening the animal will pass through ahead of it and have the rifle on the opening ready to shoot when it walks, trots, or runs into the open. If the deer is already in the open, try not to lead it too far.

Strategies at a Glance:

- Never even contemplate touching off a shot at a running deer if you have not practiced the shot.
- By swinging on a moving deer, you risk hitting unseen brush or trees. Rather, find an opening the deer is likely to run through and fire once he gets there.
- At 100 yards, very little lead is required even on a deer moving at full speed.
- Confidence is the key at hitting deer on the run. By practicing, you'll gain the much-needed edge.

46 Long-Range
Muzzleloading

BY RALPH LERMAYER

Some hunters consider all muzzleloaders to be 100-yard firearms. They've got a lot to learn.

The subject of effective range is guaranteed to stir debate among hunters, but it's doubly controversial when it comes to muzzleloading. Many shooters consider muzzleloaders close range, low power propositions, good for thin-skinned whitetails and almost a stunt on bigger game. Compared to today's magnums, muzzleloader power levels may pale, but when muzzleloaders and blackpowder cartridges were the only game in town, they did the job on the biggest and meanest of game at practical ranges. For first-hand comments on that adequacy, follow me to a frigid December morning in 1876.

On a lonely hill above the North Concho, just south of what is now Big Spring, Texas, a buffalo hunter by the name of P.C. Bicknell and his partner earned the day's wage by shooting 30 buffalo from a single stand. They were shooting blackpowder cartridges and from that stand they killed large, mature buffalo at ranges well over 200 yards. Solid lead projectiles, driven by blackpowder, chalked up kill numbers often exceeding 100 animals a day—an event repeated throughout the west until the herds of buffalo were gone.

That evening, after the skinning was done, P.C. sat in a teepee made of buffalo hides and by the light of a burning piece of cotton cord hanging from a plate of buffalo tallow, he wrote a letter to a friend and fellow buffalo hunter named Dave. That letter found its way to the archives of the Sharps Rifle Company, and surfaced in 1978. It gives us a strong insight into the guns and loads used to perform these shooting feats that by today's blackpowder standards seem incredible, yet to them were just another day's work.

Interest in muzzleloading has grown at a phenomenal rate since 1983. Much of the interest has been stimulated by big game other than whitetails. Colorado, New Mexico, Utah, Alaska and other western states have created separate seasons for muzzleloaders. Drawing chances for these premium hunts is better than for certain centerfire rifle permits. These hunts are for big western game, and unlike the eastern whitetail hunter, for western hunters 100 yards is a close shot. Plains hunters need to stretch the performance of their rifles, but reasonable range and adequate knockdown power have always been there, as attested to by the buffalo hunters of a century ago. We just have to re-apply the basics that they knew back then.

For the first clue, take a look at P.C.'s letter. His grammar and punctuation are a little rough, but his message is clear. His reference to balls is a comment on long conical, pure lead bullets, not roundballs. Back then they called all bullets balls. Ring balls refer to the lubrication grooves. He discusses the skill, experience and equipment of choice of his hunting companions and I quote directly from his letter: *"These men are men who have hunted and trapped all over the west from the Black-Hills south to Texas. The gun they swear by is Sharps .44 caliber just like yours they shoot 90 grains powder—some use the .50 caliber & 120 grains. The best gun in this part of the country is a Sharps .40 caliber with 90 grains of powder, the ball weighs 420 grains. The hunter who has it, says he can hit and kill a bull as far almost as he can see it. It holds up wonderfully. The .44 caliber day before yesterday, loaded with 85 grains 420 grains lead shot through several bulls in succession at 500 yards. My partner shoots a Maynard .40 caliber ring ball 70 grainpowder 340 grains lead. He shot a bull last week just to one side below the tail—the ball lodged in the tongue. The bull was 250 yards distant. Shooting from one side the balls mostly go through & frequently kill two at once."*

A .40 caliber rifle, shooting a 340-grain conical bullet driven by 70 grains of blackpowder, shooting clear through (lengthwise) a bull buffalo at 250 yards?! A .44 caliber shooting a 420 grain pure lead bullet, shooting through bull buffalo at 500 yards and frequently killing two at once?! Were these men exaggerating? While the ranges may have been enhanced after the fact (a practice common today), most are close to accurate. There are reams of correspondences, diaries and narratives that buffalo hunters left behind. What they did can be duplicated by today's muzzleloader hunters, and I doubt that there's a bull elk, moose or mule deer that's tougher than a mature bull buffalo weighing over 1,000 pounds on the hoof. Nowhere in the files is there mention of .54 or .58 calibers. Just the opposite; .50, .44 and .40 caliber rifles were the top choices. Again I quote P.C.'s letter: *"That .40 caliber Sharps must be the Boss gun. You see it shoots the same amount of powder as the .44 with a longer ball."* And here, the clue to the range effectiveness is in the words, 'longer ball'."

What they were dealing with then was the effects of bullet form on performance or, as we know it today, ballistic coefficient. Small diameter heavy, long bullets hold up better, shoot flatter and deliver bone smashing energy at ranges most modern muzzleloader hunters won't even consider. Within ranges that are practical, out to 200 yards, high quality muzzleloaders with the right bullets can deliver the goods as well as P.C.'s .40 caliber did a century ago. I'm aware that the rifles referred to were Sharps single-shot breech loaders using a cased cartridge. Nonetheless, they shot a moderate charge of blackpowder and fired a long, conical bullet. The case offered little ballistically, but it helped contain pressures. Most muzzleloading rifles of a century ago couldn't stand the pressures the cased Sharps could handle, although custom rifles were around that duplicated and often surpassed the Sharps performance. Muzzleloader barrels and rifles built by Pope were highly sought after, and won many a 1,000 yard match but they were not the run of the mill rifles.

Today's hunters are fortunate. While not every muzzleloader on the market (and certainly no antiques!) is built for long range work, modern steel and manufacturing techniques make possible a level of performance in some in-line and sidelock rifles that duplicates the best that Pope ever built. The Remington 700ML, the Knight rifles, the new Thompson Center Black Mountain and Encore, and the Colt Gamemaster are examples that are more than up to the task and have served me well from antelope to grizzly beyond 100 yards, as long as I used the right bullet. Lower priced rifles, especially some imported models, should be confined to the short range, low pressure work they were designed for.

Besides their strength, these rifles share design features that make them ideal long range prospects. All have a crisp trigger, fast lock time, and most importantly, the rate of twist in the barrels is always 1:38 or faster with shallow lands and grooves. Slow twist barrels (1:48 or slower) were designed for roundballs or short maxi's and simply will not stabilize a long conical bullet. Try to shoot long conicals from a slow twist barrel and you'll be lucky to group inside a Stetson hat at 75 yards. Fast twist barrels and small bores are the key to long range muzzleloader performance.

The market hunter's preference for long .40, .44, and .50 caliber bullets is sound. When bullets of this diameter are made approximately two times bore diameter (resulting in the weights indicated in P.C.'s letter) the ballistic coefficient and flattened trajectory are maximized. Unfortunately, due to bad experiences with roundball performance, many states dictate .45 caliber as the minimum bore size for big game but, where allowed, a fast twist .40 or .45 caliber muzzleloader is at the top of the list for long range, big game performance because as P.C. Bicknell so aptly stated: *"That .40 caliber Sharps must be the Boss gun . . . it shoots the same amount of powder with a longer ball . . . It holds up wonderfully."* A .40 caliber, 400 grain, pure lead bullet pushed to 1,500 fps, offers hunters an effective point on range with no holdover or compensation to 200 yards and delivers 1,360 pounds of energy when it gets there.

.45 and .50 calibers give up very little to the .40s with the selection of bullet and sabot combinations now available. Sabots are plastic cups that allow you to shoot sub-caliber bullets in your rifle. Muzzleloader sabots made of wood and leather have been around for centuries. Polymer sabots appeared in the early 80s, and were initially intended to allow deer hunters to use lightweight, jacketed handgun bullets in muzzleloaders. The breakthrough in long distance performance is coming from the use of sabots coupled with long, pure lead bullets. With the bullet protected by the sabot, it can be pushed harder and faster than an unprotected bullet. Buffalo Bullet Company's .50 caliber SSB's are available in 375 and 435 grain spire point designs. Ballistic coefficient for the 435 is .342 and for the 375 is .296—high enough to hold up within 200 yards, and heavy enough to do the job when they get there, just like they did for P.C. and his buddies. If you shoot a .50 caliber you can, with a sabot, use these .45 caliber bullets effectively. If you shoot a .45 caliber, you can use a sabot to shoot a .40 and gain the advantage of the superb flight characteristics of that long bullet with its high B.C. Those who hunt states like Colorado that don't allow sabots can still get fine long range performance with the solid lead bullets sized to just under two times bore diameter, approximately 480 grains depending on shape. You won't get the high velocity, but these are adequate on large game to 150 yards.

Chart A illustrates how effective you can be with the right muzzleloader/ bullet combination. These were all fired with heavy but safe and allowable powder charges. Included for reference is the typical roundball performance. Note how fast the roundball sheds velocity and how paltry the energy levels are. Maximum point on range is most cases is 200 yards before the drop exceeds 10 inches, well inside the heart/lung area for elk and mule deer and lethal with a top-of-the-back hold on pronghorn. To achieve these trajectories, sight your rifle in to hit the specified distance above zero at 100 yards. Hold in the center of the target and adjust to hit that high. Be sure and testfire at 25, 50 and 200 yards to make sure of your rifle's exact drop figures.

Adequate energy downrange is only half the equation. If you can't see the target clearly, you have no business shooting. Nothing ruins a hunt faster than tracking wounded game. Some will extoll the benefit of a good blood trail, but I infinitely prefer a gut pile. Make sure you precisely pick your spot and can deliver the bullet to it, or don't shoot. Many states don't allow scopes on muzzleloaders. When limited to iron sights even the mighty 300 Win Mag becomes a 90 to 100-yard rifle, and that is a long shot for most eyes. The factory sights found on muzzleloaders today have a front bead that blocks out a deer-size target at ranges over 75 yards, making bullet placement chancy and risking wounded game. Where iron sights are required, the unquestionable best choice is a narrow, highly visible front blade, matched to a large aperture peep.

Peeps are an aftermarket option on most muzzleloaders. Usually, the rear sight is changed to a peep and the front blade is left as issued. This works better than a notch but to maximize the distance potential of metallic sights, the front blade and rear peep should be matched. Quality peep systems are available from firms like Millett, or Ashley Outdoors of Fort Worth, Texas (Phone 1-888-744-4880). Colt makes these sights standard on their Gamemaster rifles, and there is a model for just about every muzzleloader. With a matched system, most shooters can hold consistent three and four-inch groups with conicals to 100 yards, even in low light. Those with excellent eyesight will no doubt do better. Where scopes are allowed, these high ballistic coefficient bullets often group two inches or better at 150 yards, and the heavy bullets handle wind well. As with any distance shooting, a steady rest and an accurate rifle that the shooter is totally familiar with are prerequisite. In the hands of a shooter who can place a bullet at that distance, muzzleloaders are effective.

They knew it a century ago and it's true today, with a little thought and preparation, the right rifle and bullet in the hands of a good shot, muzzleloaders can definitely take you out to practical hunting ranges.

Muzzleloader/Bullet Combinations

Rifle	Bullet	Muzzle Velocity FPS	Trajectory 100 200 300	200 Yard Energy Ft. Lbs.
T/C System 1 .50 cal 1:38 twist	Buffalo conical .50 cal, 490 gr. base protected with felt wad	1,456	+4.5 0 × 10	1,373
Remington 700ML 50 cal. 1:28 twist	SSB .45 cal., 435 gr. in black sabot	1,450	+4.6 0 × 10.5	1,268
White G-91 .45 cal. 1:28 twist	.40 cal (.409) 350 gr. in tan sabot	1,592	+3.6 0 × 8.5	1,232
Import .50 cal 1:48 twist	.490 180 gr. .010 patch	1,450	+3 × 5 × 20	378

Muzzle velocities measured with the Oehler model 33P. Drop figures are the average of those derived from actual shooting at Avalon Ranch. Powder charges did not exceed manufacturers maximum allowable charge.